Student Support and Benefits Handbook: England, Wales and Northern Ireland

8th edition

David Malcolm

Child Poverty Actio

CPAG promotes action for the prevention and relief of poverty among children and families with children. To achieve this, CPAG aims to raise awareness of the causes, extent, nature and impact of poverty, and strategies for its eradication and prevention; bring about positive policy changes for families with children in poverty; and enable those eligible for income maintenance to have access to their full entitlement. If you are not already supporting us, please consider making a donation, or ask for details of our membership schemes, training courses and publications.

Published by Child Poverty Action Group
94 White Lion Street, London N1 9PF
Tel: 020 7837 7979
staff@cpag.org.uk
www.cpag.org.uk

A CIP record for this book is available from the British Library

ISBN: 978 1 906076 44 3

Child Poverty Action Group is a charity registered in England and Wales (registration number 294841) and in Scotland (registration number SC039339), and is a company limited by guarantee, registered in England (registration number 1993854). VAT number: 690 808117

Cover design by Devious Designs
Typeset by David Lewis XML Associates Ltd
Printed in the UK by CPI William Clowes, Beccles NR34 7TL
Cover photo by Steve Eason/Photofusion

The author

David Malcolm is the Head of Social Policy at NUS, responsible for its work on student finance, student welfare and equalities. He has worked in student welfare for 14 years, including a year as the sabbatical Vice President Welfare at the University of Strathclyde Students' Association.

Acknowledgements

The author would particularly like to thank Alison Key, Lindsey Fidler, Jayne Aldridge, Jeanette Jones and Carolyn George for their work on previous editions of this *Handbook*.

Grateful thanks are due to Keith Houghton, Angela Toal, Connie Craig, Elaine Robinson, Gareth Davies, Sarah Wayman, Kelly Sizer, David Brookes and Barry Hansford for lending their time and expertise in checking and advising on this *Handbook*.

Many thanks also go to Judith Paterson for providing a framework for developing this *Handbook* in England, Wales and Northern Ireland.

For her swift and efficient editing and production management, thanks go to Kathleen Armstrong. Thanks also to Alison Key for producing the index and Paula McDiarmid for proofreading the text.

The law covered in this book was correct on 1 September 2010 and includes Regulations laid up to this date.

iv

Contents

Foreword

As this, the eighth edition of the *Student Support and Benefits Handbook*, is published, the fight continues to end child poverty and to enable access to a fairly funded education system across the UK.

Funding for education will remain a major political issue in the coming year. The Browne Review of higher education funding will report shortly after the publication of this *Handbook*, and could result in higher fees and higher debt for higher education students. At the same time, funding for adult learners in further education in England has been cut, and many postgraduates struggle to find any funding whatsoever. With the new Government set on reducing the deficit, further cuts seem inevitable.

Yet despite the fact that we are a rich country, one in three children in the UK still lives in poverty. Rightly, politicians see education and work as crucial routes out of poverty, and vital to the economic health of the nation. Yet students from the poorest backgrounds are still hugely underrepresented in further and higher education, even more so in the elite institutions.

Although we know that over the last decade there has been a significant improvement – for the first time, the majority of school leavers now continue in education – this expansion does not extend in anywhere near the same proportion to families living in poverty.

Many policies introduced to try and bridge the gap are welcomed: the New Deal; the minimum wage; investment in childcare; increases in child benefit and income support for families; a new tax credits system; and education maintenance allowances. These are the kinds of social policies that improve the living standards of poorer families and act as a first step in helping them make the difficult transition into education.

However, low-income students still face formidable barriers to their participation and to their achievement. Students from low-income families tend to have to work more during term time, are able to rely less on family support (both financial and otherwise), and must navigate the ever-changing and quite bewildering student support and social security benefits systems, often with little or no guidance. The ongoing reductions in income support entitlement for lone parents are likely to make matters worse.

Furthermore, when people on low incomes do enter education they tend to follow a more complicated path, taking more breaks, deferring enrolment, and switching, repeating or restarting their courses for non-academic reasons. We know these people are also more likely to drop out or forego opportunities to progress to more advanced courses. All this complicates even further their financial support and adds to the pressures they face in determining their entitlements.

'How will study affect my benefits?' is a key question for anyone who is living on benefits and thinking about going into education. No one can make a decision to start or continue studying without knowing they can support themselves and their family. Good advice is critical. Student support across England, Wales, Northern Ireland and Scotland differs and, as a devolved issue, these differences are ever more apparent. Advisers, therefore, need information that relates specifically to the different nations across the UK.

Fair access to education – indeed, education itself – is about much more than money, but clear, relevant information on financial support for students is vital. This is why the NUS is proud to collaborate with CPAG in producing this *Handbook*.

This book covers students in England, Wales and Northern Ireland, complementing CPAG's *Benefits for Students in Scotland Handbook*. We hope it will aid advisers, act as a tool to help break down barriers and, in the process, help people from disadvantaged backgrounds enter and complete further and higher education courses.

Of course, this *Handbook* is no silver bullet. If the Government is serious about its pledge to eradicate child poverty through education, it must commit seriously on a number of levels: fairer access to student support; increased capacity in the student advice sector; further development in childcare services; a wholesale change in attitude in some of our older and larger educational institutions; a raising of aspirations and achievement in schools in disadvantaged areas; and more resources channeled into our community support services. All remain substantial challenges.

When we see an entirely equal proportion of people from poor and rich backgrounds entering the higher and further education system, we will know that poverty is on its way to being eradicated. Until then, NUS is fully committed to supporting our members, breaking down financial barriers and fighting injustice throughout the education funding system.

NUS would like to thank the author, checkers and production staff for their hard work and dedication throughout this project.

Aaron Porter, NUS President
Ben Whittaker, NUS Vice President Welfare

How to use this *Handbook*

This *Handbook* is intended for those who advise students in England, Wales and Northern Ireland about their entitlement to student support, benefits, tax credits and other financial issues, such as tax and health benefits. It covers both further and higher education.

The *Handbook* covers rules affecting students studying in England, Wales and Northern Ireland who are eligible for support through English, Welsh and Northern Irish funding bodies such as the Department for Business, Innovation and Skills and the National Assembly for Wales. It does not cover the rules for students getting support from Scotland or elsewhere outside England, Wales or Northern Ireland.

CPAG publishes a companion volume entitled *Benefits for Students in Scotland Handbook*. Details can be found in Appendix 1.

Rates of government support

The *Handbook* is up to date at 1 September 2010 and is intended to be used for the academic year 2010/11.

Rates of student support, benefits and tax credits used are those for the 2010/11 academic year. Please note that benefit and tax credit rates are uprated in April 2011 (these rates are usually available from January or February), whereas student support rates are uprated in September 2011.

Definitions

Most full-time students are excluded from benefits – mainly those benefits for which entitlement relies on a means test. There is one set of definitions of 'full-time student' used for means-tested benefits: income support, jobseeker's allowance, housing benefit and council tax benefit. But other definitions are used for council tax, carer's allowance, employment and support allowance and incapacity benefit. And even for the means-tested benefits, some students can claim despite being classed as full time. It is best not to assume that because a student is excluded from one benefit, s/he is excluded from them all. Who counts as a 'full-time student' is explained in detail in the relevant chapters.

Means testing students

Government support systems do not necessarily treat student income in the same way. Different means tests apply to means-tested benefits, tax credits, health benefits and student support. It is always worth checking across these systems when calculating a student's total entitlement to government support. To help students and their advisers do this, these systems are addressed separately in their respective chapters covering treatment of income.

Structure of the *Handbook*

Part 1 looks at students' entitlement to student support. **Part 2** covers students' entitlement to benefits and tax credits. **Part 3** considers how income affects the amount of benefits or tax credits, with a particular focus on how student support is treated. **Part 4** covers other matters, such as tax and taking time out from studying.

Chapters are footnoted with references to the legal authorities. Where an abbreviation is used in the footnotes or in the text this is explained in Appendix 3 and on pxiv. If you are appealing against a benefit or tax credit decision, you may want to refer to the law. Appendix 1 suggests where you can obtain copies of Acts, Regulations and caselaw.

Your feedback counts

NUS and CPAG hope that this publication will serve as a useful resource for students and their advisers to help them deal with the complexity of financial support. We are aiming for a publication that is clear and that responds to the needs of its audience. The eighth edition of the book is set to be the largest yet, and we would appreciate any comments on how it may be improved for future years. Please contact CPAG's publications department or David Malcolm at NUS: david.malcolm@nus.org.uk.

Abbreviations

AHRC	Arts and Humanities Research Council
ALG	adult learning grant
AVCE	advanced vocational certificate of education
BBSRC	Biotechnology and Biological Sciences Research Council
BEd	Bachelor of Education
BIS	Department for Business, Innovation and Skills
BL	budgeting loan
BPA	blind person's allowance
BSA	NHS Business Services Authority
BTEC	Business and Technology Education Council
CA	carer's allowance
CCG	community care grant
CCW	Care Council for Wales
CTB	council tax benefit
CTC	child tax credit
DARD	Department of Agriculture and Rural Development
DCELLS	Department for Children, Education, Lifelong Learning and Skills in Wales
DELNI	Department for Employment and Learning Northern Ireland
DfE	Department for Education
DHSSPS	Department of Health, Social Services and Public Safety
DipHE	diploma of higher education
DLA	disability living allowance
DSA	disabled students' allowance
DSD	Department for Social Development
DWP	Department for Work and Pensions
EEA	European Economic Area
EGAS	Educational Grants Advisory Service
EGSA	Educational Guidance Service for Adults
ELB	education and library board
EMA	education maintenance allowance
EPSRC	Engineering and Physical Sciences Research Council
ESA	employment and support allowance
ESOL	English for speakers of other languages
ESRC	Economic and Social Research Council
EU	European Union
FE	further education
HB	housing benefit
HE	higher education
the Revenue	Her Majesty's Revenue and Customs
HNC	higher national certificate
HND	higher national diploma
IB	incapacity benefit
ICT	information and communication technology
IS	income support
ITT	initial teacher training
JP	justice of the peace
JSA	jobseeker's allowance
MA	maternity allowance
MRC	Medical Research Council
NERC	Natural Environment Research Council
NHS	National Health Service
NI	national insurance
NPTC	National Proficiency Tests Council
NUS	National Union of Students
NVQ	National Vocational Qualification
Ofsted	Office for Standards in Education
OSS	Office of Social Services
PAYE	pay as you earn
PC	pension credit
PGCE	Postgraduate Certificate in Education
PPMS	Professional Preparation Master's Scheme
QTA	qualified teacher status
the Revenue	Her Majesty's Revenue and Customs
SAP	statutory adoption pay
SCITT	school-centred initial teacher training
SFA	Skills Funding Agency
SFE	Student Finance England
SKE	subject knowledge enhancement
SLC	Student Loans Company
SMP	statutory maternity pay
SPP	statutory paternity pay
SSP	statutory sick pay
STFC	Science and Technology Facilities Council
TDA	Training and Development Agency for Schools
UKCISA	UK Council for International Student Affairs
WTC	working tax credit
YPLA	Young People's Learning Agency

Means-tested benefit rates 2010/11

Income support and income-based jobseeker's allowance

Personal allowances

		£pw
Single	Under 25	51.85
	25 or over	65.45
Lone parent	Under 18	51.85
	18 or over	65.45
Couple	Both under 18 (maximum)	78.30
	One 18 or over (maximum)	102.75
	Both 18 or over	102.75

Premiums

Carer		30.05
Pensioner	Single (JSA only)	67.15
	Couple	99.65
Disability	Single	28.00
	Couple	39.85
Enhanced disability	Single	13.65
	Couple	19.65
Severe disability	One qualifies	53.65
	Two qualify	106.30

Children (pre-6 April 2004 claims with no child tax credit)

Dependent children	Under 20	57.57
Family premium		17.40
Disabled child premium		52.08
Enhanced disability premium		21.00

Pension credit

		£pw
Standard minimum guarantee	Single	132.60
	Couple	202.40
Severe disability addition	One qualifies	53.65
	Two qualify	107.30
Carer's addition		30.05
Savings credit threshold	Single	98.40
	Couple	157.25

Income-related employment and support allowance

Personal allowances

		Assessment phase	Main phase
Single	Under 25	51.85	65.45
	25 or over	65.45	65.45
Lone parent	Under 18	51.85	65.45
	18 or over	65.45	65.45
Couple	Both under 18 (maximum)	78.30	102.75
	Both 18 or over	102.75	102.75

Premiums

Carer		30.05	30.05
Severe disability – one qualifies		53.65	53.65
Severe disability – two qualify		107.30	107.30
Enhanced disability	Single	13.65	13.65
	Couple	19.65	19.65
Pensioner	Single, usual rate	67.15	41.20
	Single, support group	67.15	35.75
	Couple, usual rate	99.65	73.70
	Couple, support group	99.65	68.25

Components

Work-related activity	–	25.95
Support	–	31.40

Housing benefit and council tax benefit

Personal allowances

Single	Under 25	51.85
	Under 25 (on main phase ESA)	65.45
	25 or over	65.45
Lone parent	Under 18	51.85
	Under 18 (on main phase ESA)	65.45
	18 or over	65.45

		£pw
Couple	Both under 18	78.30
	Both under 18 (claimant on main phase ESA)	102.75
	One or both 18 or over	102.75
Children	Under 20	57.57
Person over qualifying age for pension credit	Single under 65	132.60
	Single 65 or over	153.15
	Couple both under 65	202.40
	Couple one or both 65 or over	229.50

Premiums

Family	Ordinary rate	17.40
	Some lone parents	22.20
	Baby addition	10.50
Carer		30.05
Disability	Single	28.00
	Couple	39.85
Disabled child		52.08
Severe disability	One qualifies	53.65
	Two qualify	107.30
Enhanced disability	Single	13.65
	Couple	19.65
	Child	21.00

Components

Work-related activity	25.95
Support	31.40

Non-means-tested benefit rates 2010/11

	Claimant £pw
Attendance allowance	
Higher rate	71.40
Lower rate	47.80
Bereavement benefits	
Bereavement payment (lump sum)	2,000.00
Bereavement allowance (maximum)	97.65
Carer's allowance	53.90
Child benefit	
Only/eldest child	20.30
Other child(ren)	13.40
Disability living allowance	
Care component	
Highest	71.40
Middle	47.80
Lowest	18.95
Mobility component	
Higher	49.85
Lower	18.95
Employment and support allowance (contributory)	
Assessment phase	
Basic allowance (under 25)	51.85
Basic allowance (25 or over)	65.45
Main phase	
Basic allowance (16 or over)	65.45
Work-related activity component	25.95
Support component	31.40
Guardian's allowance	14.30
Incapacity benefit (short-term)	
Lower rate	68.95
Higher rate	81.60

	Claimant £pw
Incapacity benefit (long-term)	91.40
Age-related additions:	
Under 35	15.00
35–44	5.80
Jobseeker's allowance (contribution-based)	
Under 25	51.85
25 or over	65.45
Maternity allowance	
Standard rate	124.88
Variable rate	90% of earnings
Retirement pension	97.65
Severe disablement allowance	59.45
Age-related additions:	
Under 40	15.00
40–49	8.40
50–59	5.45
Statutory adoption pay	124.88
Statutory maternity pay	
Lower rate	124.88
Higher rate	90% of earnings
Statutory paternity pay	124.88
Statutory sick pay	79.15

Tax credit rates 2010/11

		£ per day	£ per year
Child tax credit			
Family element	Basic	1.50	545
	Including baby element	3.00	1,090
Child element		6.31	2,300
Disability element		7.44	2,715
Severe disability element		3.00	1,095
Working tax credit			
Basic element		5.27	1,920
Couple element		5.18	1,890
Lone parent element		5.18	1,890
30-hour element		2.17	790
Disability element		7.05	2,570
Severe disability element		3.00	1,095
50-plus element	Working 16–29 hours	3.62	1,320
	Working 30 hours or more	5.39	1,965
Childcare element	Eligible childcare costs to a maximum of:		
	One child (weekly rate)		80% of 175
	Two or more children (weekly rate)		80% of 300
Income thresholds			
First income threshold	WTC alone or with CTC		6,420
	CTC alone		16,190
Second income threshold			50,000

Student support rates 2010/11

per year

Further education
Adult learning grant (England) — up to £30 per week

Care to Learn childcare bursary
England (London) — up to £175 per child per week
England (outside London) — up to £160 per child per week
Northern Ireland — up to £165 per child per week

Education maintenance allowance
England — up to £30 per week
Wales/Northern Ireland — up to £60 per fortnight

Further education awards (Northern Ireland)
Tuition fee grant — up to £930 per year
Maintenance bursary — up to £2,092 per year

Individual learning accounts (Wales) — up to £200 per year
Welsh Assembly learning grant — up to £1,500 per year

Higher education

Full-time undergraduates

Adult dependants' grant
England — up to £2,642 per year
Northern Ireland — up to £2,695 per year
Wales — up to £2,647 per year

Childcare grant
One child (England/Northern Ireland) — up to £148.75 per week
Two or more children (England/Northern Ireland) — up to £255 per week
One child (Wales) — up to £161.50 per week
Two or more children (Wales) — up to £274.55 per week

Disabled students' allowance (England)
Non-medical personal helper — up to £20,520 per academic year
Major items of specialist equipment — up to £5,161 for duration of course
Other expenditure — up to £1,724 per academic year
Additional expenditure on travel — full reimbursement

per year

Disabled students' allowance (Northern Ireland)

Non-medical personal helper	up to £20,938 per academic year
Major items of specialist equipment	up to £5,266 for duration of course
Other expenditure	up to £1,759 per academic year
Additional expenditure on travel	full reimbursement

Disabled students' allowance (Wales)

Non-medical personal helper	up to £20,520 per academic year
Major items of specialist equipment	up to £5,166 for duration of course
Other expenditure	up to £1,729 per academic year

Higher education bursary (Northern Ireland)	up to £2,000 per year
Higher education grant (England and Wales)	up to £1,000 per year
Maintenance grant (England)	up to £2,906 per year
Maintenance grant (Northern Ireland)	up to £3,475 per year
Parents' learning allowance (England and Wales)	up to £1,508 per year
Parents' learning allowance (Northern Ireland)	up to £1,538 per year
Special support grant (England and pre-2010 cohort in Wales)	up to £2,906 per year
Special support grant (2010 cohort in Wales)	up to £5,000 per year
Special support grant (Northern Ireland)	up to £3,475 per year

Student loan (England, 2009 and 2010 cohorts)	*Full year*	*Final year*
Living away from home, studying in London	£6,928	£6,307
Living away from home, studying outside London	£4,950	£4,583
Living at home	£3,838	£3,483

Note: 28% of the student loan is means tested. The rate of loan may be reduced if you are eligible for a maintenance grant.

Student loan (England, pre-2009 cohort students, and Wales)	*Full year*	*Final year*
Living away from home, studying in London	£6,643	£6,048
Living away from home, studying outside London	£4,745	£4,391
Living at home	£3,673	£3,319

Note: 25% of the student loan is means tested. The rate of loan may be reduced if you are eligible for a maintenance grant or Welsh Assembly learning grant.

Student loan (Northern Ireland)	*Full year*	*Final year*
Living away from home, studying in London	£6,780	£6,170
Living away from home, studying outside London	£4,840	£4,480
Living at home	£3,750	£3,390

per year

Note: 25% of the student loan is means tested. The rate of loan may be reduced if you are eligible for a higher education bursary or maintenance grant.

Tuition fee grant (old system students)	up to £1,310 per year
Tuition fee grant (new system, pre-2010 cohort Welsh-domiciled students in Wales)	up to £1,980 per year
Tuition fee loan	up to £3,290 per year
Welsh Assembly learning grant (Wales)	
Old system students	up to £1,500 per year
New system students, pre-2010 cohort	up to £2,906 per year
New system students, 2010 cohort	
Part-time undergraduates	up to £5,000 per year
Course costs grant (England and Northern Ireland)	up to £265 per year
Tuition fee grant (England and Northern Ireland)	
Course intensity equivalent to:	
50–59% of a full-time course	up to £820 per year
60–74%	up to £985 per year
75%+	up to £1,230 per year
Tuition fee grant (Wales)	
Course intensity equivalent to:	
50–59% of a full-time course	up to £650 per year
60–74%	up to £780 per year
75%+	up to £975 per year
Welsh Assembly learning grant	up to £1,095 per year

Healthcare students

Means-tested bursary (England and Wales)	Old system	New system
Studying in London	up to £3,129 per year	up to £3,392 per year
Studying elsewhere	up to £2,548 per year	up to £2,810 per year
Living in parental home (London or elsewhere)	up to £2,084 per year	up to £2,346 per year

Means-tested bursary (Northern Ireland)	
Living away from parental home	up to £2,355 per year
Living in parental home	up to £1,920 per year

Non-means-tested bursary (England and Wales)	Old system	New system
Studying in London	£7,566 per year	£7,827
Studying elsewhere	£6,438 per year	£6,701

		per year
Living in parental home (London or elsewhere)	£6,438 per year	£6,701

Non-means-tested bursary (Northern Ireland)

Old system – aged under 26 at start of course	£6,055 per year
Old system – aged over 26 at start of course	£6,820 per year
New system	£6,055 per year

Reduced-rate student loan (England and Wales)	*Full year*	*Final year*
Studying in London	£3,263	£2,498
Studying outside London	£2,324	£1,811
Living in parental home (London or elsewhere)	£1,744	£1,324

Student loan (Northern Ireland)	*Full year*	*Final year*
Living away from parental home	£2,324	£1,811
Living in parental home	£1,744	£1,324

Note: there are a range of supplementary grants for healthcare students not listed here. See Chapter 6 for further details.

Social work students

NHS BSA social work bursary (England)

Studying in London	up to £4,975 per year
Studying elsewhere	up to £4,575 per year
CCW social work bursary (Wales)	£2,500 per year
OSS social work bursary (Northern Ireland)	£4,000 per year

Teacher training students

Graduate teacher programme (England)

Salary	minimum £15,461 per year
Training grant (to school)	up to £5,630 per year

Registered teacher programme (England)

Salary	minimum £15,461 per year
Training grant (to school)	£9,100 per year

Secondary undergraduate placement grants (Wales)

Shortage subjects	£1,200 per year
Non-shortage subjects	£600 per year

Teacher training bursary (England and Wales)

There are three levels of teacher training	£4,000 per year
bursary paid. The level you receive depends	£9,000 per year
on the subject you are training to teach. See	£6,000 per year

www.tda.gov.uk for which subjects attract which level.

Welsh medium improvement supplement (Wales)

Science and maths	£1,800 per year
Other subjects	£1,500 per year

per year

Postgraduates

See p63 for a table of research council and research board stipend rates.

Other sources

Professional and career development loans

£300 to £10,000
for duration of course

Part 1

Student support

Chapter 1

Further education student support

This chapter covers:
1. Student support in England (below)
2. Student support in Wales (p12)
3. Student support in Northern Ireland (p15)

Financial support available for further education students is generally split between those aged 16 to 19 and those aged 19 and over. Most of the statutory funding available is for the former group; a range of discretionary support is available for both.

1. Student support in England

Support for learners in England is funded by the Young People's Learning Agency (YPLA) and the Skills Funding Agency (SFA). However, most of the administration of learner support for both age groups is provided through one central learner support service, the Learner Support Directorate.

Support for 16–19-year-olds

Tuition fees

Subject to certain residency conditions, if you are under 19 on 31 August prior to your enrolment and beginning either a full- or part-time further education (FE) course funded by the YPLA, you do not have to pay tuition fees. Some private colleges, however, may ask for a fee.

Schools' access funds

Local authorities administer a needs-based fund for school pupils aged 16 or over but under 19. The funds are aimed at groups with low staying-on rates, but high achievers should not be excluded. Payments are in the form of grants and each local authority has its own eligibility criteria.

Education maintenance allowances

The education maintenance allowance[1] (EMA) is a statutory financial award aimed at supporting young people from low-income households who undertake a full-time FE course in college, school or certain work-based learning programmes, such as Foundation Learning.

It consists of a weekly payment of £10, £20 or £30 (income dependent) during term time only. Prior to the 2010/11 academic year, certain additional bonuses were also awarded periodically but they have now been withdrawn.

EMA is generally paid for two years, although a third year may be possible depending on your circumstances.

Who is eligible

In order to apply for an education maintenance allowance, you must meet the course and personal eligibility criteria.

You must be participating in a programme of full-time education (at least 12 guided learning hours for at least 10 weeks) at a recognised school, sixth form college, FE college or work-based learning provider. You must not be receiving any Department for Education (DfE), Department for Business, Innovation and Skills (BIS) or other government funding that would prevent you from receiving an education maintenance allowance – eg, a dance and drama award, jobseeker's allowance (JSA) or NHS bursary.

You must also fulfil certain residency requirements. You must be:

- a UK citizen or a person who is 'settled' in the UK within the meaning of the Immigration Act 1971 (ie, you have the right of abode or indefinite leave to enter or remain in the UK), and ordinarily resident in the UK for the three years prior to the start of the course; *or*
- a citizen of the European Union (EU) (or the spouse, civil partner or child of an EU citizen), and ordinarily resident in the European Economic Area (EEA – ie, the countries of the EU plus Norway, Liechtenstein and Iceland) or Switzerland for three years prior to the start of the course; *or*
- an EEA or Turkish migrant worker (or the spouse, civil partner or child of such a person) ordinarily resident in the UK at the start of the course and ordinarily resident in the EEA for the three years prior to the start of the course; *or*
- an officially recognised refugee or her/his spouse, civil partner or child, or have been granted humanitarian protection, or have EU temporary protection.

Note: some temporary absences abroad may be disregarded when assessing your entitlement. Rules on residency are complicated, so if you are in doubt, speak to an adviser in the student services department in your college or contact the National Union of Students (NUS – see Appendix 2).

You are eligible to apply for an education maintenance allowance if you turn 17, 18 or 19 between 1 September 2010 and 31 August 2011. An allowance may be available if you turned 20 between 1 September 2009 and 31 August 2010 and have a letter from a Connexions personal adviser stating that you should be eligible.

Payments

Payments are available for up to three full academic years and are dependent on your fulfilling the conditions laid out in your contract (see p6). How much you receive depends on your household income, which is assessed at the start of the year.

The income assessed is usually that of your parents, guardians or other main carers. If you live with only one parent, your other parent will not be assessed and any maintenance s/he pays will not be counted as income. The income assessed is that earned in the preceding full tax year – eg, for applications made for autumn 2010, this is the 2009/10 tax year. Any income you have (eg, from a part-time job) is not included. If you are a parent and you care for a child yourself, you are assessed on your own income.

If you live with foster parents or are in the care of the local authority, you automatically receive the full allowance, although you will have to provide proof of your status, such as a letter from the local authority. If you do not live with your parents or other carers and receive income support (IS), you will also automatically receive the full allowance.

You can also apply for 'estrangement' status if your relationship with your parents has broken down. Receipt of IS will be accepted as proof of this, otherwise a letter from a senior manager at your learning provider should be included with your application.

If your household has applied for tax credits, all you need to submit is the tax credit award notice, otherwise you, or your parents or carers, must send appropriate evidence, such as a P60 form from an employer. Photocopies of these documents will be accepted as evidence. Social security benefits, including child benefit, are disregarded when calculating your household income. The education maintenance allowance payments are disregarded for the purpose of calculating your family's entitlement to means-tested benefits. Therefore, if you or your family are claiming benefits, you can receive an education maintenance allowance in addition to them.

You are eligible for the full payment of £30 a week if your gross (before-tax) annual household income is £20,817 or less. A payment of £20 a week is made if your gross household income is between £20,818 and £25,521. A payment of £10 a week is made if your gross household income is between £25,522 and £30,810. If your gross household income is over £30,810 a year, you are not eligible for an allowance.

Applications made after the start of the course can only be backdated for 28 days, so it is crucial that applicants apply within 28 days of the start of their course.

Education maintenance allowance agreement

In order to receive your weekly payments you are required to sign an education maintenance allowance agreement. This is provided by your school, college or learning provider and sets out what you are expected to achieve in terms of attendance and academic work. This document is signed by you, your parents (or another responsible adult) and the learning provider. If you fail to meet part of the contract in any week (eg, fail to attend classes or hand in homework), you will not be paid your allowance for that week.

Although weekly payments are dependent on 100 per cent attendance, some types of absence are permitted or 'authorised'. However, it is advisable to notify the college of any absences if you want to be considered for your payment and any bonuses, particularly if you know in advance that you will be absent.

These authorised absences can include such events as sickness, unavoidable medical appointments, religious holidays, emergency caring duties, a driving test, a family funeral, or representative duties such as a college governors' meeting or official business of NUS.

Note that jury service would not normally be considered an authorised absence, as the guidance states you should seek deferral of your service to a holiday period or until after the course.

Holidays are not generally considered acceptable reasons for absence, but if you are on a Foundation Learning employment-based course, you may be able to accrue 'authorised absences' as a form of holiday entitlement. Speak to your provider for more information.

Colleges make the final decision on authorised absences and you should discuss with your own provider any absence you may have to take.

Applications

To apply for the scheme, contact your school, college, learning provider or local authority and request an education maintenance allowance application pack. Further details can also be found at http://ema.direct.gov.uk or telephone 0800 121 8989.

Care to Learn

Care to Learn is a scheme funded by the YPLA to help young parents in England pay for childcare costs while in full-time or part-time further education, Foundation Learning or other non-employed work-based learning schemes. If you are eligible, the scheme will pay for the costs of registered childcare while you are at school, college or on placement, including fees that must be paid during holidays, plus the cost of transport to and from the childcare provider. You can claim up to a maximum of £175 a week per child if you live in any of the 31 London boroughs or the City of London, or up to £160 a week per child if you live elsewhere. It does not affect, nor is it affected by, social security benefits.

The scheme does not allow double funding, so if you are in receipt of government childcare help through working tax credit or a learning programme funded by the European Social Fund, you cannot claim Care to Learn.

You can apply if you were aged under 20 on 1 August 2010, living in England and caring for your own child(ren). You must want to start or continue a publicly funded course at school or sixth-form college, or to start a course at an FE college. If you are studying on a course in Scotland or Wales, you can receive Care to Learn but your normal place of residence must be in England.

The scheme only funds registered or approved childcare. If you are uncertain whether or not your childcare is registered or approved, speak to your college's student services department. If you have informal childcare arrangements, you may still apply for support through the discretionary support funds (see p8).

You will have to meet residency conditions similar to those for education maintenance allowances (see p4). However, there are some differences: asylum seekers under the age of 18 are able to receive Care to Learn (but not EMA). Asylum seekers aged 18 or 19 can only receive Care to Learn if they are care leavers.

Further information (including how to apply) can be found at www.direct.gov.uk/caretolearn or by phoning the helpline on 0800 121 8989.

Transport

Local authorities have responsibility for ensuring appropriate provision of home-to-school or -college transport for those aged 16 to 18,[2] although this might not be free of charge. Contact your college or local authority for further information, or go to http://moneytolearn.direct.gov.uk for details of local policies. Many colleges and sixth-form colleges provide subsidised transport and you should also ask them for details.

Residential bursaries

If a course you want to do is not available locally, you may be able to get help with accommodation for a course further afield. Some specialist colleges which concentrate on agriculture, horticulture or art and design offer residential bursaries through the discretionary support funds. There are 50 of these colleges and a list is available at http://moneytolearn.direct.gov.uk – see p8 for more details about assistance from the discretionary support funds. The bursaries are available for full-time study and are also available for travel costs if you have to live at home but travel significant distances to college.

If you wish to study a course not on the list mentioned above, but which is not available locally, you may be able to receive help under the Residential Support Scheme. This offers up to £3,458 per year (£4,079 in London) for accommodation costs if the course you want to do is your first level 2 or level 3 qualification, requires 15 hours' attendance a week, is at least 10 weeks long and is not available within 15 miles or a two-hour return journey from your home. What you receive will depend on your family income, and you must be ordinarily resident in England. More information and an application pack are available from http://moneytolearn.direct.gov.uk, telephone 0800 121 8989.

Disabled students

Colleges administer additional support for disabled students locally. If you have additional needs or costs related to your disability, speak to your college's disability support officer for information about how to access extra help.

Asylum seekers

Although most public funds are not available, if you are an asylum seeker aged under 19 you can apply to the college's discretionary support funds (see below) for financial assistance. If you are under 18 (or under 20 and a care leaver) and have childcare costs, you can also apply to Care to Learn (see p6). Asylum seekers are *not* eligible for EMA.

For other sources of funding, you may also wish to contact the Educational Grants Advisory Service at www.family-action.org.uk/grants or the Ruth Hayman Trust at www.ruthhaymantrust.com.

Discretionary support funds

If you are studying at a college, including sixth-form colleges, you may be able to get additional help for your living or course costs through the discretionary support funds. These are amounts of money given to colleges by the YPLA and the Skills Funding Agency for students in need and are administered differently from higher education funds. There are three types of payments:

- hardship funds;
- residential bursaries (see p7); *and*
- childcare support.

Hardship funds

These are open to all students studying at some colleges who meet the personal, residential and course conditions (see p53). The funds are used to 'anticipate need', to act as a safety net for students and for innovative initiatives. Examples of payments include:

- means-tested bursaries;
- purchasing 'benefits' or support, or offering equipment or services at low cost;
- small payments to meet the costs of equipment;
- childcare costs for over-19-year-olds only (under-19-year-olds must use the Care to Learn scheme – see p6);
- tuition fees for ESOL (English for speakers of other languages) courses or otherwise in exceptional circumstances.

Local colleges have the discretion to decide how to prioritise spending and to stipulate their assessment criteria, which means the exact nature and levels of support available to you will depend on your college. The college must, nevertheless, have an appeals procedure to challenge decisions.

If you are receiving an education maintenance allowance, you can still receive payments from the hardship funds if you can demonstrate you have additional costs not provided for by your EMA payment. If you are in exceptional need, a loan may be provided from the funds.

Childcare support

Support can be used to meet the costs of any registered childcare for learners aged 20 or over. The support available is highly unlikely to be more than that available through the Care to Learn scheme (approximately £5,000 per child), but this may differ from college to college. Funds can be paid directly to the childcare provider or directly to you. Again, this depends on college policy. If you are aged under 20 and starting a new course, you should apply to the Care to Learn scheme (see p6) for help with registered childcare.

Support for students aged 19 and over

Tuition fees

Unlike learners under the age of 19, adult learners aged 19 or over do not have universal free tuition in further education.

Adult entitlement to learning

Adult learners in England do have a legal entitlement to free tuition in certain circumstances.[3] These include courses for basic literacy and numeracy, vocational training that leads to their first Level 2 qualification (the equivalent of five GCSEs at grades A*–C, although note that GCSEs themselves are not funded under this entitlement) or, if you are under age 25 at the start of the course, your first full Level 3 qualification.

If you qualify, the SFA will pay your tuition fees for the course. Check with your college or learning provider that you and your course are both eligible; there are residency conditions.

Tuition fee remission

Where an adult does not qualify under the legal entitlement, s/he may still be able to qualify for fee remission. Colleges can opt into a voluntary system of fee remission for anyone who is aged 19 and over and who is:

- on means-tested benefits or contribution-based JSA;
- an unwaged dependant of anyone in receipt of means-tested benefits, pension credit or contribution-based JSA;
- in receipt of working tax credit and with a gross (before-tax) income of £15,276;
- undertaking an English course because s/he is not currently fluent in that language.

When a college opts into this system, you are exempt from fee payment and the YPLA or SFA compensates the college for 100 per cent of your fees. Check whether your college offers fee remission through this system.

If you are not in any of the above groups, you may have to pay tuition fees. If you are having problems meeting the costs of fees, you should approach the college's student services to inquire about help through the discretionary support funds (see p8).

Adult learning grants

Adult learning grants are available across England.[4] These are grants of up to £30 a week for full-time learners aged over 19 who are studying for their first full Level 2 or Level 3 qualification.

Course requirements

Your course must lead to either your first Level 2 or Level 3 qualification. Your college will be able to tell you if this is the case. It must involve at least 450 hours of guided learning in the year, or at least 12 hours a week. It also has to be approved by the SFA – again, your college can tell you if this is the case.

Residence requirements

You must fulfil certain residency requirements. You must be either:

- a UK citizen or a person who is 'settled' in the UK within the meaning of the Immigration Act 1971 (ie, you have the right of abode or indefinite leave to enter or remain in the UK), and ordinarily resident in the UK for the three years prior to the start of the course; *or*
- a citizen of the EU or Switzerland (or her/his spouse, civil partner or child), and ordinarily resident in the EEA (the countries of the EU plus Norway, Liechtenstein and Iceland) or Switzerland for three years prior to the start of the course; *or*
- an EEA or Swiss migrant worker (or the spouse, civil partner or child of such a person) ordinarily resident in the UK at the start of the course and ordinarily resident in the EEA or Switzerland for the three years prior to the start of the course; *or*
- an officially recognised refugee or her/his spouse, civil partner or child, or have been granted humanitarian protection, or have EU temporary protection.

Note: some temporary absences abroad may be disregarded when assessing your entitlement. Rules on residency are complicated, so if you are in doubt, speak to an adviser in your college's student services department or contact the NUS.

Applications

You can get an application form from the student services department at your college, or by calling 0800 121 8989.

Income assessment

The grants are means tested and if you are in receipt of any out-of-work benefits, such as IS, incapacity benefit or JSA, you cannot claim an additional adult learning grant. However, other benefits such as housing benefit, child benefit and disability benefits do not affect your entitlement to a grant.

The income of any cohabiting partner (of the same or opposite sex, whether or not you are married or in a civil partnership) will also be taken into account when assessing your entitlement. Grants are available to single students with an income in the 2009/10 tax year of less than £19,513 and to students with cohabiting partners with a joint income of less than £30,810.

Note that if you are on an apprenticeship programme or in receipt of Train to Gain funding, you cannot claim the grant.

Payments

In order to receive adult learning grant payments, your attendance on your course must be satisfactory. Your weekly payment may be stopped if you are absent without authorisation. Authorised absences can include events such as sickness, unavoidable medical appointments, religious holidays, emergency caring duties or a family funeral. The college or learning provider has discretion over which absences are considered authorised – where possible, you should inform them in advance of any expected absence.

Sixth-form childcare

This allowance has been withdrawn for the 2010/11 academic year. Adult learners in sixth-form colleges who have childcare costs should apply to the discretionary support funds for additional support.

If you previously received this funding and remain on the course, transitional arrangements should be put in place by your learning provider – discuss these with them.

Free Childcare for Training and Learning for Work

This allowance has also been withdrawn for the 2010/11 academic year. Adult learners who qualified for childcare support through this scheme should apply to the discretionary support funds for additional support.

If you previously received this funding and remain on the course, transitional arrangements should be put in place by your learning provider – discuss these with them.

Disabled students

The system for students over 19 is the same as for younger students. See p8.

Discretionary support funds

If you are studying at a college, you may be able to get additional help for your living or course costs, including childcare, through the discretionary support funds. See p8 for more details.

Other grants

City and Guilds bursaries

For students on qualifying City and Guilds or National Proficiency Tests Council (NPTC) courses, a small number of bursaries are available to help with the costs of study.

Applicants must be living in the UK and intend to study in the UK to qualify. Applications are considered twice a year, in April and September. For more information, see www.cityandguilds.com/bursaries.

New Deal education and training option

If you are placed on the New Deal scheme by your Jobcentre Plus office, it may be possible for you to take advantage of the education and training option to gain qualifications which will enhance your employability while still receiving an allowance equivalent to the benefits you would otherwise receive. The maximum permitted length of the course is one year. Those aged 18 to 24 can study up to NVQ Level 2, while those aged 24 and over may study up to NVQ Level 3. There is some discretion on the part of your New Deal adviser to allow you to study a more advanced qualification if you already possess these levels at the 'maximum' level. The option is not available to those on the 50-plus scheme.

National traineeships and apprenticeships

Both these schemes are designed to allow 16–24-year-olds to enter work-based education and gain an NVQ while earning. More information is available from the National Apprenticeship Service website at www.apprenticeships.org.uk.

Professional and career development loans

Students on further education courses can apply for professional and career development loans (see p86). However, you should consider carefully whether or not this is the most affordable option for you and seek financial advice where possible.

2. **Student support in Wales**

Support for 16–19-year-olds

Tuition fees

Subject to certain residency conditions, if you are under 19 on 31 August prior to your enrolment and beginning either a full- or part-time further education (FE) course funded by the Welsh Assembly, you do not have to pay tuition fees. Some private colleges, however, may ask for a fee.

Education maintenance allowances

In Wales, the education maintenance allowance scheme (EMA) is similar to that in England (see p4), and the same residency rules apply. However, due to recent policy changes, there are various differences between the schemes, which are outlined below.

Course eligibility

The EMA in Wales is not available to learners on work-based learning programmes.

Weekly payments

Learners in Wales are paid fortnightly instead of weekly.

The income bands are also different. In Wales, you are eligible for the full payment of £30 a week if your gross (before tax) annual household income is £21,885 or less. A payment of £20 a week is made if your gross household income is between £21,886 and £26,840. A payment of £10 a week is made if your gross household income is between £26,841 and £32,400. If your gross household income is over £32,400 a year, you are not eligible for an allowance.

The Welsh Assembly has announced that it plans to scrap the £10 and £20 bands in the 2011/12 academic year, and align the income threshold for the £30 band with other student finance products (exact details of this were unavailable at time of writing).

Bonuses

While periodic bonuses have been scrapped in England, they remain in Wales.

In January and July of each year, a £100 bonus is available for learners in receipt of EMA if you have met the goals set by the school or college in your EMA contract (see p6). Note that the Welsh Assembly intends to scrap bonuses from the 2011/12 academic year.

More information on Welsh EMAs can be found at www.studentfinancewales.co.uk.

Passport to Study grants

Some local authorities in Wales offer extra funding for young people in further education whose parents are out of work, or receiving benefits because of having a low income or a disability. These are usually called Passport to Study grants and normally come in the form of assistance with travel costs. Contact your local authority to see if it offers any such funding, and what terms and conditions apply.

Financial Contingency Fund

If you are studying at a college, you may be able to get additional help for your living or course costs from the Financial Contingency Fund. This operates in a broadly similar manner to the discretionary support funds in England. See p8 for more details.

Support for students aged 19 and over

Tuition fees

There is no statutory fee remission if you are aged 19 or over. However, some colleges may run schemes that provide full or partial remission if, for example, you are on a low income or in receipt of means-tested benefits. Ask your college what it provides.

Individual learning accounts

The Welsh Assembly has a scheme for individual learning accounts for students in Wales who have no or low qualifications.[5] If you do not hold a qualification above Level 2 (ie, above GCSE level, GNVQ intermediate or NVQ Level 2), you may be entitled to a grant of up to £200 to help pay tuition fees or for certain materials on courses that lead to qualifications up to Level 3 – ie, A level, GNVQ higher or NVQ Level 3. How much you receive depends on your personal circumstances. More information can be found at www.ilawales.co.uk or from Careers Advice on 0800 100 900.

The Welsh Assembly intends to close this scheme from 30 March 2011 and the last applications will be taken on 24 September 2010.

Welsh Assembly learning grants

If you are aged 19 or over and on a low income, you may be eligible for a means-tested Welsh Assembly learning grant for further education of up to £1,500.[6] A grant of at least £450 is available if you are on a full-time course (500 contact hours or more a year) and your family income is below £17,700. If your household income is below £11,791, £750 is available. The full £1,500 will be offered if your household income is less than £5,896. Part-time students (those who have between 275 and 499 contact hours a year) can receive a reduced grant of £300, £450 or £750 on the same salary bands.

The grants are administered through Welsh local authorities, but students may attend any institution in the UK. More information is available at www.studentfinancewales.co.uk.

Financial Contingency Fund

If you are studying at a college, you may be able to get additional help for your living or course costs from the Financial Contingency Fund. This operates in a broadly similar manner to the discretionary support funds in England. See p8 for more details.

Other grants

New Deal education and training option

Welsh students may be able to receive the New Deal education and training option. See p12 for details.

Modern apprenticeships

Both these schemes are designed to allow 16–24-year-olds to enter work-based education and gain an NVQ while earning. More information is available from Careers Wales at www.careerswales.com.

3. Student support in Northern Ireland

Support for 16–19-year-olds

Tuition fees

If you are a full-time student, you will have your tuition fees paid in full. If you are a part-time student, concessionary tuition fees may apply.

Education maintenance allowances

In Northern Ireland the education maintenance allowance (EMA) scheme is similar to that in England (see p4). However, with recent policy changes there are now differences.

Course eligibility

In Northern Ireland your course must consist of at least 15 guided learning hours per week rather than 12, and EMAs are not available to students on work-based learning programmes. Students in Northern Ireland are entitled to an education maintenance allowance if they turned 16, 17, 18 or 19 between 2 July 2009 and 1 July 2010.

Weekly payments

In Northern Ireland, you are paid EMAs fortnightly instead of weekly.

The thresholds for payment are also different. In Northern Ireland, you are eligible for the full payment of £30 a week if your gross (before tax) annual household income is £22,331 or less. A payment of £20 a week is made if your gross household income is between £22,332 and £27,338. A payment of £10 a week is made if your gross household income is between £27,339 and £33,062. If your gross household income is over £33,062 a year, you are not eligible for an allowance.

Bonuses

Periodic bonuses have been scrapped in England; however they remain in Northern Ireland.

In January and July of each year, a £100 bonus is available for learners in receipt of EMA, if you have met the goals set by the school or college in your EMA contract (see p6).

More information on Northern Irish EMAs can be found at www.emani.gov.uk.

Care to Learn

The Department for Employment and Learning's Care to Learn scheme is designed to help young parents in Northern Ireland pay for childcare costs while in full- or part-time further education. If you are eligible, the scheme will pay for the costs of registered childcare while you are at school, college or on placement, including fees that must be paid during holidays, plus the cost of transport to and from the childcare provider, up to a maximum of £165 per child per week. It does not affect, nor is it affected by, social security benefits.

You can apply if you are aged 16 or over but under 19 at the start of your course of study, live in Northern Ireland and fulfil certain residency requirements, and you care for your own child(ren). You must wish to start or continue a publicly funded course at school or sixth-form college, or to start a course at a further education (FE) college. If you are already receiving childcare funding from other government sources, you are not eligible for this scheme and should apply to the college's support fund if that funding is inadequate.

The scheme will only fund childcare from a provider registered with the Health and Social Care Board. If you have informal childcare arrangements, you can still apply for support through your college's support fund.

Further information (including details of how to apply) should be available from your college.

Support for students aged 19 and over

Tuition fees

Tuition fee remission is provided if you are studying a full-time eligible vocational course up to Level 3 – ie, GNVQ higher or NVQ Level 3.

A '**full-time course**' is defined as a course lasting a minimum of 30 weeks and consisting of at least 15 hours and at least seven sessions per week, or 21 hours per week with no sessional requirement. GCSE, A level or AS level subjects are not eligible except when studied in combination with a relevant vocational qualification at a similar level. If your course does not qualify for tuition fee remission, you may be able to receive help from your college support fund.

Further education awards

If you are on a full-time FE course, you can apply to the local education and library board (ELB) for a non-repayable maintenance grant called a further education award (previously known as discretionary awards). These awards can also provide additional help with tuition fees if required. There are also extra allowances similar to those available for higher education students (see pp58–59) to students with dependants, disabled students and care leavers. All parts of these grants (apart from the disabled students' allowances) are means tested.

There are residency requirements, and you cannot be in receipt of another award, such as an education maintenance allowance or Department of Agriculture and Rural Development grant (see p18), at the same time. Although the awards are no longer being referred to as 'discretionary', they remain so – funds are insufficient to provide all applicants with grants and you should apply as soon as possible.

Note: the closing date for applications for each year is the end of June prior to the start of the course for full-time students and the end of September for part-time students.

Most courses in further education study in Northern Ireland do not attract a fee (see p16). However, you may be charged a fee if, for example, you study in mainland Britain. In 2010/11, tuition fees of up to £930 can be paid as part of the FE award.

You may qualify for a means-tested bursary for maintenance of up to £2,092. The maximum amount is available if your household income is less than £21,331, and a partial amount on incomes between £21,331 and £38,805. No maintenance grant is payable if your household income exceeds £38,805.

Support for dependants

If you have children or an adult dependant, you can claim for a childcare grant, parents' learning allowance or adult dependant's grant on the same basis as higher education students in Northern Ireland (see p59).

Disabled students

Disabled students who require additional support should apply to their college or learning provider for assistance. Contact the disability adviser at the college in the first instance.

Part-time courses

Part-time courses attract funding at lower levels. If a fee is charged, you may qualify for fee support of up to £465 a year. A means-tested course costs grant of up to £265 is available for students with an income of up to £25,000.

For further information on FE awards, see www.education-support.org.uk/students/feaa, or contact the Further Education Awards Section, Western Education and Library Board, 1 Hospital Road, Omagh, Co Tyrone BT79 0AW, tel: 028 8225 4546 or email: feawards@welbni.org.

Support funds

There are two discretionary funds administered by colleges that offer additional help if you are a part-time or full-time FE student aged 19 or over. Support funds are aimed at those experiencing financial difficulties and may include help with living costs and/or fees (eligibility criteria apply). The additional support funds are aimed at students with learning difficulties who are not in receipt of other help for disabled students, such as a disabled students' allowance, and can be used to pay for additional human or technical support, such as IT hardware.

Other grants

Department of Agriculture and Rural Development grant

If you are attending an FE course at the Enniskillen, Greenmount or Loughry campuses of the College of Agriculture, Food and Rural Enterprise, you may be eligible for financial support from the Department of Agriculture and Rural Development.

To be eligible, you must be ordinarily resident in Northern Ireland and fulfil certain other residency requirements. You can be any age.

Support comes in the form of a means-tested living costs grant of up to £1,659 if you live in your parents' home or up to £2,362 if you do not. Further allowances may be available if you have children or adult dependants, or if you are a care leaver or have a disability which means you have extra costs associated with study.

Further information can be found at www.education-support.org.uk/students/feaa. Applications should be made to: Further Education Awards Section, Western Education and Library Board, 1 Hospital Road, Omagh, Co Tyrone BT79 0AW, tel: 028 8225 4546 or email: feawards@welbni.org.

Notes

1. **Student support in England**
   1 While the power to provide education maintenance allowances is in s14 Education Act 2002, DfE does not make detailed regulations for the national scheme. However, the full guidance can be found at http://ema.ypla.gov.uk/resources/guidance.
   2 s509 EA 1996
   3 s86 ESA 2008
   4 Adult Learning Grant Guidance, SFA, June 2010

2. **Student support in Wales**
   5 ILA(W) Regs
   6 E(ALGS)(W) Regs

Chapter 2

....

Undergraduate student support: England

This chapter covers:
1. Full-time undergraduates (below)
2. Part-time undergraduates (p35)
3. Discretionary funds (p37)

....

Basic facts

– Undergraduate students can apply for a mixture of grants and loans, depending on their personal circumstances.

– The support available in England differs to that available in Wales, Northern Ireland and Scotland.

– Separate provision applies to healthcare and initial teacher training students.

– Social work students may be eligible for a social work bursary in addition to the standard package of grants and loans.

– Access to Learning funds are available for those in financial difficulty.

....

The type of financial support you can receive when you are learning depends on several factors, including when you begin your course, the length of the course, the discipline you are studying, whether the course is full time or part time, and your age.

---

1. Full-time undergraduates

Full-time undergraduates in England on eligible courses (see p53) and who are personally eligible (see p23) can apply for financial assistance from the Department for Business, Innovation and Skills (BIS). Separate provision is available for part-time undergraduates (see p35) and those studying degree or higher diploma courses in healthcare (see p67).

Support in Wales, Northern Ireland and Scotland

Welsh, Northern Irish and Scottish-domiciled students are funded under separate systems. See Chapter 3 for details of the system in Wales, Chapter 4 for details of the system in Northern Ireland and CPAG's *Benefits for Students in Scotland Handbook* for details in Scotland.

Students domiciled in England, but who wish to study in Wales, Northern Ireland or Scotland, receive the same package of support as for study in England, although fees in Scotland are charged in a different way (see p26).

Changes to student support in 2010/11 and 2011/12

Changes for 2010/11 are limited, with the main changes of substance being the withdrawal of eligibility for support for students on some types of flexible initial teacher training courses starting after 1 September 2010. The proposed repayment holiday for students graduating in 2010 or later, which would have allowed students to postpone their first loan repayments for up to five years (it was later amended to up to two years), has been cancelled.

Otherwise, student support rates have been frozen for 2010/11, with the exception of loans and grants for tuition fees, which will rise to match the increase in the maximum rates of fees.

Note also that since the 2009/10 academic year the Student Loans Company (SLC) has been responsible for assessing and processing student finance applications from all new students. The new service is known as Student Finance England (SFE) and prospective students intending to enter higher education (HE) should apply to SFE for support. Students who started their course in the 2008/09 academic year or earlier, and who are continuing on that course in 2010/11, should continue to apply to their local authority, except where that local authority is participating in a pilot scheme that previously transferred this function to the SLC.

From the 2011/12 academic year all student finance applications will go through Student Finance England, regardless of when the student started her/his course.

Old system and current system students

This chapter refers to 'old system' and 'current system' students. Whether you are classed as one or the other depends on when you started your course.

Students who entered higher education between 1 September 1998 and 1 September 2006

If you began your course between 1 September 1998 and 1 September 2006 and do not fit into the gap year provision explained below, you will receive financial help for student support as an 'old system' student.[1] Your university or college should charge you no more than £1,310 tuition fees in 2010/11 and you may be entitled to fee remission (see below).

Gap year students

Some gap year students who began in the 2006/07 academic year are treated as 'old system' students if they deferred entry to higher education from the 2005/06 academic year and had confirmed their place at their institution by 1 August 2005.[2] You must still be on that course or a course with similar content to qualify. If you think you should qualify, speak to an adviser.

Students who entered higher education on or after 1 September 2006

You qualify for support as a 'current system' student[3] if:

- you entered (or are entering) higher education for the first time in 2006 or later and do not fall under the gap year provisions outlined above;
- you started a Postgraduate Certificate in Education course on or after 1 September 2006;
- you have withdrawn from a previous course of study and did not arrange a transfer before leaving your previous course.

Some changes to student support made in 2008 affect only those students who started their course in the 2008/09 academic year. Such students are referred to as '2008 cohort' students in this chapter.

Similarly, some changes made in 2009 affect only those students who started their course in the 2009/10 academic year or later, and such students are referred to as '2009 cohort' students in this chapter.

Impact on fees and student support

In 2010/11, colleges and universities can charge fees of up to £3,290 a year in certain circumstances.[4] These circumstances are not necessarily the same as those for receiving student support for fees to that level, so it is important to check the amount of tuition fees you will be charged by your institution.

For example, if you began a course before 1 September 2006 and transfer to a similar course at the same institution, you will be charged no more than £1,310 tuition fees in 2010/11. If, however, you transfer to a similar course at a different institution or a different course at the same institution, you can be charged up to £3,290 each year. However, because you were receiving student support before 1 September 2006 and have not withdrawn from education, you will receive the student support package that you have always received – eg, an income-assessed tuition fee grant of a maximum of £1,310 and up to £1,000 HE grant, in addition to the maintenance loan and other supplementary grants for which you may be eligible.

Who is eligible for support

In order to receive help under any system you must be 'personally eligible' (see below) and studying an eligible course (see p23).

Personal eligibility

To be personally eligible for support you must meet the residence condition.[5] This usually means that you must:

- be settled in the UK within the meaning of the 1971 Immigration Act (this includes those with British citizenship, right of abode, or indefinite leave to enter/remain in the UK);
- be resident in England on the first day of the first academic year;
- have lived in the 'UK and Islands'[6] for three years immediately before the start of the course, although temporary absences for reasons such as vacations or temporary employment abroad can be disregarded. Service abroad in the regular UK armed forces is always disregarded;
- not have spent any of the three years in the 'UK and Islands' mainly for the purpose of receiving full-time education. If you were in full-time education during the three years, you can still receive support if you can prove this was not the main reason for your being in the UK.

Note: there are exceptions to these rules, many of which are complex. You may wish to speak to an adviser in your institution or students' union.

European Union nationals

Broadly, if you are a European Union (EU) national, you can qualify for 'home student' status (see below) if you have been resident in the UK for three years immediately before the start of the course and you are resident in England or Wales on the first day of the first academic year. If any of that time was spent mainly for the purpose of receiving full-time education, you must have been ordinarily resident in the UK, elsewhere in the European Economic Area (EEA) and/or Switzerland immediately before the three-year period. The EEA consists of the 27 member states of the EU plus Norway, Iceland and Liechtenstein.

Alternatively, if you have the 'right of permanent residence' after having become settled in the UK, you may qualify for 'home student' status. This can also be granted if you are a 'relevant family member' of a person with the right of permanent residence and you have been resident in the UK for three years or more.[7] However, if any of that time was spent mainly for the purpose of full-time education, you must have been resident in the UK or elsewhere in the EEA and/or Switzerland immediately before the three-year period.

If you are a national of an EU member state, or a 'relevant family member' of such a national, and coming to the UK to undertake higher education, you may be eligible for help with fees only. You must have lived in the EEA and/or Switzerland for three years prior to the start of your course, and no part of the three years can have been mainly for the purposes of full-time education. If a new country joins the EU, it is considered to have always been in the EEA when determining the three years' residency. Consequently, following Bulgaria and Romania's accession to the EU on 1 January 2007, for the purposes of assessing support they are regarded as having always been part of the EEA.

Migrant workers

If you are an EEA or Swiss migrant worker and are, or have been, working in the UK, or you are a 'relevant family member' of such a migrant worker, you may be eligible for support as a 'home student'. A **'home student'** is eligible for help with both tuition fees and living costs (subject to an income assessment). You must also have three years' residence in the EEA and/or Switzerland.

A 'relevant family member' includes children, a spouse or civil partner or, for EEA workers only, dependent direct ascendants such as parents or grandparents.

If you are a UK national and have been living in another EEA country or Switzerland and you return to the UK to study, you may be eligible for support as a 'home student'. You must apply for support in the part of the UK in which you were living before you left the country.[8]

Children of Turkish migrant workers can also receive home fees and support if their parents have been ordinarily resident in the UK and lawfully employed, and if the child is ordinarily resident in the UK on the first day of the first academic year of the course and has been ordinarily resident in the EEA, Switzerland and/or Turkey for the three years prior to the start of the course.[9]

Refugees

If you are recognised as a refugee by the UK Government and have lived in the 'UK and Islands' since being granted this status, or you are a 'relevant family member' of such a person (defined in this case as the person's spouse, civil partner or child), you should be treated as a 'home student' (see p22).[10]

If you applied for asylum and have been granted humanitarian protection or discretionary leave (or exceptional leave), you may be treated as a 'home student' for support if you received this leave before the start of the first day of the first academic year of your course and you meet the three-year residency criteria (see above).

Course eligibility

Broadly, the course must be full time (as defined by the education provider) and be:[11]

- a first degree (including foundation degrees);
- a diploma of higher education (DipHE);
- a BTEC higher national certificate (HNC) or higher national diploma (HND);
- a course of initial teacher training;
- a course for the further training of teachers, or youth or community workers;

- a course to prepare for certain professional examinations of a standard higher than A level, or BTEC HNC/HND where a first degree is not required for entry;
- a course not higher than a first degree, but higher than those described in the above bullet point.

Note that some courses, particularly in art and design, can require the student to undertake a 'foundation' year or course, which is different to a foundation degree. This is normally a course of one academic year in length which precedes the main higher education degree course.

Support for these courses is often much more limited as they usually do not fall within the definition of 'higher education'. You may be eligible for support as a further education student (see Chapter 1) – speak to an adviser in your students' union or institution for further guidance.

Confusingly, some courses in science, engineering or technology can have an integrated foundation year which will form part of the HE course and consequently attract HE funding. If in doubt about your entitlement, speak to an adviser.

Previous study

If you have previously attended an HE course, the amount of support you can receive may be affected by the rules on 'previous study'.[12]

If you are a new system student and hold an honours degree, support for any new qualification will be restricted to supplementary grants for travel costs, students with dependants and disabled students.[13]

Some exceptions apply: students who hold an honours degree and who are undertaking a Postgraduate Certificate in Education (PGCE) course receive full funding, while those undertaking a further undergraduate course in certain professional subjects such as medicine, veterinary science, architecture and social work can receive a maintenance loan for that course,[14] although not a loan for tuition fees or a maintenance or special support grant.

Note that financial support for students who wish to study a qualification of an equivalent or lower level to one that they already hold may be further restricted, as the Higher Education Funding Council for England will not provide funding to the higher education institution in the form of a teaching grant and tuition fees may therefore exceed the £3,290 cap. Again, some professional courses are exempted, but you should check entitlement with an adviser.

If you do not already hold an honours degree, then, in general, the maximum number of years of tuition fee loan and maintenance or special support grant funding you can receive is equivalent to the ordinary length of your course plus one year, less any years of study previously undertaken.[15] If you have studied part of a year, you will be treated as if you have undertaken a full year of study. Maintenance loan funding is, however, unaffected.

If you are transferring courses, or undertaking an 'end-on' course, these previous study rules will affect you. You may be able to secure additional years of 'full' funding if you were unable to complete a previous year or course for 'compelling personal reasons' such as illness or caring responsibilities[16] – you will have to provide evidence of this to Student Finance England.

Rules for old system students are slightly different but have broadly the same effect.

Further information on previous study is available from www.direct.gov.uk/studentfinance or from your student adviser.

Student support – old system students

Old system students (see p20), including those regarded as 'gap year students' in the 2006/07 academic year (see p21) are eligible to apply for a package of support which includes grants and loans for tuition fees and a higher education grant (see below). They can also apply for a student loan for living costs (see p27) and for supplementary grants in particular circumstances (see p29).

Tuition fees and loans

If you are an old system student you may be liable to pay a contribution towards your tuition fees, up to a maximum of £1,310 per academic year (rising each year with inflation). However, students with a low household income can receive help with all or some of this contribution.[17] Any help you receive from your local authority or Student Finance England towards your fees is subject to an assessment of your own and (where appropriate) your parents' or partner's income.

Any eligible continuing student who is liable for fees after the income assessment for the tuition fee grant has been carried out can take out a loan for the fees.[18] For example, if the local authority has agreed to pay £600 towards your fees, you can apply for a tuition fee loan for the remaining £710. Any such loan is repaid on the same basis as the loans for living costs (see p28).

Higher education grant

Students who started new courses between September 2004 and August 2006 (or who are treated as 'old system' students if they started their course in the 2006/07 academic year) are eligible for an HE grant of up to £1,000.[19] Students on full-time, sandwich and part-time initial teacher training courses are eligible to apply. However, if you started your course before September 2004, you are not eligible for this grant.

Student support – current system students

Current system students (see p21) are eligible to apply for a package of support which includes student loans for tuition fees and either a maintenance grant or special support grant (see p26). They can also apply for a student loan for living costs (see p27) and for supplementary grants in particular circumstances (see p29).

Tuition fees and loans

A current system student will fall within the variable fees regime in England. This means you may be liable for fees of up to £3,290 per academic year (rising each year with inflation).

Providing you are a home or EU student, you can apply for a non-income-assessed tuition fee loan to cover all or part of the cost of the fees.[20] The repayment terms are the same as for an income-contingent maintenance loan (see p28). In addition, you may be eligible for a grant of up to £2,906 and, in some circumstances, a bursary from your institution (see p35).

If you choose to study in Wales or Northern Ireland, the same arrangements apply. In Scotland, fees are fixed at £1,820 per year in 2010/11 for all courses other than medicine, for which the fees are £2,895 per year. Although these fees are lower, Scottish courses are normally one year longer than their English counterparts. As with study in England, you can take out a non-income-assessed tuition fee loan to pay for all or part of the fee charged.

If you wish to pay all or part of the fee in cash in advance, you can do so. Your institution will generally expect some indication of how you intend to pay your fees when you register.

Maintenance grant

The maintenance grant is available to students from low-income backgrounds who commenced their studies on or after 1 September 2006.[21] This grant is payable for maintenance costs and the maximum rate in 2010/11 is £2,906.

Part of the grant substitutes part of the loan for living costs. For students who started their courses before the 2009/10 academic year, the loan is substituted pound for pound up to a maximum of £1,292 in 2010/11 – eg, if you receive a £900 maintenance grant, the maximum rate of loan you can borrow is reduced by £900. Any maintenance grant in excess of £1,292 does not further reduce the loan.

For 2009 cohort students, 50 pence of the loan is substituted for every pound of maintenance grant paid, so that the maximum substitution is £1,453 where the full maintenance grant is paid.[22]

If you are eligible for means-tested benefits, you should apply for the special support grant.

Special support grant

The special support grant is available to students from low-income backgrounds who commenced their studies on or after 1 September 2006 and who are eligible to receive means-tested benefits, such as income support or housing benefit.[23] The maximum rate is £2,906 in 2010/11. This grant is payable for course-related costs and is not taken into account as income when working out entitlement to means-tested benefits.

This grant is payable in addition to the full maintenance loan.

Student maintenance loans

Student maintenance loans are available to eligible 'old' and 'current' system students to help with living costs, such as food and rent. There are two different types of loan in existence.

Mortgage-style loans were available to those students who were eligible to receive mandatory awards (the system in place before 1998). These are no longer available to students currently in higher education, but see p28 for information on repayment.

Income-contingent loans form part of the help available to students under the present student support regulations. Part of the loan – 28 per cent for 2009 cohort students, 25 per cent for other students – is subject to an income assessment. The remaining 72 or 75 per cent is not income assessed. You may be entitled to an additional amount if your course exceeds 30 weeks and three days in the year (see below).

The rates for 2009 cohort students are different from those for other students – both sets of rates are set out below.

Maximum amount of income-contingent loan 2010/11 – 2009 cohort students[24]

	Full year	Final year
London	£6,928	£6,307
Elsewhere	£4,950	£4,583
Parental home	£3,838	£3,483
Overseas rate	£5,895	£5,125

Maximum amount of income-contingent loan 2010/11 – other students[25]

	Full year	Final year
London	£6,643	£6,048
Elsewhere	£4,745	£4,391
Parental home	£3,673	£3,319
Overseas rate	£5,653	£4,915

Long courses loan

You may be entitled to additional amounts of loan for any extra weeks of attendance over the standard 30 weeks and three days.

For students who started before 1 September 2008, this will simply be added to the standard loan amount paid. For 2008 and 2009 cohort students this additional amount is known specifically as the 'long courses loan' and is treated differently in the income assessment. In both cases, however, any additional amount is paid along with other forms of support at the start of each term, and is repaid along with other student loan debt.

The table below outlines the amount paid for each week your course exceeds the standard length. If your course year lasts 45 weeks or more, you will be paid for a full 52 weeks of attendance.

Amount of long courses loan 2010/11[26]

	Weekly amount
London	£106
Elsewhere	£83
Parental home	£54
Overseas rate	£115

Repayment

Both mortgage-style and income-contingent loans are repayable at the end of your studies. The repayment method differs for each type of loan. **Mortgage-style loans** are normally paid over 60 fixed monthly instalments from the April following your graduation or the point you otherwise leave your course, or 84 fixed monthly instalments if you had loans for five or more years.[27] However, you can request that repayments be deferred if you earn less than 85 per cent of the national average wage. In 2010/11 repayments can be deferred if your gross earnings do not exceed £2,204 a month.

Liability to repay mortgage-style loans can be cancelled in certain circumstances.[28] These are if:

- you die;
- you are permanently incapacitated from work because of a disability;
- you reach the age of 50 (or 60 if you were 40 or over when you last took out a loan);
- 25 years after the April following your graduation or the point at which you otherwise left your course,

whichever comes first.

The amount of money you pay back each month on an **income-contingent loan** depends on your earnings. From the April after you graduate or otherwise leave your course, you will begin to make repayments once you earn above £15,000 a year. Repayments start at a rate of 9 per cent of all income above that threshold.[29] For example, if you earn £16,000 a year, you will pay back 9 per cent of £1,000 – ie, £90 a year or £7.50 a month.

Liability to repay income-contingent loans can also be cancelled if you die or are permanently incapacitated from work because of a disability. If you are an 'old system' student, they are also cancelled if you reach the age of 65. 'Current system' students have their liability cancelled 25 years after the April following their graduation or when they otherwise left the course.[30]

Supplementary grants

A number of additional grants is available to both old and current system students in certain circumstances.

Adult dependants' grant

If you have an adult dependant(s) 'wholly or mainly financially dependent' on you, you may be eligible for an adult dependants' grant.[31] Eligible adult dependants include your spouse or civil partner, or (if you are aged 25 or over) a cohabiting partner. The maximum grant is £2,642 in 2010/11, but the amount you receive depends on your situation and the income of your dependant(s). The amount you are eligible to receive is halved if your spouse/partner receives full-time student support from BIS.

Parents' learning allowance

If you are a parent with dependent children, you may be eligible for a parents' learning allowance.[32] This is intended to help cover your course-related costs. How much you get depends on your income and that of your partner, spouse and any other dependants. It is not counted as income when assessing your social security benefit entitlement.

The maximum entitlement is £1,508 in 2010/11. If a couple are both full-time students, both can claim the full allowance, subject to their household income.

Childcare grant

If you have responsibility for a child under the age of 15 (or 17 if s/he has special educational needs) and you use registered or approved childcare, you can apply for a childcare grant.[33] You cannot receive the childcare grant if you receive the childcare element of working tax credit (WTC – see Chapter 19). You can choose to change your funding from WTC to the childcare grant if you wish.

A 'registered childcare provider' is a person who is registered under the Children Act[34] and who provides daycare. The person must care for one or more children aged under eight for more than two hours a day for payment. The care must be provided on domestic premises used wholly or mainly as a private dwelling. A relative who provides childcare for your child would qualify as long as s/he is registered with the Office for Standards in Education (Ofsted) and s/he is also looking after other children who are unrelated to her/him. Nurseries, out-of-hours school clubs and holiday playschemes also count as registered childcare.

'Approved childcare' covers provision for children aged eight or over. The childcare must be approved by an accredited organisation under the Working Tax Credit (Entitlement and Maximum Rate) Regulations 2002 (as amended). This definition includes carers who are approved under the voluntary Childcare Approval Scheme. This scheme covers childcare in the parent's home for children of any age and childcare for children aged eight or over provided by a childminder in her/his own home or other domestic premises.

The grant can cover up to 85 per cent of your actual costs of childcare, with a maximum payment of £148.75 a week for one child or £255 a week for two or more children. The maximum amount of grant available annually is £7,735 for one child and £13,260 for two or more children.

The childcare grant is income assessed; the amount you receive depends on your income and the income of any dependants.

Disabled students' allowance

If you incur additional course-related costs as a consequence of a disability, you can apply for a disabled students' allowance.[35] This is a needs-based allowance, and if you apply to your local authority or Student Finance England (SFE) for assistance under this scheme, you will need to provide medical proof of your disability, such as a letter from your doctor, educational psychologist or other specialist. If the local authority accepts this proof, it will help you arrange a needs assessment with a recognised assessor who will recommend what additional support or equipment you should be supplied with.

Maximum amounts approved by the local authority or SFE 2010/11[36]

Non-medical personal helper(s)	£20,520 per academic year
Major items of specialist equipment	£5,161 for duration of the course
Other expenditure	Up to £1,724 per academic year
Extra travel expenditure resulting from disability	Full reimbursement

---

Assessment of income – who is assessed

Most elements of student support for both current and old system students are subject to an income assessment.[37] You may be assessed as either a dependant or an independent student (see p31).

Your own income is always assessed, plus that of your:

- parent(s), if you do not have 'independent' status (see p31); *or*
- spouse, if you are married; *or*
- civil partner, if you have entered into a civil partnership; *or*
- cohabiting partner of the opposite sex, if you are aged 25 or over and started your course in September 2000 or later; *or*
- cohabiting partner of the same sex, if you are aged 25 or over and started your course in September 2005 or later.

Dependent students

If your parents are separated, divorced or widowed and you are not deemed independent, the income of the parent with whom you live is taken into account. If you do not live with either parent, SFE will decide which parent's income is most appropriate to use.

If you started your course after September 2004, the income of a parent's new spouse, civil or cohabiting partner will also be assessed, even if that person is not your own natural parent.

If you are considered a dependent student, the local authority or SFE looks at your parents' gross taxable income over the previous full tax year (so for the academic year 2010/11, this is 6 April 2008 to 5 April 2009), then subtracts pension scheme and superannuation payments which attract tax relief. A further £1,130 is deducted for each additional dependent child or if your parent is a student her/himself.[38]

The remaining amount is added to your estimated gross taxable income for the 2010/11 academic year (if any, and subject to various disregards, including all earnings from part-time or casual work) to form your household income figure.[39]

The household income figure is then used to determine how much the household is expected to contribute to your costs and, therefore, how much support you will receive from the government.

Note: if the level of your parents' income falls by at least 15 per cent during the academic year, you can request a reassessment from the local authority or SFE.[40]

Independent students

You are assessed as an **'independent student'** if:[41]
- you are either aged 25 before the beginning of the academic year in which your course begins or you become 25 during the academic year (in which case you will have independent status from the beginning of the following academic year); *or*
- you are married or in a civil partnership before the course begins or you marry or enter a civil partnership during the course (in which case you will become independent from the beginning of the following academic year); *or*
- you have been financially self-reliant for any three years before the academic year in which your course begins (this qualifying period can include periods of unemployment and participation in training schemes for the unemployed, such as modern apprenticeships or the New Deal); *or*
- you have responsibility for one or more children; *or*
- you have received a pension, allowance or other benefit as a result of your sickness, disability or injury (including maternity allowance); *or*
- you are irreconcilably estranged from your parents (see p32); *or*
- you have been in custody or care; *or*
- your parents cannot be found; *or*

- it is not reasonably practicable for your parents to send parental contributions to the UK, or they would be placed in jeopardy if they did so; *or*
- you are an orphan; *or*
- you are a member of a religious order living in a house of that order, if you started your course before 1 September 2009.

If you are considered an independent student, your parents' income will not be taken into account. Your gross taxable income for the academic year, less various disregards (including earnings from part-time work), is taken into account, and if you have a spouse, civil partner or cohabiting partner, their income may be taken into account (see below).

Estrangement

Where your relationship with your parents has completely broken down, and you do not meet the any of the other criteria for independent status, you can apply for 'estrangement' status so that their income is not taken into account.

If you can provide evidence that you have had no contact with your parents for at least a year, you should be classed as estranged. If you have become estranged but have had contact within the last 12 months, you can still use other evidence to prove your estrangement[42] – this could include, for example, letters from social services or medical or other professionals.

Your students' union or institution advice centre will be able to assist you in making an application for estrangement status.

Students with spouses, civil partners, or cohabiting partners

If your spouse or civil/cohabiting partner is considered part of the assessable household, her/his income is assessed in a similar way to that of parents (see p30).[43]

Any income from your spouse or civil/cohabiting partner is added to your income to form the household income to be taken into account. However, if you have separated from your spouse or civil partner, their income will not be assessed.

As with dependent students, the household income figure is used to determine how much the household is expected to contribute to your costs and, therefore, how much support you will receive from the Government.

Assessment of income – how assessment works

'Current system' students: pre-2008 cohorts

If you started your course in the 2006/07 or 2007/08 academic years, and are not subject to any of the gap year provisions (see p21), the assessed income will first reduce any maintenance grant or special support grant you are due to receive.

In 2010/11, if your household income is £18,360 or less, you will receive the maximum maintenance or special support grant. If your income is between

£18,361 and £39,333 you will receive a reduced amount of the applicable grant (the minimum amount is £50). For every £5.86 of household income between £18,360 and £27,819, £1 is deducted from the grant. For every £9.27 of household income above £27,819, £1 is deducted from the grant until the maximum household income of £39,333 is reached. No grant is payable if household income is more than £39,333.[44]

Income above £39,796 reduces other support at a rate of £1 for every £9.27 of income above £39,796.[45] Any supplementary grants for dependants will be reduced first, then the 25 per cent of the student loan that is means tested and finally any grant for travel costs.[46]

This assessment also applies if you started a course in the 2008/09 academic year or later but have previously studied at HE level.

'Current system' students: 2008 cohort

If you started your course in the 2008/09 academic year and have not previously studied at HE level, the assessed income will first reduce any maintenance grant or special support grant you are due to receive.

If your household income is £25,000 or less, you will receive the maximum maintenance or special support grant. If your income is between £25,001 and £60,032 you will receive a reduced amount of the applicable grant (the minimum amount is £50). For every £5.86 of household income between £25,001 and £34,459, £1 is deducted from the grant. For every £20.59 of household income above £34,459, £1 is deducted from the grant until the maximum household income of £60,032 is reached. No grant is payable if household income is more than £60,032.[47]

Income above £61,062 will reduce the income-assessed 25 per cent of the applicable basic rate of student loan at a rate of £1 for every £9.27 of additional income.[48]

Other income-assessed support is reduced in a different way. Support is reduced at a rate of £1 for every £9.27 of income above £39,796.[49] Any supplementary grants for dependants will be reduced first, then any long courses loan payable, and finally any grant for travel costs.[50]

'Current system' students: 2009 cohort

If you start your course in the 2009/10 academic year or later and have not previously studied at HE level, the assessed income will first reduce any maintenance grant or special support grant you are due to receive.

If your household income is £25,000 or less, you will receive the maximum maintenance or special support grant. If your income is between £25,001 and £50,020 you will receive a reduced amount of the applicable grant (the minimum amount is £50). For every £5 of household income between £25,001 and £34,000, £1 is deducted from the grant. For every £15.17 of household income above £34,000, £1 is deducted from the grant until the maximum household income of

£50,020 is reached. No grant is payable if household income is more than £50,020.[51]

Income above £50,778 will reduce the income-assessed 25 per cent of the applicable basic rate of student loan (see p25) at a rate of £1 for every £5 of additional income.[52]

Other income-assessed support is reduced in a different way. Support is reduced at a rate of £1 for every £9.27 of income above £39,796.[53] Any supplementary grants for dependants will be reduced first, then any long courses loan payable, and finally any grant for travel costs.[54]

'Old system' students

If you are funded under the system available to students who started courses between 1998 and 2005, the following income assessments are applied.

Higher education grant

The income assessment for the HE grant is separate from that for other support.[55] If your household income is £16,750 or less, you will receive the maximum grant. If your income is between £16,751 and £22,735 you will receive a reduced amount of the grant (the minimum amount is £50). For every £6.30 of household income above £16,751, £1 will be deducted from the grant until the maximum household income of £22,735 is reached. No grant is payable if household income is £22,736 or more.

Dependent students

If you are a dependent student (see p31), or your spouse, civil partner or cohabiting partner's income is taken into account, your household income is calculated as for 'current system' students.

If your household income is less than £23,660, no contribution applies. Once household income reaches £23,660, a £45 contribution towards your support becomes payable. After this, £1 is deducted from your support for every £9.27 of household income above this amount.[56]

The contribution is applied first to the grant for tuition fees, then to any grants for dependants, then to the income-assessed portion of the student loan, and finally to any grant for tuition fees, until all income-assessed support is eliminated.[57]

Independent students

If you are a single independent student (see p31 for the definition of independent), the income thresholds are different. As with 'current system' students, only your own estimated gross taxable income (less various disregards) for the current academic year is taken into account. If your income is less than £11,020 no contribution is payable, but your student support is reduced by £1 for every £9.27 of income above this level in the same order as for dependent students.[58]

Institutional bursaries

A 'current system' student who is receiving the full maintenance or special support grant of £2,906 and whose university or college charges fees of more than £2,906 should be eligible for a minimum non-repayable bursary.

For 2010/11, the Office for Fair Access, which governs bursary rules, has stated that the minimum mandatory bursary must be equivalent to 10 per cent of the tuition fee charged by the university or college. Therefore, in 2010/11, where the fee charged is £3,290, the mandatory minimum bursary is £329.[59]

However, many institutions offer more than this minimum mandatory bursary. You should contact your university or college for more information.

Overpayments

If you are overpaid support by your local authority or Student Finance England, the regulations give these agencies the power to recover the overpayment.[60] This remains the case even if the overpayment was the result of a mistake made by SFE or the local authority.

Usually, any overpayment of student support will be recovered by reducing the support you are due to receive in future instalments. If you are not due to receive any further instalments, the regulations allow for the agency concerned to use any other methods open to them. In practice, this means either asking for you to repay the money in full directly, or it may mean adding the overpayment to your student loan debt.

If you have been overpaid fee support, this will usually be reclaimed from the academic institution and the institution will then discuss any amount of fees owed with you directly.

If you have received equipment through the disabled students' allowance which it is subsequently determined you have, in effect, been 'overpaid', it may be acceptable to return the equipment rather than repay its cash value.[61]

It is important to ensure that the agency concerned is correct in assessing any overpayment. You should ask your students' union or institutional advice service for their assistance in checking if an overpayment has been made, and help negotiating with SFE, the local authority or your institution if this is the case.

2. Part-time undergraduates

Support for part-time students is different from that for full-time students. The support offered is the same for both new and existing part-time undergraduate students. The course and personal eligibility requirements apply as for full-time students (see pp23 and 22).[62] To be eligible for this package, a student must be studying a course that is at least 50 per cent of a full-time course – ie, it takes no longer than twice the time of the equivalent full-time course to complete.[63]

Grant for fees

If you are a part-time undergraduate student (including students from the European Union (EU) – see p22), you may be eligible for an income-assessed grant.[64] The maximum amount of grant for which you are eligible depends on the intensity of study for each academic year of the course.

Maximum grant for part-time fees 2010/11

Course intensity	Maximum grant available 2010/11[65]
Less than 60%	£820
60–74%	£985
75% or more	£1,230

Grant for course costs

A grant for course costs of up to £265 is available to students from low-income backgrounds to help with the costs of books, equipment and travel.[66] The amount of grant available is not affected by the intensity of study. This is not available to EU students.

Additional Fee Support Scheme

Part-time students whose tuition fees are higher than the amount covered by the grant for fees are able to apply for help from the Additional Fee Support Scheme, a part of the Access to Learning Fund (see p37 for more details).

Assessment of income

In 2010/11, if your income is below £16,845, you are eligible for the maximum grant for fees and course costs. If your income is between £16,845 and £24,420, you will receive some help with fees and course costs. If your income is between £25,421 and £28,065 you will receive some help with course costs, but not with fees. The exact amount you receive depends on your income. If your income is £28,065, you will receive a course grant of £50. Only your and your partner's (if you have one) income is taken into account as household income. Your parents' income is ignored regardless of your age.[67]

If you are married or in a civil partnership, or aged 25 or over and living with a partner (including a same-sex partner) or have dependent children, the following amounts will be deducted from your income:[68]

- £2,000 for your partner;
- £2,000 for your eldest child;
- £1,000 for every other child.

Disabled students' allowance

If you are studying at an intensity of at least 50 per cent of an equivalent full-time course and have a disability, you can apply for a disabled students' allowance. The amount a local authority can award for non-medical help and other general expenditure is, however, reduced according to the workload of a part-time course.

Maximum amounts approved by the funding authority 2010/11[69]

Non-medical personal helper(s)	£15,390 per academic year
Major items of specialist equipment	£5,161 for duration of the course
Other expenditure	Up to £1,293 per academic year
Extra travel expenditure resulting from disability	Full reimbursement

---

Part-time taster modules

If you are studying between 10 and 49 per cent of an equivalent full-time course and have no previous experience of higher education, you may be eligible for help with tuition fees for a module or academic year (whichever is the shorter). The maximum amount payable is at the discretion of your university or college. You should contact the Access to Learning Fund administrator at your college or university. EU students are also eligible to apply for this help.

---

3. **Discretionary funds**

Higher education institutions are allocated money to provide discretionary hardship funds for 'home' (see p23) undergraduate and postgraduate students in financial difficulty, as well as part-time undergraduate fee support. Repayable loans and non-repayable grants can both be issued by the funds.

Access to Learning Fund

Non-repayable grants are available on a needs-assessed basis if you are experiencing financial difficulty serious enough to mean you may have to leave your course. The funds can help with living and study costs such as childcare, rent, books and utility bills, or with large one-off and exceptional costs such as major housing repairs, and emergency situations such as fire or bereavement.

Priority is given to students with children, mature students, students from low-income families, disabled students, final year students and those who have left care. However, all students who meet the personal and course requirements for undergraduate student support are eligible, including healthcare students and those in receipt of dance and drama awards. You must, however, have applied for your full entitlement of a student maintenance loan and have received the first instalment, where you are eligible for one.

The funds cannot be used to meet the costs of tuition fees charged to full-time undergraduate students or to make up for non-receipt of a parental contribution to a grant or loan.

A grant would not normally exceed £3,500, although institutions have some discretion in exceptional circumstances. Individual institutions have different application processes and different pressures on the funds and no sum is guaranteed. However, there is an appeals process should you need to challenge the fund administrator's decision.

Additional Fee Support Scheme

This scheme is available to help 'home' and European Union students meet the costs of their part-time fees while studying. Local fund administrators have discretion on how much assistance to pay and to whom. Students should contact the fund administrator at their institution for further information.

Notes

1. **1. Full-time undergraduates**
   1. Reg 2 E(SS) Regs
   2. Reg 2 E(SS) Regs
   3. Reg 2 E(SS) Regs
   4. s25 HEA 2004
   5. Sch 1 Part 2 E(SS) Regs
   6. 'Islands' in this context are the Channel Islands or the Isle of Man
   7. For a definition of 'relevant family member' see Sch 1 para 1 E(SS) Regs
   8. Sch 1 para 8 E(SS) Regs
   9. Sch 1 para 12 E(SS) Regs
   10. Sch 1 para 4 E(SS) Regs
   11. Reg 6 and Sch 2 E(SS) Regs
   12. Regs 21-23 E(SS) Regs
   13. Regs 20, 56, 60 and 67 E(SS) Regs
   14. Reg 67 E(SS) Regs
   15. Regs 20 and 21 E(SS) Regs
   16. Reg 20(9) E(SS) Regs
   17. Reg 25 E(SS) Regs
   18. Reg 34 E(SS) Regs
   19. Reg 64 E(SS) Regs
   20. Reg 20 E(SS) Regs
   21. Reg 56 E(SS) Regs
   22. Reg 72(8)-(10) E(SS) Regs
   23. Reg 60 E(SS) Regs
   24. Reg 72 E(SS) Regs
   25. Reg 70 E(SS) Regs
   26. Regs 78 and 84 E(SS) Regs
   27. Sch 2 para 5 E(SL) Regs – note that if you have taken out more than five student loans, you will repay your loan in 84 monthly instalments.
   28. Sch 2 para 12 E(SL) Regs
   29. Reg 44 E(SL)(R) Regs
   30. Reg 19 E(SL)(R) Regs
   31. Reg 44 E(SS) Regs
   32. Reg 46 E(SS) Regs

33 Reg 45 E(SS) Regs
34 s79(f) CA 1989
35 Reg 40 E(SS) Regs
36 Reg 41 E(SS) Regs
37 Sch 4 E(SS) Regs
38 Sch 4 para 3 E(SS) Regs
39 Sch 4 paras 3 and 4 E(SS) Regs
40 Sch 4 para 5(3)-(4) E(SS) Regs
41 Sch 4 para 2 E(SS) Regs
42 Sch 4 para 2(1)(e) E(SS) Regs
43 Sch 4 para 6 E(SS) Regs
44 Reg 59 E(SS) Regs
45 Sch 4 para 9 E(SS) Regs
46 Regs 98 and 101 E(SS) Regs
47 Reg 57 E(SS) Regs
48 Reg 70 E(SS) Regs
49 Sch 4 para 9 E(SS) Regs
50 Regs 97 and 100 E(SS) Regs
51 Reg 58 E(SS) Regs
52 Reg 72 E(SS) Regs
53 Sch 4 para 9 E(SS) Regs
54 Regs 97 and 100 E(SS) Regs
55 Reg 65 E(SS) Regs
56 Sch 4 para 8(1) E(SS) Regs
57 Reg 99 E(SS) Regs
58 Sch 4 para 8(2) E(SS) Regs
59 Letter from OFFA to HEIs, 23 July 2009
60 Regs 113-115 E(SS) Regs
61 Reg 115(9) E(SS) Regs

2. Part-time undergraduates
62 Reg 133 E(SS) Regs
63 Reg 135(1)(c) E(SS) Regs
64 Reg 137 E(SS) Regs
65 Reg 138 E(SS) Regs
66 Reg 137(1)(b) E(SS) Regs
67 Reg 138 E(SS) Regs
68 Reg 139 E(SS) Regs
69 Reg 141 E(SS) Regs

Chapter 3

Undergraduate student support: Wales

This chapter covers:
1. Full-time undergraduates (below)
2. Part-time undergraduates (p48)
3. Discretionary funds (p49)

Basic facts
- Undergraduate students are able to apply for a mixture of grants and loans for fees and living costs, depending on their personal circumstances.
- Support differs for full- and part-time students.
- The support available in England and Northern Ireland is different to that available in Wales.
- Separate provisions apply to healthcare, social work and initial teacher training students.
- A Financial Contingency Fund is available for those in financial difficulty.

The type of financial support you can receive when you are learning depends on several factors, including when you begin your course, the length of the course, the discipline you are studying, whether the course is full time or part time, where you normally live when you apply for support, where you will be studying, your age and if you have previously received funding for a course.

If you are a student on an NHS-funded healthcare course, a course of initial teacher training or a course leading to a qualification in social work, your support will vary (see Chapter 6).

1. Full-time undergraduates

Full-time undergraduates in Wales on eligible courses (see p42) and who are personally eligible (see p41) can apply for financial assistance from the Welsh Assembly. Separate provision is available for part-time undergraduates (see p48).

Support in England, Northern Ireland and Scotland

English, Northern Irish and Scottish-domiciled students are funded under separate systems. See Chapter 2 for details of the system in England, Chapter 4 for details of the system in Northern Ireland and CPAG's *Benefits for Students in Scotland Handbook* for details in Scotland.

Students domiciled in Wales, but who wish to study in England, Northern Ireland or Scotland, receive the same package of support for living costs as for study in Wales, and can take out loans to cover the cost of tuition fees. The fee grant for current system students is not available. In addition, fees in Scotland are charged in a different way (see p26).

Changes to student support in 2010/11 and 2011/12

There are a number of changes for 2010/11 for Welsh-domiciled students. Students starting their courses on or after 1 September 2010 (other than students classed as 'gap year' students – see p21) will no longer receive the tuition fee grant of £1,980. However, they will be entitled to a higher rate of Assembly learning grant or special support grant – up to £5,000 for students with the lowest household incomes.

Students who take out a student loan for maintenance in 2010/11 will also have £1,500 of this 'written off' at the point where repayments begin, although, at the time of writing, details of this provision have still to be announced by the Welsh Assembly Government.

The regulations also withdraw eligibility for support for students on some types of flexible initial teacher training courses starting after 1 September 2010.

Otherwise, student support rates have been frozen for 2010/11, with the exception of loans and grants for tuition fees, which will rise to match the increase in the maximum rates of fees.

In 2011/12, a new national bursary scheme is due to be introduced, which will give Welsh-domiciled students with household incomes below £34,000 per year an additional £600 per year, to be paid alongside their Assembly learning grant or special support grant. This will be available whether the student chooses to study in Wales or elsewhere in the UK, but will not be available to English, Scottish or Northern Irish-domiciled students studying in Wales. Full details will be set out in the 2011/12 edition of this handbook.

Who is eligible for support

In order to receive financial support you must be 'personally eligible' (see below) and studying an eligible course (see p42).

Personal eligibility

To be personally eligible for support from the Welsh Assembly you must meet the residency rules.[1] These are the same as for England (see p22), except that, where

3

appropriate, you must be normally resident in Wales on the first day of the first academic year.

Course eligibility

Broadly, the course must be full time (as defined by the education provider) and be:[2]

- a first degree;
- a higher education (HE) diploma;
- a BTEC higher national certificate (HNC) or higher national diploma (HND);
- a course of initial teacher training;
- a course for the further training of teachers, or youth or community workers;
- a course to prepare for certain professional examinations of a standard higher than A level, or BTEC or HNC/HND where a first degree is not required for entry;
- a course not higher than a first degree, but higher than those described in the above bullet point.

Note that some courses, particularly in art and design, can require the student to undertake a 'foundation' year or course, which is different to a foundation degree. This is normally a course of one academic year in length which precedes the main higher education degree course.

Support for these courses is often much more limited as they usually do not fall within the definition of 'higher education'. You may be eligible for support as a further education student (see Chapter 1) – speak to an adviser in your students' union or institution for further guidance.

Previous study

If you have previously attended an HE course, the amount of support you can receive may be affected by the rules on 'previous study'.[3]

If you are a current system student (see p44) and hold an honours degree from a UK institution, support for any new qualification will be restricted to supplementary grants for travel costs, students with dependants and disabled students.[4]

Some exceptions apply: students who hold an honours degree and who are undertaking a Postgraduate Certificate in Education (PGCE) course receive full funding, while those undertaking a further undergraduate course in certain professional subjects, such as medicine or veterinary science, can receive a maintenance loan for that course,[5] although not a loan for tuition fees or a maintenance or special support grant.

If you do not already hold an honours degree then, in general, the maximum number of years of tuition fee loan and maintenance or special support grant funding you can receive is equivalent to the ordinary length of your course plus one year, less any years of study previously undertaken.[6] If you have studied part of a year, you will be treated as if you have undertaken a full year of study. Maintenance loan funding is, however, unaffected.

If you are transferring courses, or undertaking an 'end-on' course, these previous study rules will affect you. You may be able to secure additional years of 'full' funding if you were unable to complete a previous year or course for 'compelling personal reasons' such as illness or caring responsibilities[7] – you will have to provide evidence of this to your local authority.

Rules for old system students (see below) are slightly different but have broadly the same effect.

Further information on previous study is available from www.studentfinancewales.co.uk or from your student adviser.

Student support

Old system and current system students

This chapter refers to 'old system' and 'current system' students. Whether you are classed as one or the other depends on when you started your course.

Students who entered higher education on or after 1 September 1998 and before 1 September 2006

If you began your course between 1 September 1998 and 1 September 2006 and do not fit into the gap year provision explained on p21, you will receive financial help for student support as an 'old system' student.[8]

In the main, the support you are entitled to is identical to the support available for 'old system' students in England (see p20).[9]

However, if you are eligible for funding under this system as a Welsh-domiciled student there are some differences. In addition to the support available for all English and Welsh students, you may be able to receive an Assembly learning grant for 'old system' students.

Assembly learning grant for 'old system' students

Students who started their education in either the 2002/03 or the 2003/04 academic years, and who are on a low income, may be eligible for a means-tested Welsh Assembly learning grant of up to £1,500.[10] A grant of at least £450 is available if you are on a full-time course and your family income is below £17,770. If your household income is below £11,791, £750 is available. The full £1,500 will be offered if your household income is less than £5,896. The grants are administered through Welsh local authorities but you can attend any institution in the UK.

If you are an 'old system' student, and you started your higher education in September 2004 or later, you should apply for the £1,000 HE grant in the first instance (see p25).[11] However, if your household income is less than £5,896, you will receive a £500 'top-up' Assembly learning grant to bring your total grant funding to £1,500.

Assessment of income

The means test for 'old system' Welsh students is broadly the same as that for English students (see p34).[12]

Students who entered higher education on or after 1 September 2006

You qualify for support as a 'current system' student[13] if:

- you entered (or are entering) higher education for the first time in September 2006 or later and do not fall under the gap year provisions outlined on p21;
- you started a PGCE course on or after 1 September 2006;
- you have withdrawn from a previous course of study and did not arrange a transfer before leaving your previous course.

Some changes to student support made in 2010 affect only those students who started their course in the 2010/11 academic year. Such students are referred to as '2010 cohort' students in this chapter.

Tuition fees

Eligible, 'current system' Welsh-domiciled students and non-UK European Union students studying in Wales will pay flexible fees of up to £3,290 in the 2010/11 academic year. If you are not a 2010 cohort student, you will also receive a tuition fee grant of up to £1,940, so that the most that you will pay is £1,310 for the year.[14] You will be eligible to take out a tuition fee loan to cover the remainder.[15] If you are a 2010 cohort student, or otherwise eligible for fee support but not for a fee grant, you can receive a fee loan up to the level of the fee charged.[16]

If you choose to study in England or Northern Ireland, you will pay up to £3,290. Fees for Welsh-domiciled students in Scotland are fixed at £1,820 a year for all courses except medicine, which is fixed at £2,895 a year. In all cases, eligible Welsh-domiciled students can take out tuition fee loans to cover the cost.

The maximum loan available will match the fee you are charged. The fee loan is not means tested on your income or the income of anyone in your household. However, the loan will be added to your total student loan debt (including any loans taken out for living costs) and you must start your repayments once you have graduated, or otherwise left the course, and are earning at least £15,000 a year (if you are working in the UK).

If you wish to pay all, or part, of the fee in cash in advance, you can do so. Your institution will generally expect some indication of how you intend to pay your fees when you register.

Help with tuition fees for part-time courses is also available (see p48).

Assembly learning grant for 2010 cohort current system students

The Assembly learning grant for 2010 cohort current system students (see above) is a non-repayable, means-tested allowance of up to £5,000.[17] The maximum amount is payable to students with a household income of less than £18,371 a year, and a partial amount is paid on a sliding scale to students with a household income of up to £50,020.

Part of the grant substitutes the student loan for living costs. If you receive an Assembly learning grant, the amount of loan for living costs you can receive is reduced by 60 pence for every £1 you receive, up to a maximum of £2,844 (see p46 for more details of loans for living costs).

Example

Rhys receives an Assembly learning grant of £1,540. The maximum amount of loan for living costs he can receive will be reduced by £924.

If you are entitled to apply for means-tested benefits, you should apply for the special support grant instead of the Assembly learning grant (see p46). If you are not entitled to apply for such benefits, but your partner is, the Assembly learning grant will be included as income in any benefits claim. See Chapter 20 for more details.

Assembly learning grant for other current system students

Other 'current system' students receive a slightly different Assembly learning grant. It is a non-repayable, means-tested allowance of up to £2,906.[18] The maximum amount is payable to students with a household income of less than £18,371 a year, and a partial amount is paid on a sliding scale to students with a household income of up to £39,329.

As for 2010 cohort students, part of the grant substitutes the student loan for living costs. In this case, if you receive an Assembly learning grant, the amount of loan for living costs you can receive is reduced, pound for pound, up to a maximum of £1,288. If you receive more than £1,288 Assembly learning grant, the student loan is not reduced further (see p46 for more details).

Example

Hadeel receives an Assembly learning grant of £1,540. The maximum amount of loan for living costs she can receive will be reduced by £1,288.

If you are entitled to apply for means-tested benefits, you should apply for the special support grant instead of the Assembly learning grant (see p46). If you are not entitled to apply, but your partner is, the Assembly learning grant will be included as income in any benefits claim. See Chapter 20 for more details.

Special support grant

In order to provide extra support for students regarded as particularly vulnerable, a separate grant is available if you are a full-time student eligible to claim means-tested social security benefits.[19]

Most full-time students cannot receive such benefits. Some students, however, can claim – eg, if you are a lone parent, or you and your partner are both full-time students and have one or more children, or you receive disability living allowance, or you are deaf. See the relevant benefits chapter for details of which students can claim means-tested benefits.

If you can claim means-tested benefits, you should claim the special support grant rather than the Assembly learning grant. Like the Assembly learning grant for 'new system' students, the special support grant is a non-repayable, means-tested allowance of up to £5,000 for 2010 cohort students,[20] or £2,906 for other current system students.[21] The special support grant is paid on the same income scales as the maintenance grants for each of the cohorts (see p45).

Unlike the Assembly learning grant, however, the special support grant does not substitute any part of the student loan, and it is not taken into account when calculating your entitlement to means-tested benefits.

Student loans for living costs

Student loans for living costs are available to eligible Welsh-domiciled students on the same terms and rates as for non-2009 cohort students in England (ie, students who started their course before the 2009/10 academic year – see p27), except that the maximum rate for study in London is slightly higher at £6,648 per year (£6,053 for final year students).

Supplementary grants

A number of other grants and allowances are available to particular groups of students, both old and current system, who have extra needs.

Students with dependants

Students with dependent children may be able to receive a parents' learning allowance[22] of up to £1,508 and/or a childcare grant[23] of 85 per cent of actual costs up to a maximum of £161.50 per week for one child or 85 per cent of actual costs up to a maximum of £274.55 per week for two or more children.

If you have an adult dependant(s) 'wholly or mainly financially dependent' on you, you may be eligible for a means-tested adult dependants' grant up to a maximum of £2,647.[24] Students with children should also apply for child tax credit (see Chapter 18).

Disabled students' allowance

If you are disabled and have extra costs associated with your course because of your disability, you may be entitled to extra help to pay for them. This is also awarded on the same basis as in England (see p30). Please note that there is a slight difference in two of the rates: the maximum general allowance in Wales is £1,729 and the maximum grant for equipment is £5,166.[25]

Grants for travel costs

Medical and dental students on placement and students who must travel abroad may be entitled to help with the cost of travel. This is awarded on the same basis as in England (see p70).[26]

Assessment of income

Much of the support you receive is based on your household income. The definition of household income in Wales is the same as that in England (see p30).

Once your household income is assessed, it will first reduce any maintenance grant or special support grant you are due to receive. The assessment is different depending on whether you are a 2010 cohort or other current system student.

2010 cohort students

In 2010/11, if your household income is £18,370 or less, you will receive the maximum maintenance or special support grant. If your income is between £18,371 and £50,020 you will receive a reduced amount of the applicable grant (the minimum amount is £50). For every £3.77 of household income between £18,371 and £26,500, £1 is deducted from the grant. For every £4.315 of household income between £26,501 and £34,000, £1 is deducted from the grant. For every £15.17 of household income above £34,000, £1 is deducted from the grant until the maximum household income of £50,020 is reached. No grant is payable if household income is £50,021 or more.[27]

Income above £50,778 reduces other support at a rate of £1 for every £5 of additional income.[28] Any supplementary grants for dependants will be reduced first, then the 25 per cent of the student loan that is means tested, and finally any grant for travel costs.[29]

Other current system students

In 2010/11, if your household income is £18,370 or less, you will receive the maximum maintenance or special support grant. If your income is between £18,371 and £39,329 you will receive a reduced amount of the applicable grant (the minimum amount is £50). For every £5.86 of household income between £18,371 and £27,852, £1 is deducted from the grant. For every £9.27 of household income above £27,852, £1 is deducted from the grant until the maximum household income of £39,329 is reached. No grant is payable if household income is £39,330 or more.[30]

Income above £39,793 reduces other support at a rate of £1 for every £9.27 of income above £39,793 until 75 per cent of the full maintenance loan remains.[31]

Any supplementary grants for dependants will be reduced first, then the 25 per cent of the student loan that is means tested, and finally any grant for travel costs.[32]

2. **Part-time undergraduates**

New and existing part-time undergraduate students can qualify for grants for fees and living costs. The course and personal eligibility requirements are the same as for full-time students (see pp41–42). To be eligible for this package, a student must be studying a course that is at least 50 per cent of a full-time course.[33]

Grant for fees

If you are a part-time undergraduate student (including students from the European Union (EU) – see p22), you may be eligible for a means-tested grant for fees.[34] The maximum amount of grant to which you are eligible depends on the intensity of study for each academic year of the course (see table below).

Grant for course costs

A grant for course costs of up to £1,095 is available to students from low-income backgrounds to help with the costs of books, equipment and travel.[35] The amount of grant available is affected by the intensity of study (see table below). This is not available to EU students. It does not affect your entitlement to means-tested benefits.

Part-time fee and course grants

Course intensity	Maximum fee grant	Maximum course grant	Total maximum support
50–59% of the equivalent full-time course	£650	£1,095	£1,745
60–74% of the equivalent full-time course	£780	£1,095	£1,875
75% or more of the equivalent full-time course	£975	£1,095	£2,070

Assessment of income

If you are single and you have no dependants, the following assessment applies to you.[36] If your income is £16,864 or less, you are eligible for the maximum grant for fees and course costs. If your income is between £16,865 and £25,435, you will receive some help with fees and course costs. If your income is between £25,436 and £28,180, you will receive some help with course costs, but not with fees. The exact amount you receive depends on your income. Only your and your partner's (if you have one) income is taken into account as household income. Your parents' income is ignored.

If you are married or in a civil partnership, or aged 25 or over and living with a partner (including a same-sex partner) or have dependent children, the following amounts are added to the above income limits:

- £2,000 for your partner;
- £2,000 for your eldest child;
- £1,000 for every other child.[37]

The Student Finance Wales booklet *A Guide to Financial Support for Part-time Students in Higher Education 2010/11* provides further details, including examples.

Disabled students' allowance

If you are studying at an intensity of at least 50 per cent of an equivalent full-time course and have a disability, you may also apply for a disabled students' allowance (DSA).[38] The amount a local authority can award for non-medical help and other general expenditure is, however, reduced according to the workload of a part-time course.

See p37 for further information on the DSA.

Grants for dependants

If you are studying at an intensity of at least 50 per cent of an equivalent full-time course and have dependent children or an adult dependant, you may also apply for the childcare allowance, parent's learning allowance or adult dependant's allowance.[39]

As with the DSA, the amount a local authority can award is reduced pro rata according to the workload of the part-time course.

See p29 for further information on the allowances.

Fee waiver

This is available to part-time students undertaking 10 credits or more who are in receipt of a means-tested benefit, whose sole income is benefits or who are registered jobseekers. Students who already have a first degree are not eligible to apply. This scheme is administered by the universities and colleges.

3. **Discretionary funds**

Higher education institutions are allocated money to provide hardship funds for 'home' (see pp22–23) undergraduate and postgraduate students in financial difficulty. Repayable loans and non-repayable grants can both be issued by the funds.

Financial Contingency Fund

Non-repayable grants are available on a needs-assessed basis if you are experiencing financial difficulty serious enough to mean you may have to leave your course. The Financial Contingency Fund can help with living and study costs such as childcare, rent, books and utility bills, or with large one-off and exceptional costs such as major housing repairs and emergency situations such as fire or bereavement.

Priority is usually given to students with children, mature students, students from low-income families, disabled students, final year students and those who have left care. However, all students who meet the personal and course requirements for undergraduate student support are eligible to apply, including healthcare students and those in receipt of dance and drama awards. You must, however, have applied for your full entitlement of a student loan if you are eligible for one.

The funds cannot be used to meet the costs of tuition fees charged to full-time undergraduate students or to make up for non-receipt of a parental contribution to a grant or loan.

A grant would not normally exceed £3,500, although institutions have some discretion in exceptional circumstances. Individual institutions have different application processes and different pressures on the funds and no sum is guaranteed. However, there is an appeals process should you need to challenge the fund administrator's decision.

Notes

1. Full-time undergraduates

1 Sch 1 ALGL(HE)(W) Regs
2 Reg 5 and Sch 2 ALGL(HE)(W) Regs
3 Regs 6-7 ALGL(HE)(W) Regs
4 Reg 7 ALGL(HE)(W) Regs
5 Reg 7(4) ALGL(HE)(W) Regs
6 Reg 6 ALGL(HE)(W) Regs
7 Reg 6 ALGL(HE)(W) Regs
8 Reg 2 ALGL(HE)(W) Regs
9 ALGL(HE)(W) Regs
10 E(ALGS)(W) Regs
11 Reg 36 ALGL(HE)(W) Regs
12 Sch 5 ALGL(HE)(W) Regs
13 Reg 2 ALGL(HE)(W) Regs
14 Reg 19 ALGL(HE)(W) Regs
15 Reg 23 ALGL(HE)(W) Regs
16 Reg 22 ALGL(HE)(W) Regs
17 Reg 39 ALGL(HE)(W) Regs
18 Reg 38 ALGL(HE)(W) Regs
19 Reg 40 ALGL(HE)(W) Regs
20 Reg 42 ALGL(HE)(W) Regs
21 Reg 41 ALGL(HE)(W) Regs
22 Reg 29 ALGL(HE)(W) Regs
23 Reg 28 ALGL(HE)(W) Regs
24 Reg 27 ALGL(HE)(W) Regs
25 Reg 25 ALGL(HE)(W) Regs
26 Regs 32-34 ALGL(HE)(W) Regs
27 Reg 39 ALGL(HE)(W) Regs
28 Sch 5 ALGL(HE)(W) Regs
29 Reg 60 ALGL(HE)(W) Regs
30 Reg 39 ALGL(HE)(W) Regs
31 Sch 5 ALGL(HE)(W) Regs
32 Reg 60 ALGL(HE)(W) Regs

2. Part-time undergraduates

33 Reg 86(1)(c) ALGL(HE)(W) Regs
34 Reg 87 ALGL(HE)(W) Regs
35 Reg 72 ALGL(HE)(W) Regs
36 Reg 82(5) ALGL(HE)(W) Regs
37 Reg 82(8) ALGL(HE)(W) Regs
38 Reg 89 ALGL(HE)(W) Regs
39 Reg 90-99 ALGL(HE)(W) Regs

Chapter 4

Undergraduate student support: Northern Ireland

This chapter covers:
1. Full-time undergraduates (below)
2. Part-time undergraduates (p60)
3. Discretionary funds (p60)

Basic facts

- Undergraduate students are able to apply for a mixture of grants and loans for fees and living costs, depending on their personal circumstances.
- There are differences in support for full- and part-time students.
- The support available in Northern Ireland is different to that in England and Wales.
- Separate provisions apply to healthcare, social work and initial teacher training students.
- Discretionary hardship funds are available for those in financial difficulty, but funding is not guaranteed.

The type of financial support you can receive when you are learning depends on several factors, including: when you begin your course, the length of the course, the discipline you are studying, whether the course is full time or part time, and your age.

If you are a student on an NHS-funded healthcare course, a course of initial teacher training or a course leading to a qualification in social work, your support will vary (see Chapter 6).

1. Full-time undergraduates

Student awards for Northern Irish-domiciled students studying in Northern Ireland, mainland Britain or the Republic of Ireland are administered by the Department for Employment and Learning (DELNI). Applications for support are processed by five education and library boards (ELBs). You should apply to the

ELB which covers the area in which you normally live, rather than where you intend to study.

Support in England, Wales and Scotland

English, Northern Irish and Scottish-domiciled students are funded under separate systems. See Chapter 2 for details of the system in England, Chapter 3 for details of the system in Wales, and CPAG's *Benefits for Students in Scotland Handbook* for details in Scotland.

Students domiciled in Northern Ireland, but who wish to study in England, Northern Ireland or Scotland, receive the same package of support as for study in Northern Ireland, although fees in Scotland are charged in a different way (see p26). Students who wish to study in the Republic of Ireland are treated as 'old system' students (see p20 for a definition).

Who is eligible for support

In order to receive financial support, you must be 'personally eligible' (see below) and studying an eligible course (see below).

Personal eligibility

To be personally eligible for support from DELNI, you must meet the residency rules.[1] These are the same as for England (see p22), except that, where appropriate, you must be normally resident in Northern Ireland on the first day of the first academic year.

Course eligibility

Broadly, the course must be full time (as defined by the education provider) and be:[2]

- a first degree;
- a higher education (HE) diploma;
- a BTEC higher national certificate (HNC) or higher national diploma (HND);
- a course of initial teacher training;
- a course for the further training of teachers, or youth or community workers;
- a course to prepare for certain professional examinations of a standard higher than A level, or BTEC or HNC/HND where a first degree is not required for entry;
- a course not higher than a first degree, but higher than those described in the above bullet point.

Note that some courses, particularly in art and design, can require the student to undertake a 'foundation' year or course, which is different to a foundation degree. This is normally a course of one academic year in length which precedes the main higher education degree course.

Support for these courses is often much more limited as they usually do not fall within the definition of 'higher education'. You may be eligible for support as a further education student (see Chapter 1) – speak to an adviser in your students' union or institution for further guidance.

Previous study

If you have previously attended an HE course, the amount of support you can receive may be affected by the rules on 'previous study'.[3]

If you are a current system student (see p21 for a definition) and hold an honours degree, support for any new qualification will be restricted to supplementary grants for travel costs, students with dependants and disabled students.[4]

Some exceptions apply: students who hold an honours degree and who are undertaking a Postgraduate Certificate in Education (PGCE) course receive full funding, while those undertaking a further undergraduate course in certain professional subjects such as medicine or veterinary science can receive a maintenance loan for that course,[5] although not a loan for tuition fees or a maintenance or special support grant.

If you do not already hold an honours degree, then, in general, the maximum number of years of tuition fee loan and maintenance or special support grant funding you can receive is equivalent to the ordinary length of your course plus one year, less any years of study previously undertaken.[6] If you have studied part of a year, you will be treated as if you have undertaken a full year of study. Maintenance loan funding is, however, unaffected. Students on social work courses are also exempt from these rules.

If you are transferring courses, or undertaking an 'end-on' course, these previous study rules will affect you. You may be able to secure additional years of 'full' funding if you were unable to complete a previous year or course for 'compelling personal reasons' such as illness or caring responsibilities[7] – you will have to provide evidence of this to your ELB.

Rules for old system students (see p20 for a definition) are slightly different but have broadly the same effect.

Further information on previous study is available from the student or financial adviser in your students' union or institution.

Student support

Definitions

This chapter refers to 'old system' and 'current system' students. Whether you are classed as one or the other depends on when you started your course.

Students who entered higher education on or after 1 September 1998 and before 1 September 2006

If you began your course on or after 1 September 1998 or were counted as a 'gap year' student in the 2006/07 academic year (see p21), you will receive financial help under the old rules for student support.[8]

This system also applies to old or new students who are attending institutions in the Republic of Ireland.

Tuition fees

The maximum fee you will have to pay in the 2010/11 academic year is £1,310.[9] The Government may pay some, or all, of the fee depending on your family's income. If you are assessed to make a contribution, you may be eligible for a student loan for fees up to the amount of the fee charged.[10] See p57 for more details.

If you are a Northern Irish student attending a course at a publicly funded college in the Republic of Ireland, you will have your tuition fees paid by the Irish Government. In addition, the college may charge a registration fee of €1,500 (2009/10 rates) to cover examination and student services fees, which can be claimed back from your ELB.[11] Note that this will not be means tested and therefore, it is important that you apply to your ELB to ensure this charge will be paid, even if you do not intend to apply for financial help towards living costs.

Higher education bursary

If you have a low income you may be eligible for a non-repayable, means-tested bursary of up to £2,000 to help with your living costs.[12]

The full amount is available if you have a household income of less than £11,805, whereas a partial amount is available on a sliding scale if your family's income is between £11,806 and £23,605. If you have a family income of more than £23,605, you are not eligible to receive the bursary.

Any bursary you receive will affect the amount of student loan you can have (see p56).

Your bursary is paid in three instalments over the course of the academic year.

Student loan

You can apply for a partially means-tested student loan to help cover living costs and other expenses. These are income-contingent loans (see p27).

Maximum amount of income-contingent loan 2010/11[13]

	Full year	Final year
London	£6,780	£6,170
Elsewhere	£4,840	£4,480
Parental home	£3,750	£3,390

You may be entitled to additional amounts of loan for any extra weeks of attendance over the standard 30 weeks and three days.

A quarter of the loan is means tested on your household income. In addition, if you are entitled to the full rate of bursary (see p55), the amount you can borrow is reduced by £1,500. If you are entitled to a partial bursary, the amount of loan you can take out is reduced by the amount of the bursary you receive.[14]

The loan is repayable at the end of your studies. The amount of money you pay back each month for an income-contingent loan depends on your earnings. Once you earn above £15,000 a year, repayments begin at the rate of 9 per cent of all income above this threshold. For example, if you earn £16,000 a year, you will pay back 9 per cent of £1,000 – ie, £90 a year or £7.50 a month.

Other support

The childcare grant, parents' learning allowance, adult dependants' grant and disabled students' allowance (DSA) are all available to Northern Irish undergraduates on the same basis as students in England (see pp29–30).[15]

With the exception of the disabled students' allowance, all of these grants are means tested. Note that in Northern Ireland, the rates for some of these grants are slightly higher than in England. The current rates in Northern Ireland are:

Grant	Northern Ireland rate (per year for 2010/11)
Parents' learning allowance	£1,538
Adult dependents' grant	£2,695
Disabled students' allowance – non-medical personal help	£20,938
Disabled students' allowance – equipment	£5,266 (for duration of course)
Disabled students' allowance – general allowance	£1,759

The childcare grant in Northern Ireland is paid at the same rates as in England. See p29 for further details.

Medical and dental students on placement and students who must travel abroad may be entitled to help with the cost of travel. This is awarded on the same basis as in England (see p70).

Students who entered higher education on or after 1 September 2006

If you began your course on or after 1 September 2006 and are not otherwise treated as if you had started before this date (eg, you had secured a deferred entry place from the 2005/06 academic year), you will receive financial help under the current rules for student support.[16] The exception to this rule is if you are studying in the Republic of Ireland, in which case you will be funded as an 'old system' student.

Tuition fees

Eligible, 'current system' Northern Irish-domiciled students studying in Northern Ireland, Wales or England will pay variable fees of up to £3,290 in the 2010/11 academic year. You are eligible for a tuition fee loan to cover these.[17]

Fees for Northern Irish-domiciled students in Scotland are fixed at £1,820 per year for all courses except medicine, in which case the fee is fixed at £2,895 per year. In all cases, eligible Northern Irish-domiciled students can take out tuition fee loans to cover this cost.

The maximum fee loan available will match the fee you are charged. The fee loan is not means tested on your income or the income of anyone in your household. However, the loan will be added to your total student loan debt (including any loans taken out for living costs – see p59) and you will start repayments once you have graduated or otherwise left the course and are earning at least £15,000 a year.

If you wish to pay all or part of the fee upfront yourself, you can do so. Your institution will expect some indication of how you intend to pay your fees when you register.

Help with tuition fees for part-time courses is also available (see p60).

If you wish to study in the Republic of Ireland, see the information for 'old system' students on p55.

Maintenance grant

The maintenance grant for 'current system' students is a non-repayable, means-tested allowance of up to £3,475. The maximum amount is payable to students with a household income of £19,203 or less a year, and a partial amount is paid on a sliding scale up to a household income of £41,065.[18]

If you are entitled to apply for means-tested benefits, you should apply for the special support grant instead of the maintenance grant (see p58). If you are not entitled to apply, but your partner is, the maintenance grant will be included in benefits claims for your household.

Part of the maintenance grant substitutes the student loan for living costs. This means that if you receive any maintenance grant, the amount of loan for living costs you can receive is reduced, up to a maximum of £1,887.[19] The formula for this can be complex, and you should seek advice from your ELB, students' union or university advice service if you are uncertain it has been applied correctly.

If you are in receipt of a full maintenance grant of £3,475, the maximum amount of student loan for living costs is reduced by £1,887.

Where you are in receipt of a maintenance grant of more than £1,318 but less than £3,475, your loan is reduced by an amount equal to £1,887 less £1 for every £17.25 that your household income exceeds £19,203. See p59 for an explanation of how your household income is calculated. If your grant is £1,318 or less, the loan is reduced by the amount of maintenance grant paid.

Teacher training students are treated slightly differently – check with your ELB, students' union or university advice service.

Examples

Gail is a single, independent student studying in Belfast. She starts her course in October 2010. She has an assessable household income of £2,000. She receives the maximum grant of £3,475 and can take out a student loan of up to £2,953 (the maximum rate of £4,840 less £1,887).

Anne is 18 and lives with her parents in Armagh. She starts her course in Belfast in October 2010. Her assessable family income is £21,500, which means she receives a maintenance grant of £2,921.

Her household income is £2,297 above the lower limit of £19,203. This £2,297 is divided by 17.25 to give £133. This is subtracted from the maximum loan deduction of £1,887 to give £1,754.

Anne's maximum loan entitlement is therefore £3,750 less £1,754 = £1,996.

John is 19 and starts his course in Coleraine in October 2010. He receives a maintenance grant of £800. The maximum amount of loan he can receive is reduced by £800.

For more details of student loans for living costs, see p59.

Special support grant

In order to provide extra support to students regarded as particularly vulnerable, a separate grant is available if you are a full-time student eligible to claim means-tested social security benefits.[20]

Most full-time students cannot receive such benefits but if, for example, you are a lone parent, or you and your partner are both full-time students and have one or more children, or you receive disability living allowance, or you are deaf, you may be able to claim one or more means-tested benefits. See Chapters 12, 14 and 15 for full details of which students can claim means-tested benefits.

If you can claim means-tested benefits, you should claim the special support grant instead of the maintenance grant. Like the maintenance grant, this is a non-repayable, means-tested allowance of up to £3,475. The maximum amount will be payable to students with a household income of £19,203 or less a year. A partial amount will be paid on a sliding scale up to a household income of £41,065.

Unlike the maintenance grant, the special support grant does not substitute any part of the student loan and it is not taken into account when calculating your entitlement to means-tested benefits.

Student loan

Student loans for living costs are available to eligible 'current system' students on the same terms and rates as for 'old system' students, except that up to £1,887 of the loan may be substituted for the maintenance grant that is paid to the student. See p55 for rates of loan and p57 for details of the loan substitution. If you receive a special support grant, no part of your loan is substituted.

Other support

The childcare grant, parents' learning allowance, adult dependants' grant and disabled students' allowance are all available to Northern Irish undergraduates on the same basis as students in England, except that rates for most grants other than the childcare grant are now slightly higher in Northern Ireland. See p56 for a table giving the Northern Irish rates (which are the same as for old system students) and pp29–30 for further details of these forms of support.

Medical and dental students on placement and students who must travel abroad may be entitled to help with the cost of travel. This is awarded on the same basis as in England (see p70).

You may also be entitled to a bursary from your institution – see p35 for details.

Assessment of income

Much of the support you receive is based on your household income. The definition of household income in Northern Ireland is the same as that in England (see p30).

Once your household income is assessed, it will first reduce any maintenance grant or special support grant you are due to receive.

In 2010/11, if your household income is £19,203 or less, you will receive the maximum maintenance or special support grant. If your household income is between £19,203 and £41,065 you will receive a reduced amount of the applicable grant (the minimum amount is £50). For every £4.55 of household income between £19,203 and £29,019, £1 is deducted from the grant. For every £9.50 of household income above £29,019, £1 is deducted from the grant until the maximum household income of £41,065 is reached. No grant is payable if household income is £41,066 or more.[21]

Income above £41,540 reduces other support at a rate of £1 for every £9.50 of income above that figure.[22] Any supplementary grants for dependants will be reduced first, then the 25 per cent of the student loan that is means tested, and finally any grant for travel costs.[23]

2. **Part-time undergraduates**

Part-time students in Northern Ireland receive funding on the same basis as part-time students in England (see p35).[24]

3. **Discretionary funds**

Higher education institutions are allocated money to provide hardship funds for 'home' (see p23) undergraduate and postgraduate students in financial difficulty. In Northern Ireland these are known as 'support funds'. Repayable loans and non-repayable grants can be issued by the funds. Such support is not guaranteed.

Some institutions may have additional hardship funds – check with your institution or students' union.

Support funds

Non-repayable grants are available on a needs-assessed basis if you are experiencing financial difficulty serious enough to mean you may have to leave your course. The funds can help with living and study costs such as childcare, rent, books and utility bills, or with large one-off and exceptional costs such as major housing repairs and emergency situations such as fire or bereavement. These are known as support funds in Northern Ireland, although similar funds are available elsewhere.

Priority is usually given to students with children, mature students, students from low-income families, disabled students, final year students and those who have left care. However, all students who meet the personal and course requirements for undergraduate student support are eligible, including healthcare students. You must, however, have applied for your full entitlement of a student loan if you are eligible for one.

The funds cannot be used to meet the costs of tuition fees or to make up for non-receipt of a parental contribution to a grant or loan.

A grant would not normally exceed £3,500, although institutions have some discretion in exceptional circumstances. Individual institutions have different application processes and different pressures on the funds and no sum is guaranteed. However, there is an appeals process should you need to challenge the fund administrator's decision.

Notes

1. Full-time undergraduates
  1 Sch 1 E(SS)(NI) Regs
  2 Reg 5 and Sch 2 E(SS)(NI) Regs
  3 Regs 14-15 E(SS)(NI) Regs
  4 Regs 20, 57, 59 and 63 E(SS)(NI) Regs
  5 Reg 63(2) E(SS)(NI) Regs
  6 Reg 23 E(SS)(NI) Regs
  7 Reg 20(10) E(SS)(NI) Regs
  8 Reg 2 E(SS)(NI) Regs
  9 Reg 32 E(SS)(NI) Regs
 10 Regs 35-36 E(SS)(NI) Regs
 11 Reg 32(7) E(SS)(NI) Regs
 12 Reg 61 E(SS)(NI) Regs
 13 Reg 68 E(SS)(NI) Regs
 14 Reg 68 (3)-(4) E(SS)(NI) Regs
 15 Regs 41-56 E(SS)(NI) Regs
 16 Reg 2 E(SS)(NI) Regs
 17 Regs 20-25 E(SS)(NI) Regs
 18 Reg 58 E(SS)(NI) Regs
 19 Reg 66 E(SS)(NI) Regs
 20 Regs 59-60 E(SS)(NI) Regs
 21 Regs 58(5) and 60(5) E(SS)(NI) Regs
 22 Sch 5 para 9 E(SS)(NI) Regs
 23 Regs 88 and 90 E(SS)(NI) Regs

2. Part-time undergraduates
 24 Regs 122-138 E(SS)(NI) Regs

Chapter 5

Postgraduate student support

This chapter covers:
1. Studentship rates (below)
2. Disabled students' allowance (p63)
3. Postgraduate student support in Northern Ireland (p64)

If you are a UK student undertaking a postgraduate course, you have a legal right to receive financial support in one situation only: if you are studying on a postgraduate course of initial teacher training – eg, a Postgraduate Certificate in Education (see p77). English and Welsh students may also be able to receive a bursary for postgraduate study in social work (see p83), but this financial help is not available to Northern Irish students undertaking such study in England or Wales.

State support for other postgraduate courses is very limited. Individual scholarships or 'studentships' are available from seven research councils but the demand far outstrips supply and funding is not guaranteed. Interdisciplinary studentships are also offered by some funders, such as the Economic and Social Research Council and the Natural Environment Research Council. See Appendix 2 for the addresses of the award-making bodies.

Some alternative sources of finance will be open to postgraduates – see Chapter 6 for more details.

Funding for postgraduate students in Northern Ireland is different to that in England and Wales – see p64 for further details.

1. Studentship rates

Research councils fund research and Masters studentships, covering fees and maintenance. The following are the basic rates for maintenance stipends in 2010/11. They do not include any grant for tuition fees, which is usually paid in addition. The rate for this in 2010/11 is £3,466. Other schemes may be available, and eligibility and residence conditions will apply – contact the relevant research council for full information on the funding it provides (see Appendix 2).

Body	Research studentships	Masters studentships	
AHRC	£15,590	£11,490	London
	£13,590	£9,490	Outside London
AHRC PPMS	–	£10,845	London
	–	£8,845	Outside London
ESRC	£15,590	–	London
	£13,590	–	Outside London
NERC	£15,590	£10,712	London
	£13,590	£8,712	Outside London
MRC[1]	£15,590	£15,740	London
	£13,590	£13,590	Outside London
EPSRC[2]	£13,590	–	
	£15,090	–	Engineering doctorates only
STFC	£15,590	–	London
	£13,590	–	Outside London
BBSRC[3]	£15,590	£15,590	London
	£13,590	£13,590	Outside London
	£20,970	£20,970	Students with veterinary degrees only

AHRC = Arts and Humanities Research Council

BBSRC = Biotechnology and Biological Sciences Research Council

EPSRC = Engineering and Physical Sciences Research Council

ESRC = Economic and Social Research Council

MRC = Medical Research Council

NERC = Natural Environment Research Council

PPMS = Professional Preparation Master's Scheme

STFC = Science and Technology Facilities Council (formerly the Partial Physics and Astronomy Research Council)

Additional allowances may be available if you have dependants, and some research councils will fund part-time study. The relevant research council can offer guidance on the full range of support available.

Note: the application deadline for almost all awards made through the research councils is usually several months in advance of the start of the course, and you should make your application as early as possible.

2. Disabled students' allowance

Both full- and part-time postgraduate students studying 'recognised' taught and research courses are eligible for a disabled students' allowance (DSA).

A recognised course is one which normally requires a first degree qualification to enter, is at least one academic year long, is provided by a publicly funded institution and is not a course of initial teacher training. Your course should be eligible for an award from a research council or be equivalent to a course which is eligible for awards, but if that course offers its own equivalent allowance, then you must apply for this (see below).

Part-time courses should be for longer than a year, but no more than twice as long as an equivalent full-time course. Existing and new students are eligible and there is no age limit, but residency conditions will apply.

One allowance of up to £10,260 a year in 2010/11[4] is available for specialist equipment, non-medical personal helpers and/or additional travel costs, subject to a needs assessment. Contact your local authority or Student Finance England (see Appendix 2) for more details.

Students funded through one of the main studentship programmes outlined in section 1 above will be eligible for more generous DSA funding through the research councils, and you should speak to the disability support office at your institution in the first instance regarding an application.

3. Postgraduate student support in Northern Ireland

There are no concessionary fees for postgraduate courses in Northern Ireland. You should contact the university or college where you want to study to check on any sources of funding for your course. **Note**: postgraduate funding is no longer available for UK students wishing to study in the Republic of Ireland.

Funding is generally in the form of studentship awards. To be considered for funding you must comply with the three-year residency requirement for undergraduates (see p22).

If you are a suitably qualified graduate you may compete for an award, but there are always more applicants than awards. Further information can be obtained in the booklet *Awards for Postgraduate Study*, available from the Department for Employment and Learning Northern Ireland (DELNI). Closing dates for the different awards vary between 1 May and 30 June and are strictly observed. Check the closing date with the postgraduate office at the university you will be attending.

Studentship awards

These grants are awarded for postgraduate research degrees (eg, MPhil, PhD) and for approved courses of advanced study – eg, Masters degrees. You can obtain approved course lists from the universities. Most students benefiting from these awards have degree classifications of 2:1 or above, although you may be accepted for a taught Masters degree in science and technology if you have a lower second-class honours degree.

Studentship awards are for fixed amounts and are not means tested. Approved fees and maintenance costs are included. The basic rate of the maintenance grant payable in 2010/11 is £13,590 for research studentships, and £6,795 for taught studentships. Additional allowances may also be paid for dependants and students with special needs.

If you are a science and technology student working on a research project, you may also apply through DELNI for a Co-operative Award in Science and Technology that involves sponsorship from industry. Details are available from DELNI. The basic maintenance grant of £13,489 is supplemented by a payment of at least 40 per cent from the collaborating body.

The Department of Agriculture and Rural Development (DARD) runs a separate scheme providing postgraduate studentships in its priority research areas. Contact DARD on 028 9052 4710 or visit www.dardni.gov.uk for more details.

Studying in Northern Ireland

If you are seeking research funding and want to study in Northern Ireland, you must apply directly to the university for a place on a course and an award. Being offered a place does not automatically mean that you will obtain funding. Closing dates for applications are at the discretion of the institution (and are generally around April/May), but late applications may be accepted subject to availability of places. Grants are awarded by DELNI for all fields except agriculture and medicine.

Studying elsewhere in the UK

If you plan to study elsewhere in the UK, you may be able to receive funding through various research councils (see p62). You need to approach the university where you want to study. The university will then advise you which research council to apply to and when application forms are available. Closing dates vary between councils.

Disabled students' allowance

A postgraduate disabled students' allowance is available to eligible postgraduate students in Northern Ireland on the same basis as for postgraduate students in England (see p63). You should apply to your education and library board.

Bursary awards for particular courses

Postgraduate Certificate in Education

See the information on initial teacher training in Northern Ireland on p81.

European Social Fund

Institutions hold updated lists of postgraduate courses (one-year vocational courses) that offer places attracting European Social Fund funding. To meet the criteria, students must be unemployed graduates under 25 years of age. Your circumstances and the class of your degree are taken into account when awards are being made. Apply directly to the institution for this funding.

Notes

1. **Studentship rates**
   1 The MRC and EPSRC have slightly different methods of funding. Individual institutions are now allocated block grants from which they then set the number of studentships and the level of stipend. A minimum level of stipend is set as indicated in the table, with institutions deciding whether to grant more than this depending on local circumstances.
   2 See note I. Note that the EPSRC sets no minimum payment for Masters studentships.
   3 The BBSRC has a similar scheme to the MRC and EPSRC for its doctoral (research) studentships only. The minimum level of bursary is set as indicated.

2. **Disabled students' allowance**
   4 Reg 157 E(SS) Regs 2009

Chapter 6

· ·

Vocational courses and other sources of student support

This chapter covers:
1. Healthcare students in England and Wales (below)
2. Healthcare students in Northern Ireland (p74)
3. Initial teacher training in England (p76)
4. Initial teacher training in Wales (p79)
5. Initial teacher training in Northern Ireland (p81)
6. Social work students (p82)
7. Dance and drama awards (p82)
8. Alternative sources of finance (p86)

1. Healthcare students in England and Wales

If you are studying an allied health profession, or a profession complementary to dentistry, nursing or midwifery, you may be eligible for an NHS bursary and any applicable supplementary allowances. You may also be eligible if you are studying medicine or dentistry, but only for the latter years of pre-registration training.

There are two types of bursary. The type you are able to receive depends on the level of course you are studying. Diploma-level students are eligible for a non-means-tested bursary, while degree-level students are eligible for a means-tested award. Each type of bursary also has additional allowances for specific groups. To be eligible for either, you must also fulfil the personal residency requirement for higher education students in England (see p22).

Both types of bursary are funded in England by NHS Student Bursaries, based in Fleetwood. In Wales nursing and midwifery students are eligible for the non-means-tested bursary and this is processed by the university. The means-tested bursary and the childcare allowance for all students are processed by the NHS Wales Student Awards Unit, based in Cardiff. In addition to receiving either of the two bursaries, all NHS students who meet the criteria are eligible for financial support from the Access to Learning Fund (see p37) for study in England and the

Financial Contingency Fund for study in Wales. In both cases, the NHS pays your tuition fees for you (see pp68 and 70).

Eligible courses
- Allied health professions: chiropody, dietetics, occupational therapy, orthoptics, physiotherapy, prosthetics and orthotics, radiography, speech and language therapy
- Professions complementary to dentistry: dental auxiliary, dental hygiene, dental therapy
- Audiology[1]
- Degree-level nursing and midwifery
- Diploma-level nursing, midwifery or operating department practice (including conversion courses for second-level nurses who have not practised for a year or more)
- Medicine and dentistry (the latter stages of pre-registration training only)

Old and new system

The bursary scheme was updated for the 2007/08 academic year in the light of age discrimination legislation. There were new provisions for NHS-funded healthcare students who require maternity leave (see p74). The changes only affect students starting their course in the 2007/08 academic year or later. Students who started before this date are covered by the previous system. This chapter therefore refers to 'old' and 'new' system students.

At the same time, provisions for all NHS-funded healthcare students who require maternity/paternity leave and adoption leave (see p74) were also introduced. Note that these new provisions affect all students enrolled onto a pre-registration course and who are in receipt of the maintenance element of the NHS bursary regardless of when they started their course – ie both old and new system students qualify.

Diploma-level students

Diploma-level students receive the non-means-tested bursary. The level of bursary you receive does not depend on your income. In England the bursary is available to students on a nursing, midwifery or operating department practice higher education diploma course. In Wales, the bursary is available to nursing and midwifery students. In Wales, operating department practice students have their tuition fees paid by the NHS and receive a training salary instead of the non-means-tested bursary.

If you are eligible for this bursary, the NHS also pays your fees. The bursary is paid in 12 equal monthly instalments across the academic year. There are three rates of bursary; the rate you receive depends on where you live.

Maximum amounts of non-means-tested bursaries 2010/11

	Old system students	New system students
London	£7,566	£7,827
Elsewhere	£6,438	£6,701
Parental home	£6,438	£6,701

There are additional allowances available if you are a diploma student.

Extra weeks' allowance

The bursary assumes that you are required to attend the course for 45 weeks a year. However, if, as part of your course, you must move to London to attend a practice placement, the bursary will be increased by £17 a week for the length of the placement.

Older students' allowance

If you are an 'old system' student and were 26 or over before the beginning of your first academic year,[2] you will receive an additional £752. If you turn 26 during your course, you do not become eligible in later years. This cannot be claimed in addition to the single parent addition (see p70). This is not available for 'new system' students.

Dependants' allowances

If you have adults or children wholly or mainly financially dependent on you, you may be eligible for extra dependants' allowances. However, the income of your dependant(s) is taken into account and so eligibility for this allowance is means tested.

Dependants' allowances 2010/11

'New system' students:

Spouse or civil partner (or other adult dependant, or first child if there is no spouse or any adult dependants)	£2,238
Each additional dependant	£539

'Old system' students:

Spouse or civil partner (or other adult dependant, or first child if there is no spouse or any adult dependants)	£2,238
Child aged under 11[3]	£473
Child aged 11–15	£940
Child aged 16–17	£1,245
Child aged 18+	£1,783

Single parent addition

If you are an 'old system' student and a lone parent, you are entitled to an additional £1,104. This is not paid in addition to the older students' allowance. 'New system' students should apply for the parents' learning allowance.

Parents' learning allowance

If you are a 'new system' student and have a dependent child(ren), you can claim an additional £1,104. This is available to all 'new system' student parents, including those with partners, but is means tested.

Childcare allowance

If you have responsibility for a child under the age of 15 (or 17 if s/he has special educational needs) and you use registered or approved childcare, you can apply for a childcare allowance. You cannot receive the childcare allowance if you also receive the childcare element of working tax credit (see Chapter 19).

The grant can cover up to 85 per cent of your actual costs of childcare, with a maximum payment of £126.65 a week for one child or £187.75 a week for two or more children (in Wales the maximum payment for two or more children is higher at £209.95 a week).

The childcare grant is means tested; the amount you receive depends on your income and that of any dependants.

Initial expenses allowance

If you are a first-year student, you are given an additional one-off payment of £55 at the beginning of your course.

Practice placement costs

The cost of travel between your home and a practice placement site that is not part of the college, plus additional residential costs where appropriate, may be reimbursed to you. Only the amount that exceeds the cost of travel between your term-time residence and place of study is reimbursed. Your college will have details of how these expenses should be claimed.

Disabled students' allowance

If you have a disability, you can claim a disabled students' allowance from the NHS on the same basis as students in other forms of higher education (see p31).

Degree-level students

A means-tested bursary is available if you are studying for a degree-level qualification in any of the healthcare disciplines outlined on p68. If you meet the personal eligibility criteria, your fees will be paid. The amount of money you receive for living costs depends on your (and your partner's) income. If you are a dependent student (see p31), your parents' income is taken into account. The living costs include a basic amount for, for instance, rent and food. A means-tested bursary-holder may also be eligible for a reduced-amount undergraduate student loan. This loan is not subject to a means test and an application should be made through your local authority or Student Finance England.

Employed students do not usually qualify for bursaries, but may qualify for student support payable by the Department for Business, Innovation and Skills or Welsh Assembly Government.

Maximum amounts of means-tested bursaries 2010/11

	'Old system' students	*'New system' students*
London	£3,129	£3,392
Elsewhere	£2,548	£2,810
Parental home	£2,084	£2,346

Reduced rate student loans 2010/11[4]

	All students – full year	*All students – final year*
London	£3,263	£2,498
Elsewhere	£2,324	£1,811
Parental home	£1,744	£1,324

As with diploma students, there is a range of additional allowances available. However, the rates for degree-level students are generally different.

Extra weeks' allowance

The bursary is paid for a notional academic year of 30 weeks and three days. However, should your course require additional attendance over and above this, further allowances are paid. The rate for each additional week is as follows, and is the same for both 'old system' and 'new system' students.

Extra weeks' allowance 2010/11

London	£106
Elsewhere	£82
Parental home	£54

If your required attendance in an academic year is 45 weeks or more, an allowance for all 52 weeks is paid.

Older students' allowance

If you are an 'old system' student, and were aged 26 or over before the beginning of your first academic year,[5] you will receive an additional allowance. If you turn

26 during your course, you do not become eligible in later years. This cannot be claimed in addition to the single parent addition. It is also payable to diploma students attending accelerated programmes for graduates, regardless of age.

Older students' allowance 2010/11

Age before first academic year

26	£448
27	£777
28	£1,152
29+	£1,524

Dependants' allowances

If you have adults or children wholly or mainly financially dependent on you, you may be eligible for extra dependants' allowances. However, the income of your dependants is taken into account and so eligibility for this allowance is means tested.

Dependants' allowances 2010/11

'New system' students:

Spouse or civil partner (or other adult dependant, or first child if there is no spouse or any adult dependants)	£2,640
Each additional dependant	£539

'Old system' students:

Spouse (or other adult dependant, or first child if there is no spouse or any adult dependants)	£2,640
Child aged under 11[6]	£552
Child aged 11–15	£1,104
Child aged 16–17	£1,468
Child aged 18+	£2,113

Single parent allowance

If you are an 'old system' student and a lone parent, you are entitled to an additional £1,303. This is not paid in addition to the older students' allowance. 'New system' students should apply for the parents' learning allowance.

Parents' learning allowance

If you are a 'new system' student and have a dependent child(ren), you can claim an additional £1,303. This is available to all student parents, including those with partners, but is means tested.

Childcare allowance

This is paid on the same basis as the childcare allowance for non-means-tested NHS bursary students. See p70 for details.

Practice placement costs

The cost of travel between your home and a practice placement site that is not part of the college, and additional residential costs where appropriate, may be reimbursed to you. Only the amount that exceeds the cost of travel between your term-time residence and place of study is reimbursed. Your college will have details of how these expenses should be claimed.

Disabled students' allowance

If you have a disability, you can claim a disabled students' allowance from the NHS on the same basis as students in other forms of higher education (see p31).

NHS hardship grant

In addition to institutional hardship funds such as the Access to Learning Fund (see p37), the NHS operates a limited hardship fund for medicine and dentistry students eligible for the means-tested bursary. You should contact NHS Student Bursaries to apply for the NHS hardship fund.

European Union nationals

If you are a national of a European Union (EU) member state, you may be eligible for NHS bursary support as follows.

Non-UK EU nationals and their children who satisfy the three-year residence criteria in the 'UK and Islands' will be treated as if they were UK students and are eligible for support for both maintenance and fees. They are not required to have settled status. If their residence in the UK was mainly for the purpose of full-time higher education, they may still be eligible for an NHS bursary (maintenance grant and tuition fees) if they can show that they were ordinarily resident in a European Economic Area country or Switzerland immediately prior to their period of ordinary residence in the UK.

EU students who are not ordinarily resident in the UK under the terms described, may be awarded an 'EU fees only' award, under which they have the cost of their tuition fees met, but are not eligible for a student loan, hardship funds or the maintenance element of the NHS bursary.

You may also qualify for support as a migrant worker – the rules are very complex, so check with your students' union or university or college advice centre.

Part-time students

Part-time students on NHS-funded degree courses are eligible for 75 per cent of the means-tested NHS bursary. The part-time diploma students' bursary is the appropriate portion of full-time study.

The full rate is paid if you have additional costs resulting from a disability and for reimbursing the costs of attending a clinical placement.

Students who are pregnant or who have recently given birth

If you are an NHS-funded student, have enrolled on your course and require maternity leave, you can be paid your bursary for a period of up to 45 weeks (known as a 'maternity allowance'). Seconded students and EU nationals on fees-only awards cannot receive this help as they are not eligible for the bursary or any of the supplementary grants.

For more information see www.nhsbsa.nhs.uk/students or contact the NHS Wales Student Awards Unit (www.nliah.wales.nhs.uk).

2. Healthcare students in Northern Ireland

If you are planning to study an allied health professions degree course in Northern Ireland, you can apply for funding from the Department of Health, Social Services and Public Safety (DHSSPS). Under these arrangements, you will not have to pay tuition fees and will be eligible to apply for an income-assessed bursary to cover living costs and a reduced-rate, non-income-assessed student loan. As in England and Wales, medical and dental students in their final years of study are also funded through this system. Students from European Union states who are studying in Northern Ireland are also exempt from paying tuition fees, but they are not eligible for a bursary or loan to cover living costs.

The amount of bursary you receive depends on your household income. Additional allowances may be available if you have dependants or a disability. Your local education and library board (ELB) will be able to advise. The rates for 2010/11 are as follows.

Bursary rates 2010/11

Full-year rates	Bursary	Loan
Living away from parental home	£2,355	£2,324
Living at parental home	£1,920	£1,744
Final-year rates		
Living away from parental home	£2,355	£1,811
Living at parental home	£1,920	£1,324

The ELBs deal with the bursary arrangements on behalf of the DHSSPS. If you are a Northern Irish student, you should, therefore, apply to your local Student Finance office. If you live in England, Scotland or Wales, you should apply to apply to Student Finance NI at the address for the North Eastern ELB.

Nursing and midwifery students

Full-time pre-registration nursing and direct entry midwifery students taking up a commissioned DHSSPS place on a course leading to entry on the Nursing and Midwifery Council register are entitled to receive a bursary while undertaking the course. Students receiving a bursary do not pay tuition fees, but they are not eligible for support from their ELB. They are now eligible for help from their institution's discretionary support fund. Speak to your students' union or university advice centre for more details.

The bursary system changed for new students after 1 September 2007, but 'old system' students who started their course before that date remained funded under the original rules.

Both schemes comprise a non-means-tested basic rate, additional means-tested allowances, travel expenses for costs incurred while on clinical placements and one-off payments of £110 for uniforms and £80 for books. Disabled students' allowances are also payable where appropriate, at the same rate as for other higher education students (see p30). The rates are determined annually.

Note: a general review of the bursary scheme is being conducted and changes may be made for this or future academic years. Contact the DHSSPS for further information (see Appendix 2).

Bursary rates 2010/11: 'old system' students

Basic award (not means tested)

Aged under 26 years at the start of the course (this rate applies for the duration of the course)	£6,055
Aged 26 years and over at the start of the course	£6,820

Additional dependants' additions (means tested)

Partner or other adult dependant (or first child if no other dependant)	£2,275
Child aged under 11	£475
Child aged 11–15	£950
Child aged 16–17	£1,260
Child aged 18+	£1,810
Single parents' allowance (not means tested)	£1,125

Bursary rates 2010/11: 'new system' students

Basic award (not means tested)	£6,055

Additional dependants' additions (means tested)

Partner or other adult dependant (or first child if no other dependant)	£2,275
Each subsequent child	£540

Parents' learning allowance (not means tested)	£1,125
Contribution to childcare	Up to £1,245

3. Initial teacher training in England

There are four main routes for initial teacher training (ITT) in England that lead to qualified teacher status (QTS):

- Bachelor of Education (BEd) – an undergraduate degree, usually for four years' full-time study or equivalent, with qualified teacher status gained after a year's successful teaching, although now there are certain two- or three-year undergraduate courses which lead to QTS;
- Postgraduate Certificate in Education (PGCE) – a postgraduate degree, usually for one year or part-time equivalent, with qualified teacher status gained after a year's successful teaching;
- school-centred initial teacher training (SCITT). This can be undertaken through two routes:
  - the graduate teacher programme – up to one year of postgraduate training while working as a teacher to gain qualified teacher status; *or*
  - the registered teacher programme – up to two years of undergraduate degree study while training and working as a teacher to gain qualified teacher status.
- subject knowledge enhancement (SKE) – students who hold undergraduate degrees in certain subjects, particularly in maths and science, and who are choosing to undertake a PGCE course some time after being awarded their original degree, may be required to undertake an SKE course before moving onto the main PGCE course. These are modular, and the number of modules required will depend on the student and her/his current level of knowledge.

Each route has a different funding mechanism.

Bachelor of Education/Bachelor of Arts with qualified teacher status

The principal financial assistance available if you are studying a BEd qualification is the basic undergraduate student support package as outlined in Chapter 2. This includes all supplementary grants and access to the hardship funds.

Students on certain two-year, full-time undergraduate ITT courses leading to QTS are able to receive a teacher training bursary of £7,000 per year if they are undertaking courses in maths, chemistry or physics. Contact the Training and Development Agency for Schools (TDA) for more information.

There are no further incentives for BEd or Bachelor of Arts with QTS study in 2010/11.

Postgraduate Certificate in Education

If you are on a full- or part-time PGCE course and meet the personal and residential eligibility criteria for undergraduate student support (see pp22–23), you are entitled to the same support package as new undergraduate students (see Chapter 2). You are also eligible for assistance from the Access to Learning Fund. There are also several incentive packages for which you may be eligible.

Tuition fees

In England, PGCE students are, like new undergraduates, liable for variable fees of up to £3,290, but eligible UK students can take out a loan to cover the cost of these.[7]

Teacher training bursary

A tax-free bursary is available if you are undertaking a postgraduate teacher training course. There are three levels of bursary: £9,000, £6,000 and £4,000. The level you receive will depend on the subject you are training to teach, and these change each year, with priority subjects attracting higher rates of bursary – a current list of subjects and the bursary they attract can be found at www.tda.gov.uk.

If you are on a one-year course, you are paid in monthly instalments between October and June. If your course is part time, you are paid in instalments in accordance with the length of your training.

If you are on a modular course, you are eligible provided you are not already employed as a teacher in a school or within further or higher education. In this instance, one payment of half the total amount (ie, £2,000, £3,000 or £4,500) is made after you have registered for the first assessment module, and the second is paid after you achieve qualified teacher status.

If you are a full-time trainee, the salary is not taxable and you do not have to pay national insurance contributions. If you are a part-time trainee, the salary may be taxable, depending on your total income for the year. It will be included in any calculation for means-tested benefits.

Students from the European Union are eligible for this incentive.

'Golden hello'

This is an incentive to encourage you to train in certain shortage subject areas (maths, science, information and communications technology, design and technology, modern languages, religious education or music). The money is paid if you have successfully achieved qualified teacher status and are entering your second year of teaching in one of the shortage areas, provided the second year is within 12 months of the induction year. The post must be in a publicly funded school in England, a non-maintained special school, or an academy. The position must also be permanent or on a fixed-term contract of more than a term's duration. The amount you receive depends on the subject. For maths and science, the payment is £5,000. The amount for other subjects is £2,500. The incentive is paid in a lump sum with your salary and is taxable. You should inform the school that you are eligible to receive the incentive.

Graduate teacher programme

If you are a graduate aged 24 or over, the graduate teacher programme allows you to train as a teacher in maintained schools while still earning a living.

Salary

When you start on the programme, you receive a salary from the school in which you are based. The level of salary to be paid by the school is agreed by the governing body and may be at a rate based on the scales for either qualified or unqualified teachers, but must be no lower than the minimum salary grade for unqualified teachers of at least £15,461. If you are on this scheme, you are not eligible for the training salary or the 'golden hello' outlined above.

Training grant

In addition, the school receives £5,630 a year for the cost of your training. This can be used to cover the cost of an initial training needs assessment, tuition fees, supply cover, mentoring training, learning resources and materials. This funding cannot be used as a wage supplement.

Registered teacher programme

This scheme is similar to the graduate teacher programme. But if you have yet to complete the necessary degree-level qualification, you can continue to study for this in addition to your teacher training within a maintained school.

Salary

The school agrees your salary level, but it must be no lower than the minimum salary grade for unqualified teachers of £15,461.

Training grant

As with the graduate teacher programme, the school receives a £9,100 training grant. This can be used for the purposes specified above, including meeting the costs of your degree course fees.

Subject knowledge enhancement courses

Students undertaking SKE courses prior to commencing a PGCE course are able to apply for a bursary to help fund the course.

SKE courses are modular. You will receive £400 per module for chemistry, maths and physics. You can also receive £300 per module for other sciences, design and technology, information and communications technology, religious education, music or modern languages, although in the case of this second group the course must be at least four modules long.

The bursary is usually paid monthly and you are not eligible for other student support. Contact your training provider or the TDA for more information on this funding.

Repayment of teachers' loans

This was a pilot scheme for newly qualified teachers who took teaching posts in the academic years 2002/03, 2003/04 or 2004/05. If you are eligible and you work in a shortage subject (see p77), you will have your student loan repaid. The scheme only applies if you spend at least half of your teaching time teaching the shortage subjects.

To be eligible you must:

- be employed in England or Wales in a teaching post at a maintained school, a non-maintained special school, a city technology college, a city college for the technology of arts or a city academy;
- have begun employment between 1 July 2002 and 30 June 2005;
- be employed to teach one or more of the shortage subjects for at least half of your teaching time within a normal school week.

More information is available at www.teachernet.gov.uk/teachersloans. The scheme has not been extended and is, therefore, unavailable to those teachers who started employment after 30 June 2005, unless they could not start work before that date because they were pregnant or had recently given birth.

4. Initial teacher training in Wales

In Wales, there are three main routes for initial teacher training (ITT) that leads to qualified teacher status.

- Bachelor of Education (BEd) – an undergraduate degree, usually for four years' full-time study or equivalent, with qualified teacher status gained after a year's successful teaching;
- Postgraduate Certificate in Education (PGCE) – a postgraduate degree, usually for one year or part-time equivalent, with qualified teacher status gained after a year's successful teaching;
- school-centred initial teacher training (SCITT), through the graduate teacher programme – up to one year of postgraduate training while working as a teacher to gain qualified teacher status.

Bachelor of Education

The principal financial assistance available if you are studying a BEd qualification is the basic undergraduate student support package for Welsh students as outlined in Chapter 3. This includes all supplementary grants and access to the hardship funds. In addition to this support, students in Wales may be eligible for certain incentive packages, which are outlined below.

Secondary undergraduate placement grants

Grants of £1,200 are available if you are on an undergraduate teacher training course in Wales and are studying one of the secondary shortage subject areas (maths, science, modern foreign languages, design and technology, information technology, Welsh, music, geography and religious education).

If you are studying in a non-shortage area, £600 is payable. The only course currently offering this is English including drama. The grant is paid to you through the teacher training provider in two instalments in each year of the course.

Welsh medium improvement supplement

In order to help those students who need additional assistance to raise their competence and confidence, a £1,500 grant is available to undergraduate or postgraduate students undertaking secondary ITT in Wales using the Welsh language.[8] This increases to £1,800 for maths, chemistry and physics courses. Once qualified, you are expected to take up a secondary school teaching post using the Welsh language. Your institution assesses your eligibility and advises you on the application process.

Postgraduate Certificate of Education

If you are on a full- or part-time PGCE course and meet the personal and residential eligibility criteria for undergraduate student support (see pp41–42), you are entitled to the same support package as new undergraduate students (see p44). You are also eligible for assistance from the Financial Contingency Fund. As with undergraduate students, there are also several incentive packages for which you may be eligible.

Tuition fees

Eligible, 'new system' (see p44) Welsh-domiciled PGCE students studying in Wales and starting their courses in September 2010 or later will pay flexible fees of up to £3,290 in the 2010/11 academic year.[9] You are eligible for a tuition fee loan to cover the remainder.[10]

Chapter 6: Vocational courses and other sources of student support
5. Initial teacher training in Northern Ireland

6

Teacher training grant

If you undertake a PGCE course in Wales, you are eligible for a teacher training grant during the period of study and may be eligible for an additional teaching grant on taking up employment as a qualified teacher.

The rate of grant depends on the subject you are training to teach. There are three levels: £9,000, £6,000 and £4,000. The level you receive will depend on the subject you are training to teach, and these change each year, with priority subjects attracting higher rates of bursary – a current list of subjects and the bursary they attract can be found at www.educationcymru.org.

If you are a full-time trainee, the salary is not taxable and you do not have to pay national insurance contributions. If you are a part-time trainee, the salary may be taxable, depending on your total income for the year. It will be included in any calculation for means-tested benefits.

Students from the European Union (EU) are eligible for this incentive.

PGCE(FE)

This is a long-running pilot scheme for full-time PGCE students training to teach in further education studying at a Welsh institution and has been extended for 2010/11. Full-time students receive a bursary of £4,000, with £7,000 available for those training to teach science or maths. It is not means tested and is open to EU students. As with other PGCE courses, if you meet the personal and residential criteria for undergraduate student support, you can apply for the same support package as undergraduate students (see p43).

Welsh medium improvement supplement

This is available on the same terms as for undergraduate students (see p80).

Graduate teacher programme

A graduate teacher programme also operates in Wales on a similar basis to England (see p78), except that the salary rate may be slightly lower.

Repayment of Teachers' Loans scheme

The Repayment of Teachers' Loans scheme has closed to new applicants. However, existing teachers on this scheme still benefit (see p79).

5. Initial teacher training in Northern Ireland

Students accepted on a course of initial teacher training in Northern Ireland in the 2010/11 academic year, including Postgraduate Certificate in Education (PGCE) courses, receive the same funding as 'new system' undergraduate students

6

Chapter 6: Vocational courses and other sources of student support
5. Initial teacher training in Northern Ireland

(see p56). This means that PGCE students are liable for tuition fees, but can take out a loan to cover these.

You can make an application for funding through an education and library board. The additional financial incentives available for undergraduate and PGCE study in England and Wales are not available in Northern Ireland, but Northern Irish students studying in England or Wales can claim these.

6. **Social work students**

England

Students studying an undergraduate diploma or degree in social work in England may be eligible for a non-means-tested bursary from the Department of Health. The NHS Business Services Authority (BSA) administers these bursaries on its behalf.

If you are a full-time undergraduate studying at an institution in England, you may be eligible to receive this assistance in addition to the Department for Business, Innovation and Skills student support package (see p19).

Undergraduate support

Support for undergraduates studying social work is made up of several elements.

Tuition fees

If you are an 'old system' student (ie, you are not required to pay variable tuition fees – see p25) and are liable to make a contribution towards your tuition fees after your local authority has made a financial assessment for your student support, this is paid on your behalf by the NHS BSA directly to your university or college.

If you are a 'new system' student (and, therefore, required to pay variable tuition fees – see p26), the NHS BSA does not pay your tuition fees on your behalf. Instead, you receive a higher rate of bursary (see p83), which you can use to pay all or part of the fee. You do not, however, have to do this.

Basic grant

This gives you additional money for living costs. The amount you receive depends on where you study and whether or not you are a 'new system' student (see p21). A fixed contribution of £575 is paid as part of the basic grant to cover the costs of travel to placements.

If you are an 'old system' student (see p20), you can get £3,075 if you are studying at an institution outside London, or £3,475 if you are studying at a university or college in London or at the University of London. Essentially, the amount of loan you receive from your local authority or Student Finance England (SFE) determines the rate of basic grant you receive.

If you are a 'new system' student, the basic grant rates rise to £4,575 outside London and £4,975 within London.

Both types of bursary are paid for 52 weeks and will be taken into account in benefits calculations. The element paid for travelling expenses should be disregarded.[11] However, this is not usually specifically identified so benefits offices may take the full bursary into account. Speak to an adviser for assistance.

Part-time students

If you are a part-time undergraduate student, you will have your tuition fees paid by the NHS BSA. You can receive the 'incentive to train' bursary at half the rate for full-time study. Students who started in 2006/07 or later academic years receive half the 'new system' students' rate. All students are also eligible for help with placement costs. You are not eligible for other forms of support.

Postgraduate support

In addition to the undergraduate bursary, the NHS BSA also administers support for students studying a postgraduate level course, such as the Masters in Social Work, or for students studying an undergraduate degree or diploma who already have a first degree. The bursary can help with extra study and living costs, and there is additional help if you have children or a disability.

Tuition fees

Your tuition fees of up to £3,390 are paid in full by the NHS BSA, direct to the institution. These are not means tested.

Basic grant

Although unable to apply for support from Student Finance England, eligible postgraduate students can receive a basic grant from the NHS. This is non-means tested, and you can get £3,362.50 if you are studying at an institution outside London, or £3,762.50 if you are studying at a university or college in London or at the University of London. As with undergraduates, this includes a placement travel expenses allowance – in this case £862.50.

Additional maintenance grant

This is a means-tested grant paid in addition to the basic grant. Up to £4,026 is available to students studying in London or at the University of London, with up to £2,608 available to those studying elsewhere.

The grant is means tested on your unearned income and any taxable income of a partner, if you have one.

Students with dependants

You can receive the adult dependants' grant, the parents' learning allowance and the childcare grant on the same basis as higher education (HE) undergraduates receiving local authority or SFE support (see p29).

Disabled students' allowance

Postgraduate social work students can apply for a disabled students' allowance at the same rates as for HE undergraduates (see p30).

Part-time students

Part-time postgraduate students have their tuition fees paid by the NHS BSA. They can receive the 'incentive to train' bursary at half the rate for full-time study, plus help with placement costs. They are not eligible for other forms of support.

How to apply

In the first instance, if you are an undergraduate, you should apply to Student Finance England for student support. When it has assessed your application and you have received notification of this (sometimes known as an award notification), you should contact the NHS BSA for an application form for the bursary. Postgraduates should apply directly to the NHS BSA.

Application forms are also available from the NHS BSA website at www.nhsbsa.nhs.uk/students.

Wales

Students in Wales studying for qualifications in social work may qualify for financial help from the Care Council for Wales (CCW).

Undergraduate support

If you are studying for an undergraduate degree or diploma in social work, you should first apply for student support through your local authority, as do other undergraduate students (see Chapter 3). CCW provides a tuition fee element of £1,285. If you study in Wales and started your course before 1 September 2010, you may be eligible for a tuition fee grant of £1,980, leaving a contribution of £40 which you can either pay in cash or borrow in the form of a tuition fee loan. If you start your course in the 2010/11 academic year, or study outside Wales, you would then need to borrow £2,005 to cover the tuition fees of £3,290.

You will also receive a non-means-tested bursary to help cover your living costs of £2,500 in 2010/11. If you are studying part time, the bursary is calculated on a pro rata basis.

In addition, a practice learning opportunity allowance is paid to help cover the costs of attending placements. This is paid at £7.50 per day of placement if you start your course in 2010/11, or £500 is added to your bursary if you started your course beforehand. In the latter case, if your travel costs to placements are more than £500, you can apply to the CCW for reimbursement of these extra costs. However, you should keep all receipts as you may be asked to submit these as proof of expenditure.

To apply, you should contact the CCW for an application form or visit www.ccwales.org.uk.

Postgraduate support

If you are on a postgraduate diploma or Masters course in Wales, you should apply in the first instance for the basic undergraduate bursary from the CCW, including the practice learning grant.

While you cannot receive undergraduate support through your local authority, the CCW may be able to offer an additional graduate bursary, of up to £2,570 in 2010/11. The exact amount will depend on your personal circumstances. You can apply for the adult dependants' grant, the parents' learning allowance and the childcare grant from CCW at the same time as the additional graduate bursary.

If you have a disability, you may be eligible for extra help through the postgraduate disabled students' allowance (see p63).

The CCW will also pay your tuition fees of up to £3,390.

Northern Ireland

If you are studying for a degree in social work in Northern Ireland, you can apply for an additional incentive grant from the Office of Social Services (see Appendix 2). Non-means-tested grants of £4,000 plus a further £500 towards placement expenses are available for each year of the course.

You will have to pay tuition fees, but the funds are in addition to any money you are entitled to through your education and library board as part of the main undergraduate support system, including loans for fees.

Students in receipt of the incentive grant are now eligible to apply to the discretionary support funds for extra help (see p60).

7. **Dance and drama awards**

The Department for Business, Innovation and Skills (BIS) has set up a scholarship programme to ensure that talented dance and drama students can attend courses at the leading dance and drama institutions in England, in cases where fees and living costs would otherwise be prohibitively expensive.[12] Dance and drama awards fund studies in higher national diploma (HND) and higher national certificate (HNC) courses in dance, drama and production. Funding is available through selected, approved specialist schools for between one and three years of study. You must be aged 16 and over for dance courses, or 18 and over for drama-related courses. There are 525 awards granted each year, and they are generally issued to those who show exceptional talent in an audition.

The residency rules for other higher education support apply (see p22) and students from England, Wales and Scotland can apply for full support, while students from Northern Ireland can apply for help with fees only. A separate scheme operates in Northern Ireland for help with other costs (see p86).

If you are a recipient of an award most of your fees will be paid, but you will have to make a contribution. In 2010/11 this is £1,275. If you have a low family income, you can apply for extra assistance with your fees. The award may also provide support for your living costs, depending on your circumstances. The maximum available is £5,460 for those living in lodgings in London, and £4,823 for those living elsewhere. Other allowances may be available if you have extra costs associated with a disability or childcare expenses. More information on the awards is available through the participating dance and drama schools or from www.direct.gov.uk/danceanddrama (where a list of the participating schools can also be found).

Northern Ireland

The dance and drama (Northern Ireland) awards form part of the Northern Ireland further education awards scheme (see p16). They provide assistance for courses at one of the 21 accredited providers in mainland Britain (as there is no provision in Northern Ireland). If a student receives a main dance and drama award which pays for the majority of the fees charged, s/he can also apply to the Western Education and Library Board for a dance and drama (Northern Ireland) award for help with the remainder of the fee and maintenance.

As on the mainland, the maximum available is £5,460 for those living in lodgings in London, and £4,823 for those living elsewhere. For more information, see www.welbni.org.

8. Alternative sources of finance

Professional and career development loans

The Department for Business, Innovation and Skills (BIS), in participation with two major banks (Barclays and the Co-operative, although the Young People's Learning Agency (YPLA), which administers the scheme, is hopeful more banks will join the scheme) operates a deferred repayment loan system.[13] You can borrow between £300 and £10,000 towards fees and other expenses if you are on a vocational full-time, part-time or distance learning course lasting up to two years (and including up to one year's practical work experience where it is part of your course). Degree and postgraduate courses are included.

The interest charged will vary depending on the bank, when you apply and the length of repayment, but currently is typically 9.9 per cent a year. You should, however, check with the bank. Throughout your period of study and up to one month after completing or leaving the course, the YPLA pays the interest on the loan for you. Repayments are fixed and can be spread between one and five years. If you are registered unemployed at the end of the first month of completing your course, you may apply to the bank for deferment of repayment for up to five months initially, and for two further extensions of six months each. More information on professional and career development loans can be found at www.direct.gov.uk/pcdl.

Professional and career development loans are now also available in Northern Ireland.

Professional Trainee Loans Scheme

One of the major high street banks, Natwest, offers professional studies loans. The schemes are specifically aimed at study in certain fields – eg, medicine, dentistry, law, veterinary science and architecture. Loans of up to £25,000 are available. Interest rates and repayment terms are variable, and you can usually defer repayment until after the completion of your course, although the debt will continue to accrue interest. Contact a local branch or visit the Natwest website for more information.

Note that some other banks had previously offered similar loans but these have become more difficult to obtain since 2008 and banks can be very cautious in their lending decisions.

The Professional Trainee Loans Scheme is not available in Northern Ireland.

Business school loan scheme

The Association of MBAs runs this scheme in conjunction with NatWest. It is available to those studying for a Masters in Business Administration or equivalent, full time, part time or by distance learning. Repayment is deferred until the completion of your course, but the debt continues to accrue interest. For further information, contact NatWest on freephone 0800 015 1166, or visit the Association's website at www.mbaworld.com. Some individual business schools also have a loan scheme with HSBC. Contact the school where you want to study to see if it participates.

The business school loan scheme is not available in Northern Ireland.

Charities

It is unlikely that a course lasting more than one year could be financed entirely by trust fund help. Educational charities and trusts are, however, in a position to provide supplementary help to students who may be without funding for part of their course or who, for various reasons, need help over and above that provided by public funds.

Educational charities and trusts often have specific, even unusual, terms of reference. They may be restricted to helping, for example, students only:

- on certain courses of study; *or*
- above or below a certain age (often 21 or 25); *or*
- from particular parts of Britain or countries of the world; *or*
- in defined occupations, professions or industries, or who have a parent working in one of these.

A student does not usually receive more than about £300 from any one charity, although higher amounts are not unknown. Charities more often make single, rather than recurrent, payments. Payments tend to be:

- for particular items – eg, tools or equipment; *or*
- for a specific purpose – eg, childcare; *or*
- those which the charity or trust believes might make the difference between completion and non-completion of the course.

Charities are more sympathetic to students whose need for assistance results from sickness or unforeseen circumstances than to students who have mismanaged their money or who have started a course knowing they had insufficient funds.

Many charities only give assistance to first-time students. Assistance is more difficult to find if you are a postgraduate or taking a second undergraduate course. Applications often take some time to process so it is wise to apply for support well in advance of the course start date.

Further information

There are a number of publications that contain details of charities and trusts, including:

- *The Educational Grants Directory* (Directory of Social Change);
- *The Guide to Grants for Individuals in Need* (Directory of Social Change);
- *The Directory of Grant Making Trusts* (Directory of Social Change);
- *Charities Digest* (Waterlow Legal and Regulatory);
- *The Grants Register* (Palgrave Macmillan) – this is particularly relevant to postgraduate student awards for both the UK and overseas;
- *British and International Music Yearbook* and the *British Music Education Yearbook* (both published by Rhinegold).

Many of these publications can be found in local public libraries, or university or college libraries. Advice centres may also carry some, particularly *The Educational Grants Directory*.

There are also some useful websites listing charities and educational grants, including:

- Hotcourses database at www.scholarship-search.org.uk;
- Funderfinder at www.funderfinder.org.uk.

Students in need should also consult their local authority, students' union, careers service, Citizens Advice Bureau, town hall and local clergy as they may know of other trusts. In addition to awarding scholarships and prizes in specific subjects, colleges may have funds available for students in financial difficulties and unable to apply to the Access to Learning Fund or discretionary support funds, so it may be useful to consult your institution's student service. Students in Northern Ireland should contact the duty information officer at the Educational Guidance Service for Adults (EGSA).

Educational Grants Advisory Service

For more advice on alternative sources of funding, contact the Educational Grants Advisory Service (EGAS). If you provide information on your personal background, course and requirements, you will be matched with any appropriate trusts or charities. Its website at www.family-action.org.uk/grants contains an online educational grants search which will link through to an application form if you meet any of the trusts' eligibility requirements. Your university or college must be affiliated to EGAS in order for you to be able to use this service.

However, EGAS generally cannot help overseas students or students wishing to study outside the UK. You can phone the advice line on 020 7241 7459, open from 2pm–4pm Tuesdays, Wednesdays and Thursdays only. You can also apply for help online. See Appendix 2 for the full contact details.

Educational Guidance Service for Adults

For further information on alternative sources of funding in Northern Ireland, you can also contact EGSA. Telephone 0845 602 6632 or email info@egsa.org.uk. See Appendix 2 for the full contact details.

Notes

1. **Healthcare students in England and Wales**
   1 Audiology courses must be recognised by the British Academy of Audiology.
   2 This is not necessarily the first day of your course.
   3 The age of the child used for determining the level of allowance is that on the day before the start of the academic year, unless s/he is born during that year.
   4 Reg 77 E(SS) Regs
   5 This is not necessarily the first day of your course.
   6 The age of the child used for determining the level of allowance is that on the day before the start of the academic year, unless s/he is born during that year.

3. **Initial teacher training in England**
   7 Reg 20 E(SS) Regs

4. **Initial teacher training in Wales**
   8 E(WMTTIS) Regs
   9 Reg 20 ALGL(HE)(W) Regs
   10 Reg 22 ALGL(HE)(W) Regs

6. **Social work students**
   11 **IS** Reg 62(2)(h) IS Regs
   HB Reg 59(2)(g) HB Regs
   CTB Reg 46(2)(g) CTB Regs
   See also para 30122, Vol 6 DMG

7. **Dance and drama awards**
   12 E(G)(DD)(E) Regs

8. **Alternative sources of finance**
   13 s2 ETA 1973

Part 2
Benefits and tax credits

Chapter 7

Carer's allowance

This chapter covers:
1. What is carer's allowance (below)
2. Who is eligible (p94)
3. Amount of benefit (p96)
4. Claiming carer's allowance (p96)
5. Challenging a decision (p96)
6. Other benefits and tax credits (p97)

Basic facts

– Carer's allowance (CA) is paid to people who care for someone with a severe disability.
– Part-time students are eligible to claim.
– Full-time students cannot claim.
– The amount of CA you get is not affected by any savings you may have, but you cannot get CA if you work and earn more than £100 a week.
– You do not need to have paid any national insurance contributions to qualify for CA, but you can receive national insurance credits while receiving it.
– Getting CA qualifies you for a carer premium with income support, income-based jobseeker's allowance, income-related employment and support allowance, housing benefit and council tax benefit, or a carer addition with pension credit.
– Claims are administered by the Department for Work and Pensions Carer's Allowance Unit. You can make your claim at local Jobcentre Plus offices.

1. What is carer's allowance

Further information

This chapter gives an outline of the carer's allowance rules and focuses on issues relevant to students. For more detailed information on the rules, see CPAG's *Welfare Benefits and Tax Credits Handbook*.

Carer's allowance is paid to people who spend at least 35 hours a week looking after a disabled person (adult or child). The disabled person must be getting attendance allowance, or the middle or highest rate of disability living allowance care component. The amount you get is not means tested, but counts as taxable income when assessing your student loan, grant or other student support income.

2. **Who is eligible**

You qualify for carer's allowance (CA) if:[1]
- you are 16 or over;
- you spend at least 35 hours a week caring for someone;
- the person for whom you care gets the middle or highest rate disability living allowance care component, attendance allowance or constant attendance allowance;
- you are not earning over £100 a week after deductions;
- you satisfy residence and presence conditions, and are not a 'person subject to immigration control' for benefit purposes (see CPAG's *Welfare Benefits and Tax Credits Handbook* for more details).

You are not eligible if you are in full-time education – ie, you are studying more than 21 hours a week (see below).

There is no upper age limit for CA.

Breaks from caring

If you have been providing care for at least 35 hours a week in 22 of the last 26 weeks (14 of the last 26 weeks if either you or the disabled person were in hospital), you can still get CA. Effectively, you can have a four-week break from caring every six months (a 12-week break if either you or the disabled person were in hospital for at least eight weeks).[2]

What is 'full-time education'

You are in full-time education if an overall consideration of the course requirements, and your performance against these requirements, suggests this. If you are on a full-time course of education, you would normally be taken to be in full-time education.[3]

You are also treated as being in **'full-time education'** if you attend a course of education at a university, college or other educational establishment for 21 hours or more a week.[4]

These 21 hours include not just classes, lectures and seminars, but also individual study for course work. Meal breaks and unsupervised study are ignored. However, you are regarded as studying under supervision if you are doing course work, whether at home or at college, alone or in the presence of a supervisor.[5]

'Unsupervised study' is work beyond the requirements of the course.

Students and carer's allowance

When you start college or university, you should inform the Department for Work and Pensions (DWP) (in Northern Ireland, the Department for Social Development). The DWP normally requires details of your course, including its length and written confirmation of exactly how many hours of study a week students are expected to do. It is advisable to send a copy of your timetable to the DWP with a letter from the head of the appropriate department at the institution, who will be asked to estimate the weekly hours of study required. It is unusual for an institution to have a fixed amount of regular hours expected on its courses; normally a timetable is issued to a student, with a requirement to study independently throughout the terms and vacations. It is, therefore, always worth checking with your department exactly how many hours are expected in addition to the college timetable.

If your college or university says that the course is full time, or that it expects students to spend 21 hours or more a week in supervised study and classes, the DWP will normally conclude that it is full-time education.

In practice, if you want to show that you spend fewer hours on coursework than the college or university expects, you will need to provide detailed evidence and be prepared to appeal. It may be that your particular circumstances mean that you are not expected to satisfy the normal requirements of the course – eg, you are exempt from certain subjects or classes.[6]

If you are not required to attend all of the modules on your full-time course because of prior accreditation, or if you have already completed some of the course requirements in advance (eg, you were previously attending the course part time, or completed extra modules in the summer vacation, or are repeating a year because you failed a module), this should be taken into account by the DWP and the appropriate time deducted from the compulsory hours.

If your course is part time but you spend more time than the standard amount expected on it, this should not exclude you from CA as long as the college or university regards your course as part time. If you have to care for someone, you may need to change your registration to that of a part-time student.

Taking a break from full-time study

'Attending' a course means being enrolled on and pursuing a course.[7] You are treated as still being in full-time education during short and long vacations and until the course ends, you abandon it or are dismissed from it. You are also still regarded as being full time during temporary interruptions.[8]

If you have to take time out to care for someone, you might not be able to get CA unless you have finally abandoned your course or have changed your mode of registration on the course from full time to part time (see p295). However, you can claim jobseeker's allowance for up to a maximum of 12 months once your caring responsibilities have ended and you are waiting to return to your course (providing you meet the other rules of entitlement – see Chapter 15).

3. **Amount of benefit**

You get £53.90 a week (2010/11 rate).

4. **Claiming carer's allowance**

You can make a claim for carer's allowance (CA) online at www.dwp.gov.uk/carersallowance. Alternatively, you can claim on Form DS700, available from local Jobcentre Plus offices, the Carer's Allowance Unit on 0845 608 4321 or from the Benefit Enquiry Line on freephone 0800 882 200. In Northern Ireland, the form is available from the Disability and Carers Service, Castle Court, Royal Avenue, Belfast BT1 1HR, telephone 028 9090 6186. Alternatively, you can use the freephone number 0800 220 674.

Your claim can be backdated for up to three months if you qualified during that earlier period. Your claim may be backdated further if you claim within three months of the person for whom you care being awarded a qualifying benefit – eg, attendance allowance or disability living allowance. In this case, your CA can be backdated to the first day from when the qualifying benefit is payable.

Getting paid

CA is usually paid directly into a bank (or similar) account. Which account it goes into is up to you. If you do not want your benefit to be paid into an account that is overdrawn, give the DWP details of an alternative account if you have access to, or can open, one.

If you are overpaid CA, you might have to repay it.

5. **Challenging a decision**

If you think a decision about your carer's allowance is wrong (eg, because the decision maker got the facts or law wrong), there are a number of ways you can try to get the decision changed.
- You can seek a revision or a supersession of the decision. In some cases you have to show specific grounds. In others, you must apply within a strict time limit.
- You can appeal to an independent tribunal. There are strict time limits for appealing – usually one month from the date you are sent or given the decision. You can make a late appeal in limited circumstances.

If you are considering challenging a decision, you should seek advice as soon as possible.

6. **Other benefits and tax credits**

The disabled person's benefit

It is not always financially prudent to claim carer's allowance (CA). Although it may be more money for you, it may result in the person for whom you care losing some income support (IS), income-based jobseeker's allowance (JSA), income-related employment and support allowance (ESA), pension credit (PC), housing benefit (HB) or council tax benefit (CTB). If s/he lives alone, s/he may also be getting a severe disability premium included in these benefits (additional amount with PC). This will be lost as soon as CA is paid to you for looking after her/him. The severe disability premium/additional amount is roughly the same amount as CA, so it is always worth checking who would be better off claiming the extra help – the carer or the disabled person.

Also, if you become a full-time student and no longer qualify for CA, check whether the disabled person can qualify for the severe disability premium.

Overlapping benefits

Although you cannot receive CA at the same time as another income-replacement benefit, such as incapacity benefit, contribution-based JSA, contributory ESA, retirement pension, bereavement benefits, maternity allowance or severe disablement allowance, if you are eligible for more than one benefit you get the one which is worth the most.

Getting a carer premium

If you are eligible for IS, income-based JSA, ESA, PC, HB or CTB as a part-time student, getting CA entitles you to a carer premium (carer's addition with PC). If you are awarded CA, you should inform the local benefit office that pays your IS, JSA, ESA or PC, or the local authority if you get HB or CTB, so that your benefit can be recalculated to include the carer premium (carer's addition with PC). There is a good chance that your benefit will increase as a result of this addition.

Notes

2. Who is eligible

1 s70 SSCBA 1992
2 Reg 4(2) SS(ICA) Regs
3 *Deane v Secretary of State for Work and Pensions* [2010] EWCA Civ 699, 23 June 2010
4 Reg 5(2) SS(ICA) Regs
5 Reg 5(2) SS(ICA) Regs
6 CG/3189/2004 *Flemming v Secretary of State for Work and Pensions* [2002] EWCA Civ 641, 10 May 2002; *Bronwyn Wright-Turner v Department for Social Development* [2002] NICA 2
8 Reg 5(3) SS(ICA) Regs

Chapter 8

Child benefit

This chapter covers:
1. What is child benefit (below)
2. Who is eligible (p100)
3. Amount of benefit (p103)
4. Claiming child benefit (p104)
5. Challenging a decision (p104)
6. Other benefits and tax credits (p105)

Basic facts
– Child benefit is paid to people who are responsible for a child or a 'qualifying young person'.
– Both full-time and part-time students can claim child benefit.
– If you are under 20, someone else may be able to claim child benefit for you if you are studying.
– Child benefit is not means tested.
– Claims are administered by HM Revenue and Customs.

1. **What is child benefit**

Further information
This chapter gives an outline of the child benefit rules and focuses on issues relevant to students. For more detailed information on the rules, see CPAG's *Welfare Benefits and Tax Credits Handbook*.

Child benefit is paid to people who are responsible for a child or 'qualifying young person'. You do not have to have paid national insurance contributions to qualify for child benefit. It is not means tested, so the amount you get is not affected by your student loan, grant or other income.

2. **Who is eligible**

You qualify for child benefit if:[1]

- you are responsible for a child or 'qualifying young person' – ie:
  - s/he lives with you; *or*
  - you contribute to the cost of supporting her/him at a rate of at least the amount of child benefit for her/him; *and*
- you have priority over other potential claimants. Only one person can get child benefit for a particular child. There is an order of priority for who receives it where two or more people would otherwise be entitled; *and*
- you and the child or 'qualifying young person' satisfy presence and residence conditions; *and*
- you are not subject to immigration control for benefit purposes.

Note that you do not have to be the child's parent to claim child benefit for her/him.

Being a student, whether full time or part time, does not affect your entitlement to child benefit.

If you are a 'qualifying young person', someone else may be able to claim child benefit if s/he is responsible for you. You cannot, however, claim child benefit for yourself.

If a qualifying young person receives incapacity benefit, income support, income-based jobseeker's allowance, employment and support allowance, working tax credit or child tax credit in her/his own right, any child benefit paid for the young person stops.

If a young person lives with a partner, or is married or in a civil partnership, you can get child benefit for the young person if s/he lives with you or you still contribute to her/his support, but only if her/his partner is in 'relevant education' or approved training. The young person's partner cannot be the claimant.

Special rules apply in some circumstances – eg, if your child is being looked after by a local authority or if s/he is in detention.

Who counts as a child

Anyone aged under 16 counts as a 'child' for child benefit purposes, whether or not s/he goes to school. As long as you meet the other qualifying conditions, child benefit can be paid for her/him.[2] Child benefit can also be paid for a child after s/he reaches 16 until at least 31 August after her/his 16th birthday and then for as long as s/he continues to count as a 'qualifying young person'.

Who counts as a qualifying young person

A 'qualifying young person' is someone who:[3]

- is aged 16 and has left 'relevant education' (see p102) or training. This only applies up to 31 August after her/his 16th birthday (but see p101); *or*

- is aged 16 or 17, has left education or training and satisfies the extension period rule (see p102); *or*
- is aged 16 or over but under 20 and either:
  - is on a course of full-time non-advanced education which was not provided as a result of her/his employment; *or*
  - is on approved training which was not provided under a contract of employment – in England, Entry to Employment, Foundation Learning or Programme-Led Apprenticeships; in Wales, Skillbuild, Skillbuild+ or Foundation Modern Apprenticeships; or in Northern Ireland, Programme-led Apprenticeships (ApprenticeshipsNI), Jobskills and Training for Success (professional and technical training).[4]

  The young person must have begun the course of full-time non-advanced education or approved training before reaching 19, or have been accepted or enrolled to undertake the education or training before that age; *or*
- is aged 16 or over but under 20 and:
  - has finished a course of full-time non-advanced education, but has been accepted or is enrolled on another such course; *or*
  - has finished a course of full-time non-advanced education or approved training, but has been accepted or is enrolled to take further approved training.

  This does not apply if the courses or training are provided as a result of her/his employment or provided under a contract of employment. Although you must have begun, or been accepted or enrolled on the training or education when you were under 19 to be a qualifying young person once the course begins, the rules do not specify this for the gap between courses.[5] If the young person was accepted or enrolled after reaching age 19, you can argue that s/he is a qualifying young person from the end of the course until the next course begins; *or*
- is aged 16 or over but under 20 and has left 'relevant education' (see p102) or approved training but has not passed her/his 'terminal date' (see p102).

If your child counts as a qualifying young person on more than one of the above grounds, s/he counts as a qualifying young person until the last date that applies.[6]

If you stop being entitled to child benefit for your child because s/he no longer counts as a qualifying young person, but s/he later satisfies one of the above conditions again and so counts as a qualifying young person once more, child benefit can again become payable for her/him. **Note:** in some cases, you can continue to claim during such an interruption – eg, if your qualifying young person is ill.

In the rest of this chapter the term 'child' is used to mean both children under 16 and qualifying young people aged 16 or over.

Relevant education

'Relevant education' is defined as education which is full time and non-advanced. For the purpose of deciding if your child is in relevant education, HM Revenue and Customs considers that the definition of 'full time' given on p169 applies, but this is not actually stated in the legislation. It may, therefore, be possible to argue, for example, that unsupervised, as well as supervised, study should be counted when assessing if such a course is full time.

The extension period rule

If your child is 16 or 17, s/he continues to count as a qualifying young person, and so child benefit can continue to be paid for her/him, during an 'extension period' if:[7]

- s/he has left education or training; *and*
- s/he is registered as available for work, education or training with the Careers Wales or Connexions service, Ministry of Defence or, in Northern Ireland, the Department for Employment and Learning or an education and library board. In some circumstances, s/he can also be registered with a corresponding body in another European Economic Area state; *and*
- s/he is not in remunerative work – ie, work of 24 hours a week or more for payment, or in expectation of payment; *and*
- you were entitled to child benefit for her/him immediately before the extension period started; *and*
- you apply in writing within three months of the date your child's education or training finished.

In this context, 'education' and 'training' are not defined and so may mean any kind of education or training.

The extension period starts from the Monday after your child's course of education or training ends and lasts for 20 weeks from that date. If your child reaches 18 during the extension period, unless s/he counts as a qualifying young person on another ground (see p100), your child benefit for her/him ends from the first child benefit payday on or after s/he reaches 18.[8]

The terminal date rule

If your child leaves 'relevant education' (see above) or approved training (see p101) before reaching 20, s/he continues to count as a qualifying young person until either:[9]

- the first Sunday on or after her/his 'terminal date' (see p103); *or*
- if s/he reaches 20 before that date, the Sunday on or after her/his 20th birthday (unless her/his 20th birthday is on a Monday, in which case s/he counts as a qualifying young person until the Sunday before her/his birthday).

This means that, unless s/he continues to count as a qualifying young person on another ground or is returning to sit an exam, the general rule is that you stop receiving child benefit for her/him on that date.

Your child's **'terminal date'** is the first of the following dates which falls after the date her/his 'relevant education' or approved training finished:

- the last day in February; *or*
- the last day in May; *or*
- the last day in August; *or*
- the last day in November.

A child who returns to sit an external examination in connection with her/his course of relevant education is treated as still being in relevant education until the date of the last exam.[10]

19-year-olds

If your child is on a course of full-time non-advanced education or approved training, s/he can only count as a qualifying young person once s/he is 19, if s/he began (or was accepted or enrolled on) that course of education or training before that age.[11] If s/he did, so long as you meet the other qualifying conditions, you continue to be entitled to child benefit for her/him until the first terminal date falling after the end of the course or training, or her/his 20th birthday if this comes first.

Even if HM Revenue and Customs does not accept that your child counts as a qualifying young person while on a new course, it may be possible to argue that s/he should count as a qualifying young person for a period after s/he leaves the new course under the terminal date rule if s/he then leaves that course or training before reaching 20.[12] If your claim is refused, seek advice.

3. **Amount of benefit**

Weekly rate from April 2010

Eldest eligible child	£20.30
Other children (each)	£13.40

If you are living with a partner and your family includes stepchildren or the children of your partner, and you each receive child benefit for your respective children, only one of you can receive the higher rate for the eldest child – ie, the one with the eldest child.

4. **Claiming child benefit**

Child benefit is administered by HM Revenue and Customs (the Revenue). You claim child benefit on Form CH2, which can be obtained from the Child Benefit Office on 0845 302 1444, any Revenue enquiry centre, the Revenue's website (www.hmrc.gov.uk) or from Jobcentre Plus offices.

You should submit your claim to the Child Benefit Office, PO Box 1, Newcastle upon Tyne NE88 1AA. In some cases, you might be able to claim child benefit online.

You should make a claim within three months of becoming eligible. This is because your claim can usually only be backdated for up to three months. You do not have to show any reason why your claim was late.

Getting paid

Child benefit is usually paid directly into your bank (or similar) account. Which account it goes into is up to you. If you do not want your benefit to go into an account that is overdrawn, give the Revenue details of an alternative account, if you have access to, or can open, one.

If you are overpaid child benefit, you might have to repay it.

5. **Challenging a decision**

If you think a decision about your child benefit is wrong (eg, because the decision maker got the facts or law wrong, or your circumstances have changed since the decision was made), there are a number of ways you can try to get the decision changed.

- You can seek a revision or a supersession of the decision. In some cases you have to show specific grounds. In others, you must apply within a strict time limit.
- You can appeal to an independent tribunal. There are strict time limits for appealing – usually one month from the date you are sent or given the decision. You can make a late appeal in limited circumstances.

If you are considering challenging a decision, you should seek advice as soon as possible.

You cannot appeal against some decisions, such as a decision on which of two people whose claims have equal priority should get child benefit. However, you can ask for a revision or a supersession of such a decision.

6. **Other benefits and tax credits**

If you qualify for child benefit, you may also qualify for tax credits and means-tested benefits. Child benefit is:

- paid in addition to non-means-tested benefits;
- ignored as income for tax credits purposes.

Child benefit is ignored as income for pension credit purposes. It is also ignored as income for income support (IS) and income-based jobseeker's allowance (JSA) if you are getting child tax credit (CTC). However, if you have been getting IS or income-based JSA since before 6 April 2004 which includes amounts for your child(ren), child benefit is taken into account as income until you are awarded CTC, unless you have a child under one, in which case £10.50 of your child benefit is ignored.

Child benefit is ignored as income for income-related employment and support allowance, housing benefit (HB) and council tax benefit (CTB).

If you receive child benefit, you count as responsible for a child for IS, income-based JSA, and, usually, for HB and CTB. This can help you qualify for these benefits while you are a full-time student in some circumstances (see Chapters 12, 14, 15 and 23).

Notes

2. **Who is eligible**
1 ss141-147 SSCBA 1992
2 s142(1) SSCBA 1992; reg 4 CB Regs
3 s142(2) SSCBA 1992; regs 2-8 CB Regs
4 Reg 1(3) CB Regs
5 Reg 3 CB Regs
6 Reg 2(2) CB Regs
7 Reg 5 CB Regs
8 Reg 14 CBGA(A) Regs; reg 5(3) CB Regs
9 Reg 7 CB Regs
10 Reg 7(2) case 2 CB Regs
11 Reg 3(4) CB Regs
12 This is because in the rules on terminal dates there is no requirement that a course of education or training must be started before a person is 19.

Chapter 9
Disability living allowance

This chapter covers:
1. What is disability living allowance (below)
2. Who is eligible (p107)
3. Amount of benefit (p111)
4. Claiming disability living allowance (p111)
5. Challenging a decision (p112)
6. Other benefits and tax credits (p113)

Basic facts

– Disability living allowance (DLA) is paid in order to assist disabled people with personal care and mobility needs.
– The amount you get is not affected by your income or capital, and all student support is ignored when working out entitlement.
– DLA has a care component and a mobility component.
– Adults, young people and children can all qualify for DLA.
– A person can receive either one or both components providing s/he meets the eligibility criteria.
– DLA is available to both full-time and part-time students who meet the basic eligibility criteria.
– Receipt of DLA enables a full-time student to be eligible for housing benefit and council tax benefit or for increased amounts of these benefits.
– Receipt of DLA enables a full-time student to be eligible for income-related ESA.
– Claims for DLA are administered by the Department for Work and Pensions or, in Northern Ireland, the Department for Social Development.

1. What is disability living allowance

Further information

This chapter gives an outline of the disability living allowance rules and focuses on issues relevant to students. For more detailed information on the rules, see CPAG's *Welfare Benefits and Tax Credits Handbook*.

Disability living allowance (DLA) is a benefit available to disabled people aged under 65 when they first claim, who require help with personal care or have mobility difficulties. You do not have to have paid national insurance contributions to qualify for DLA. It is not means tested, so the amount you get is not affected by your student grant or loan, or any other income you receive. It is available to both full- and part-time students who meet the basic eligibility criteria.

DLA has two components.

- **Care component.** This is for help with personal care needs and is payable at three different rates.
- **Mobility component.** This is payable at two different rates depending upon the severity of your walking problems.

DLA is payable to the person with the disability rather than her/his carer. The carer may be eligible to receive carer's allowance, providing that the disabled person receives the middle or highest rate care component of DLA (see Chapter 7).

2. **Who is eligible**

To qualify for disability living allowance (DLA) you must:

- be under the age of 65 when you make the claim (attendance allowance is available to people above this age for care needs only);
- meet the disability test for the care and/or mobility component;
- unless you are terminally ill (see below), you must have satisfied the disability test for a continuous period of three months immediately before the start of the award and be likely to satisfy it for the next six months; *and*
- satisfy residence and presence tests and not be a 'person subject to immigration control' for benefit purposes. You can get further advice from the UK Council for International Student Affairs (UKCISA – see Appendix 2).

You are regarded as **'terminally ill'** if you have a progressive disease and can reasonably be expected to die within six months as a result of that disease. If this is the case, you can claim under what are known as the 'special rules', or someone can claim under these rules on your behalf.

Care component

To get the care component you must have a physical or mental disability that means you need care from another person as outlined below. What is important is the help you need rather than the help you actually get.

You can get either the lowest, middle or highest rate.

Lowest rate

You can qualify for this if you require care in connection with your bodily functions for a 'significant' period of the day (whether during a single period or a number of periods) or you meet the 'cooking test'.

You should count as requiring care for a significant portion of the day if it would take an hour in total to provide the help you need. This can be continuous or made up of short periods of time – eg, if you need help for 20 minutes three times a day.[1]

For the cooking test you have to be 16 or over and show that you are so severely physically or mentally disabled that you cannot prepare a cooked meal for yourself, assuming you had the ingredients. Your ability to chop food, use taps, carry pans or use a cooker are all relevant.

Middle rate

You can qualify for this if you require:
- frequent daytime attention in connection with your bodily functions (several times throughout the day);[2] *or*
- continual daytime supervision in order to avoid substantial danger to yourself or others;[3] *or*
- prolonged (20 minutes or more) or repeated night-time attention; *or*
- supervision at night in order to prevent danger to yourself or others that requires another person to be awake for a prolonged period or at frequent intervals to watch over you.

Highest rate

You can qualify for this if you need care or supervision during the day and the night, and you meet both a daytime *and* a night-time middle rate criteria, or if you are terminally ill (see p107) and claiming under the special rules (see p111).[4]

Attention and bodily functions

'Attention' is active help from another person to assist you with personal tasks concerning your bodily functions that you are unable to do for yourself. '**Bodily functions**' include breathing, sitting, seeing, hearing, eating, drinking, washing, going to the toilet, getting out of bed or a chair, taking medication and communicating. Any help in connection with impaired bodily function can count if it involves personal contact (physical or verbal in your presence) and it is reasonably required.

For example, a blind student might need the help of a notetaker or reader, or a guide around campus or around town. A deaf student might need an interpreter. A student with arthritis might need help getting in and out of chairs. However, you must need the help of another person to qualify for DLA; if you need to use artificial aids only, you will not qualify.

You cannot get help for domestic chores, unless someone is helping you do them for yourself.

If you have dyslexia, you could argue that you qualify for DLA but only if you need someone to be with you to help you read and write – ie, someone sitting beside you reading to you, or helping you develop writing skills.[5]

Continual supervision

'Continual supervision' is regular or frequent supervision, but does not necessarily have to be non-stop. The supervision does not have to stop the danger to the disabled person, but should reduce the risk of harm. You must show that there is a real risk of danger without the help of the other person. The person providing the supervision need not always be active or awake, but needs to be ready to act should help be required.

Having a social life

The kind of help you need must be reasonably required. This means you need it to enable you as far as possible to live a normal life. You can include help needed to take part in social activities, sport, recreation, cultural or political activities, so long as the help is required in connection with a bodily function.

Mobility component

To qualify for DLA mobility component you must be able to benefit from 'enhanced facilities for locomotion' – ie, that you are interested in going out, can get out from time to time and would benefit from outdoor journeys. There are two rates of mobility component and the level you receive depends on the severity of your disability.

Lower rate

You can qualify for this if you can walk but are so severely mentally or physically disabled that, disregarding your ability to use familiar routes, you cannot take advantage of your ability to walk outdoors without the guidance or supervision of another person most of the time.

You can still qualify if you are able to manage on familiar routes. If you cannot manage without guidance or supervision on unfamiliar routes or if you cannot manage anywhere, you should qualify. For example, a student with learning difficulties may qualify even though s/he has learned the route to and from home and college, if s/he still needs guidance in other places.[6]

Higher rate

You can qualify for this if:
- you are unable to walk; *or*

- you are virtually unable to walk outdoors;[7] *or*
- you are totally blind and have an 80 per cent hearing loss;[8] *or*
- (from April 2011) you have a severe visual impairment; *or*
- you have no legs or feet (from birth or because of amputation); *or*
- the exertion required to walk would constitute a danger to your life or be likely to lead to a serious deterioration in your health; *or*
- you have a severe mental impairment and highly disruptive and dangerous behavioural problems, and you are in receipt of the highest rate of DLA care component.[9]

Unable/virtually unable to walk

Being '**unable to walk**' means that you cannot literally put one foot in front of another.

Most disputes about mobility component involve the interpretation of '**virtually unable to walk**'. You have to show that your ability to walk out of doors is so limited, taking into account the distance, speed, length of time and manner in which you walk without feeling severe discomfort that you are virtually unable to walk. Any walking done when you are suffering pain or severe discomfort must be discounted.

Exertion required to walk

You can qualify for the higher rate mobility component if the '**exertion required to walk**' could lead to a danger to your life or a serious deterioration in your health. You need to show that you would never recover, or that recovery would take a significant period of time or require some medical intervention. For example, if you have a serious lung, heart or chest condition you may qualify.

Students and disability living allowance

Full-time and part-time disabled students are eligible to claim DLA. It does not affect your eligibility for, or the amount of, student support income. In addition, entitlement to DLA can help you qualify for means-tested benefits.

If you become a student, this may result in the Department for Work and Pensions (DWP) reconsidering whether you are still entitled to DLA, although this is not standard practice. However, the DWP might assume that, if you are now capable of a full-time course, your health has improved and you no longer have the same care or mobility needs. If this happens and your DLA is affected, see p112 for information about challenging the decision.

3. **Amount of benefit**

Weekly rate from April 2010	£
Care component (lowest rate)	18.95
Care component (middle rate)	47.80
Care component (highest rate)	71.40
Mobility component (lower rate)	18.95
Mobility component (higher rate)	49.85

4. **Claiming disability living allowance**

You can make a claim for disability living allowance (DLA) online at www.direct.gov.uk.

Alternatively, you can request an application pack from the Benefit Enquiry Line on 0800 882 200 (textphone 0800 243 355) or your local Jobcentre Plus office, or in Northern Ireland, by calling 0800 220 674. Providing you make the claim within six weeks of requesting the form, if eligible, you will receive DLA for all of this period.

The claim pack is extensive and repetitive in places, but it is important to give as much information as you can about your disability. Give examples of all the things you cannot do or have difficulties with. You will be asked about your leisure activities and hobbies, and the help you need. Make sure to put down all the help you need, whether you undertake hobbies or not and any help you need with studying. It does not matter whether or not you are already receiving the help; it is what you need that counts.

Claiming under the special rules

You are allowed to claim under the special rules if you are regarded as 'terminally ill' – ie, if you have a progressive disease and could reasonably be expected to die within six months as a result.

In these circumstances there is no requirement to satisfy the disability test for the three-month qualifying period (see p107) and the highest rate care component of DLA is paid straight away. Claims should be dealt with within eight working days.

Note: you do not qualify for the mobility component automatically. However, you should claim this based on your mobility needs.

Awards are made for a fixed period of three years but, if there is already a mobility component award in place, the period of the special rules award may be adjusted to end at the same time.

Getting paid

DLA is usually paid directly into your bank (or similar) account. Which account it goes into is up to you. If you do not want your benefit to go into an account that is overdrawn, give the Department for Work and Pensions (or the Department for Social Development) details of an alternative account if you have access to, or can open, one.

If you have been overpaid DLA, you might have to repay it.

5. **Challenging a decision**

If you think a decision about your disability living allowance (DLA) is wrong (eg, because the decision maker got the facts or the law wrong), there are a number of ways you can try to get the decision changed.
- You can seek a revision or a supersession of the decision. In some cases, you have to show specific grounds. In others, you must apply within a strict time limit.
- You can appeal to an independent tribunal. There are strict time limits for appealing – usually one month from the date you are sent or given the decision. You can make a late appeal in limited circumstances.

If you are considering challenging a decision, you should seek specialist advice as soon as possible.

Note: when you ask for an award of DLA to be revised or you appeal (in respect of one or both components), the Department for Work and Pensions (DWP), Department for Social Development (DSD) or tribunal can look at your entitlement to both components of DLA, whether or not you want it to. You run the risk of having your award reduced or of one or both components being removed altogether. You should, therefore, seek advice or consider fully all the circumstances before applying for a revision or appealing. If you have only been awarded DLA for a set period, it may instead be worth waiting to apply for a higher rate when you make your next (renewal) claim.

If the DWP or DSD assumes that, because you are a student, you no longer have the same care or mobility needs and your DLA is affected, you can challenge the decision. See above for what you should consider before you do so. If you do challenge the decision, bear the following in mind.
- Let the DWP or DSD (or appeal tribunal) know if you took up the course for therapeutic reasons and are only able to do it with the support of disability services or the disabled students' allowance.
- It is sometimes worth providing a copy of the disabled students' allowance report as evidence of the difficulties you have with studying and the support you need if your DLA entitlement is in dispute.

6. **Other benefits and tax credits**

Disability living allowance (DLA) is usually paid in full in addition to any other social security benefits or tax credits. Constant attendance allowance overlaps with the care component, and the war pension mobility supplement overlaps with the mobility component. You are paid the higher of these.

If you are in receipt of DLA, you are eligible for housing benefit (HB) and council tax benefit (CTB) even if you are a full-time student. You are also eligible for income support (IS) if you made a claim before 27 October 2008. After this date, you are eligible to claim income-related employment and support allowance (ESA) if you are not already in receipt of IS.

If you are in receipt of income support as a result of receiving DLA prior to 27 October 2008, then the current proposal is that you will be transferred to the employment and support allowance system between 2011 and 2014.

Receiving DLA may entitle you to additional premiums in IS, income-related ESA, HB and CTB. The amount of the premium depends on the rate and the components of DLA you receive.

If your child receives DLA (at any rate), your HB/CTB will include a disabled child premium, and an enhanced disability premium if s/he receives the highest rate care component. If you have two children receiving DLA, you should receive one of these premiums for each child, depending on how many they qualify for. You can also get the disability/severe disability element of child tax credit.

If you are receiving working tax credit, DLA enables you to qualify for the disability element only if you are working more than 16 hours per week and pass the disability test as well, and the severe disability element only if you get highest rate care component of DLA.

If you are still receiving allowances for your children with your IS or income-based jobseeker's allowance, you can also get a disabled child premium if your child gets any rate of DLA, and possibly an enhanced disability premium if your child receives the highest rate care component.

When you make a claim for a means-tested benefit or tax credits, it is, therefore, important to inform the local Department for Work and Pensions office, the Department for Social Development, local authority or HM Revenue and Customs that you, your partner or child are receiving DLA.

Notes

2. Who is eligible

1 CDLA/58/1993
2 s72(1)(b)(i) SSCBA 1992 and CA/281/ 1989
3 s72(1)(b)(ii) SSCBA 1992 and R(A) 2/75
4 s72(4)(a) SSCBA 1992
5 CDLA/1983/2006; CDLA/3204/2006
6 s73(1)(d) SSCBA 1992
7 s73(1)(a) SSCBA 1992; reg 12 SS(DLA) Regs
8 s73(2)SSCBA 1992
9 s73(3) SSCBA 1992; reg 12(5) and (6) SS(DLA) Regs

Chapter 10

Employment and support allowance

This chapter covers:
1. What is employment and support allowance (p116)
2. Who is eligible (p116)
3. Limited capability for work (p120)
4. Amount of benefit (p120)
5. Claiming employment and support allowance (p125)
6. Challenging a decision (p125)
7. Other benefits and tax credits (p126)

Basic facts

– Employment and support allowance replaced incapacity benefit and income support for people making a new claim on grounds of disability from 27 October 2008.

– It is for people who have limited capability for work, according to a work capability assessment.

– There is an income-related and a contributory employment and support allowance, including a contributory 'employment and support allowance in youth'.

– Part-time students who have limited capability for work and full-time students who get disability living allowance are eligible for income-related employment and support allowance.

– Part-time and full-time students can claim contributory employment and support allowance if they have paid sufficient national insurance contributions.

– Full-time students aged 19 or over and part-time students can claim employment and support allowance in youth after 28 weeks of limited capability for work, which began when they were under 20 (or sometimes 25) without having any national insurance contributions.

– In some circumstances, full-time students under 19 can get employment and support allowance in youth.

1. What is employment and support allowance

Further information

This chapter gives an outline of the employment and support allowance rules and focuses on issues relevant to students. For more detailed information on the rules, see CPAG's *Welfare Benefits and Tax Credits Handbook*.

There are two types of employment and support allowance (ESA) – contributory ESA and income-related ESA. Contributory ESA is for people who have paid national insurance contributions, or whose period of limited capability for work starts when they are young. Income-related ESA is means tested and is for people who have limited capability for work and are on a low income. It is possible to receive one or both types of ESA.

2. Who is eligible

To qualify for employment and support allowance (ESA) you must meet all the basic conditions.[1]

- You have limited capability for work (see p120).
- You are aged 16 or over and under qualifying age for pension credit (see p165).
- You are in the UK (although some absences are allowed – see CPAG's *Welfare Benefits and Tax Credits Handbook*).
- You satisfy the rules for contributory ESA (see below) or income-related ESA (see p118).
- You are not working, although some 'permitted work' is allowed (see CPAG's *Welfare Benefits and Tax Credits Handbook*).

Contributory employment and support allowance

Contributory ESA is not means tested. To qualify, you must meet the basic conditions above and either:[2]

- have paid sufficient national insurance (NI) contributions (see CPAG's *Welfare Benefits and Tax Credits Handbook* for details); *or*
- you can get ESA in youth (see p117). This depends on:
  - your age when you began your period of limited capability for work;
  - your age when you make your first claim; *and*
  - whether or not you are a full-time student (see p117).

Employment and support allowance in youth

You can get ESA in youth if you meet the basic conditions (see p116) and:
- you were aged under 20 (or under 25 if covered by the age exception) when your period of limited capability began, and, if you are under 19, you are not in full-time education (see below);
- you have had 196 days (28 weeks) of limited capability for work; *and*
- you satisfy residence and presence tests and are not a 'person subject to immigration control' (see CPAG's *Welfare Benefits and Tax Credits Handbook* for details).

Under age 19

Students in full-time education under age 19 are not eligible for contributory ESA, except a very small minority who can qualify through their NI contributions and those whose course is not counted because it is designed for disabled people (see below).

You can get ESA in youth as soon as you reach your 19th birthday if you are still in full-time education. You must have had limited capability for work for 28 weeks before benefit can be paid, but these weeks can fall before your 19th birthday.

Students under age 19 in part-time education are eligible for ESA in youth. You can claim from age 16. You can serve the 28-week qualifying period before you reach age 16, so your benefit can start from your 16th birthday.

Full-time education

You are treated as being in **'full-time education'** if you attend a course of education for 21 hours or more a week. Count classes, lectures, seminars and periods of supervised study. Do not count lunch breaks, private unsupervised study or work at home.[3] You continue to be treated as being in full-time education during any temporary interruption of your studies.

Disabled students should ignore any hours of tuition that would not be received by someone of the same age who is not disabled. Any such special teaching does not count towards the 21 hours.[4]

Aged 19

At age 19 students can get ESA in youth regardless of whether they are studying full or part time. If you have already had limited capability for work for 28 weeks when you reach your 19th birthday, you can claim and be paid ESA straight away.

Aged 20 or over

If you already get ESA in youth, you can continue to get it after age 20. If you have not already claimed, you must start your claim no later than the end of a continuous period of 196 days (28 weeks) of limited capability for work that began before your 20th birthday. You have a further three months to send in your claim form. After that, you can only make a new claim for contributory ESA if:

- you have paid sufficient NI contributions; *or*
- you are 25 or under and a former student. There is an age exception that allows certain people to claim up to age 25 when they have left their course (see below).

Age exception

Normally, to claim contributory ESA after age 20 you must have sufficient NI contributions, but there is an age exception for students. You can claim if you are under 25 and give up or finish a course that you started before your 20th birthday and you have had limited capability for work for 28 weeks. The following rules specify when your course must have started and finished, and by when you need to claim. You claim once you have left your course.[5]

- You were registered on a course of full-time education, or certain kinds of training, three months or more before your 20th birthday. Any course counts, from secondary school education to university undergraduate or postgraduate degrees. If you are studying part time because your disability prevents you from doing a full-time course, you are regarded as full time for this rule. The law does not say what 'full time' means or give a set number of hours. The Department for Work and Pensions (DWP) may ask you for evidence from the educational institution.
- You attended the course in the first academic term after registration.
- You were still attending the course within the last two complete tax years before the benefit year in which you claim ESA. A tax year runs from 6 April and a benefit year runs from the first Sunday in January. For example, if you claim ESA in 2010, you must have attended the course at some point on or after 6 April 2007. You are regarded as still attending the course while taking time off temporarily because of illness or a domestic emergency.
- You start your claim no later than the end of a continuous period of 196 days (28 weeks) of incapacity that started before your 25th birthday. You have another three months to send in your claim form.

Income-related employment and support allowance

Income-related ESA is means tested. You are eligible if you are a part-time student and have limited capability for work. If you are a full-time student, you are only eligible if you get disability living allowance (DLA).

To qualify for income-related ESA while studying, you must satisfy the basic conditions on p116 and all the following conditions:[6]

- you are either a full-time student (see p119) who is entitled to DLA (either component, at any rate – see Chapter 9) or a part-time student.[7] However, if you are a full-time student who has been transferred to ESA from income

support (IS), which you were receiving because you were a disabled student, you do not have to get DLA to qualify for income-related ESA; *and*
- your income is less than the set amount the law says you need to live on (known as your 'applicable amount' – see p122); *and*
- you have no more than £16,000 capital; *and*
- your partner (if you have one) is not working 24 hours or more a week; *and*
- you are 'habitually resident' in the UK, Ireland, Channel Islands or Isle of Man, have a 'right to reside' in the UK, and are not a 'person subject to immigration control'. These terms are explained in CPAG's *Welfare Benefits and Tax Credits Handbook*. Further advice is available from UKCISA (see Appendix 2).

Full-time student

You are a full-time student if you are:[8]
- under 20 and a 'qualifying young person' (see below); *or*
- 19 or over and a full-time student (unless you are aged 19 and count as being a qualifying young person – see below); *or*
- under 19 in full-time advanced education (see p120).

Under 20 and a qualifying young person

You are a qualifying young person if you are 19 or under and attending a full-time course of non-advanced education which you were accepted on, enrolled on or started when you were under 19. If you are accepted on, enrol on or start the course on or after your 19th birthday, you are not a qualifying young person (see below). 'Non-advanced education' is anything below degree, higher national certificate (HNC) or higher national diploma (HND) level, and includes school-level courses. Your course is classed as full time for income-related ESA if it is for more than 12 hours a week during term time. These 12 hours include classes and supervised study, but not meal breaks or unsupervised study either at home or at college. You may count as a qualifying young person in a gap between courses or for a period after you have finished a course (see p100).

19 or over and a full-time student

You count as a full-time student if you are undertaking a full-time course of study at an educational establishment.[9]

If you attend a **further education** college and your course is government funded, you will usually count as a part-time student as long as your course comprises 16 guided learning hours or less a week. 'Guided learning hours' include all supervised study – eg, classes, lectures, tutorials and structured assessment periods. They do not include unstructured or unsupervised study time – eg, studying at home or in a library. A document called a 'learning agreement' is used to provide proof of course hours. It is important to use the official learning agreement. The hours on this document are calculated as an average figure and may differ from the hours on your timetable. Ask about your learning agreement at your college or check with your course tutor. The local authority uses your learning agreement to decide whether or not you are studying full time.

In Northern Ireland, the definition of a full-time course depends on the institution's definition of 'full time'. A letter from the institution stating that your course is part time should be sufficient when applying for ESA.

Students in **higher education** are counted as full-time students if the college or university says the course is full time. Ask at your college, or check with the course tutor or the registry department for evidence of whether you are registered on a full- or part-time course.

If your course is only for a few hours each week, you should argue that it is not full time. But a course could be full time even if you only attend a few lectures a week.

Under 19 in full-time advanced education

If you are under 19 and in full-time advanced education rather than in non-advanced education, the rules on when you count as full time are the same as for those aged 19 or over (see p119).

3. Limited capability for work

One of the basic rules of entitlement to employment and support allowance (ESA) is that you must be assessed as having 'limited capability for work'.

Full-time students who get disability living allowance (DLA) and who are claiming income-related ESA are treated as having limited capability for work and do not have to satisfy this part of the test.[10] However, this does not apply to all full-time students. If you are a qualifying young person under 20 and claiming income-related ESA (see p119), you have to satisfy this test. Similarly, if you are claiming contributory ESA (including ESA in youth), but not income-related ESA, you still have to pass the limited capability for work test, even if you get DLA. All students, unless they get the support component, have to attend work-focused interviews. These include agreeing an action plan of activities to help you find work. At present, your benefit will not be reduced if you do not undertake any of these. However, this may become a requirement of entitlement to benefit at the full rate in the future.[11]

4. Amount of benefit

Employment and support allowance (ESA) is payable after three 'waiting days' (apart from ESA in youth, which has a 196-day qualifying period). You are paid a limited amount of ESA during an initial 'assessment phase' (in most cases, this is expected to last 13 weeks) and are paid more in the 'main phase' that follows.

The exact amount of ESA you are paid depends on:
- whether you are claiming contributory ESA or income-related ESA;
- whether you are in the assessment or the main phase;
- which of the two possible additional components you get after the assessment phase. These are a support component of £31.40 a week and a work-related activity component of £25.95 a week.

In the assessment phase, for **contributory ESA** you get a basic allowance. For **income-related ESA**, the amount you get depends on your needs (your applicable amount) and how much income you have.

In the main phase, an additional component (either the work-related activity component or the support component) is added. In income-related ESA, it is added to your applicable amount and, as in the assessment phase, your income is subtracted from your applicable amount. In contributory ESA, it is added to the basic allowance.

Contributory employment and support allowance

Weekly rate from April 2010[12]	£
Assessment phase, basic allowance (under 25)	51.85
Assessment phase, basic allowance (25 or over)	65.45
Main phase, basic allowance (16 or over)	65.45
Main phase, support component	31.40
Main phase, work-related activity component	25.95

Income-related employment and support allowance

The amount of income-related ESA you get depends on your circumstances and the circumstances of your partner, if you have one.[13] The amount also depends on your income and capital. You should go through the following steps to work out the amount of ESA to which you are entitled.

Step 1: capital

If your capital is over £16,000 you cannot get income-related ESA (see p119). Some kinds of capital are ignored. For details, see CPAG's *Welfare Benefits and Tax Credits Handbook*.

Step 2: work out your applicable amount

This is an amount for basic weekly needs. It is made up of:[14]
- personal allowances (see p122);
- premiums (see p123);
- work-related activity or support component (see p124);
- housing costs (see p124).

Step 3: work out your weekly income

Chapter 20 explains how your loan, grant or other income is taken into account and how to work out your weekly income.

Step 4: deduct weekly income from applicable amount

If your income is less than your applicable amount, ESA equals the difference between the two.

If your income is the same as or more than your applicable amount, you cannot get ESA. You can claim again if your income goes down – eg, during the long vacation.

Income-related ESA tops up contributory ESA if you are entitled to both and the income-related amount is higher.

Applicable amount

Work out your applicable amount by adding together your personal allowances, premiums, the component that applies to you in the main phase, and eligible housing costs. Note that benefit rates are uprated in April each year, but it is usually possible to find out what the new rates will be from the beginning of December. Check the Department for Work and Pensions website at www.dwp.gov.uk for a press release on social security uprating.

Personal allowance

Your personal allowance is made up of one personal allowance at either the single, lone parent or couple rate depending on your situation. The amount depends on your age and whether you are in the assessment phase or the main phase.

Circumstances	Assessment phase £ per week	Main phase £ per week
Single		
Under 25	51.85	65.45
25 or over	65.45	65.45
Lone parent		
Under 18	51.85	65.45
18 or over	65.45	65.45
Couple		
Both under 18 (higher rate)	78.30	102.75
Both under 18 (if not eligible for higher rate)	51.85	65.45
One under 18, one 18 or over (higher rate)	102.75	102.75
One under 18, one 18–24 (if not eligible for higher rate)	51.85	65.45

| One under 18, one 25 or over (if not eligible for higher rate) | 65.45 | 65.45 |
| Both 18 or over | 102.75 | 102.75 |

If you are both under 18, you get the higher rate if:
- one of you is responsible for a child; *or*
- you and your partner would both be eligible to claim income-related ESA if you were single; *or*
- your partner would qualify for income support (IS) if s/he were single; *or*
- your partner would qualify for income-based jobseeker's allowance (JSA) or severe hardship payments of JSA.

If one of you is under 18 and the other is 18 or over, you get the higher rate if the younger person would:
- qualify for IS or income-related ESA if s/he were single; *or*
- qualify for income-based or severe hardship payments of JSA.

Premiums

Qualifying for premiums depends on your circumstances. You can qualify for a:
- pensioner premium (see below for amounts);
- carer premium of £30.05;
- enhanced disability premium for an adult of £13.65 (£19.65 for a couple);
- severe disability premium of £53.65.

If you or your partner have reached the qualifying age for pension credit, you qualify for a **pensioner premium**. If you are single you get £67.15 and if you are in a couple you get £99.65. In the main phase, these amounts are reduced by the amount of the work-related activity component or support component that you qualify for.

You qualify for a **carer premium** in the same way as you qualify for a carer premium in IS (see p97).

You qualify for an **enhanced disability premium** if you or your partner get the highest rate disability living allowance (DLA) care component or you get the support component of ESA.

The **severe disability premium** is for severely disabled people who live alone, or can be treated as living alone. You qualify for this premium if you get the middle or highest rate DLA care component and no one gets carer's allowance for looking after you. You will not get it if you live with another person aged 18 or over (eg, a friend or parent), unless they are separately liable for rent, or you only share a bathroom or hallway, or in some other circumstances. See CPAG's *Welfare Benefits and Tax Credits Handbook* for details.

If you have a partner, you will not qualify unless s/he also qualifies in her/his own right or is registered blind. If you both qualify, you get two premiums.

Components

In the main phase, you receive one of either the work-related activity or support components. The work-related activity component is £25.95. The support component is £31.40. It is possible to lose the whole of the work-related activity component if you do not take part in the required assessments/interviews.

Housing costs

If you own your own home, income-related ESA can help with the cost of mortgage interest payments. Normally, help only starts once you have been getting ESA for 13 weeks, although it can be as much as 39 weeks in some cases. For help with your rent, you need to claim housing benefit (HB – see Chapter 12). For an outline of the rules, see p179 and for full details, see CPAG's *Welfare Benefits and Tax Credits Handbook*.

Example
Doreen is 19 and has cerebral palsy. She gets the lowest rate DLA care component and lives with her parents. In January 2011 she starts a full-time NVQ Level 3 course. She claims ESA. She is eligible for contributory ESA in youth and income-related ESA.

Assessment phase:
Contributory ESA
Doreen gets £51.85 basic allowance.

Income-related ESA
Step 1 Doreen has no savings or capital.
Step 2 Her applicable amount is:
Basic allowance for herself = £51.85.
Step 3 Her weekly income is:
Contributory ESA = £51.85 (DLA is disregarded).
Step 4 The amount of contributory ESA is the same as the amount of income-related ESA to which she is entitled, so she gets contributory ESA of £51.85.

Main phase:
Contributory ESA
Doreen is assessed as having limited capability for work and as being in the work-related activity group. In the main phase of ESA, she gets £65.45 basic allowance and £25.95 work-related activity component (£91.40 in total).

Income-related ESA
Step 2 Her applicable amount is:
Basic allowance for herself (£65.45) and work-related activity component (£25.95) = £91.40

Step 3 Her weekly income is:
Contributory ESA = £91.40 (DLA is disregarded).
Step 4 The amount of contributory ESA is the same as the amount of income-related ESA to which she is entitled, so she gets contributory ESA of £91.40.

5. **Claiming employment and support allowance**

You start your claim by phoning a Jobcentre Plus contact centre (although paper claim forms should also be available if it is not suitable for you to use the telephone). Phone the national number on 0800 055 6688 (textphone 0800 023 4888) and your call will be routed to your local centre.

In Northern Ireland, phone 0800 085 6318 (textphone 0800 328 3419).

You are usually interviewed after you claim. You need to send in medical certificates from your GP until you are assessed under the work capability assessment. If you need to serve a 28-week qualifying period before you can get employment and support allowance (ESA), ask your doctor for a backdated medical certificate and send this with your claim.

Either member of a couple can make a claim for income-related ESA for both, but whoever claims must be eligible in her/his own right. You claim contributory ESA for yourself only.

Claims for ESA can be backdated for up to three months.

6. **Challenging a decision**

If you think a decision about your employment and support allowance (ESA) is wrong (eg, because the decision maker got the facts or law wrong), there are a number of ways you can try to get the decision changed.

- You can seek a revision or a supersession of the decision. In some cases you have to show specific grounds. In others, you must apply within a strict time limit.
- You can appeal to an independent tribunal. There are strict time limits for appealing – usually one month from the date you are sent or given the decision. You can make a late appeal in limited circumstances.

As ESA is a relatively new benefit, and students are subject to specific rules, you should look closely at any decision to make sure it is correct. If you are considering challenging a decision, you should seek advice as soon as possible.

7. **Other benefits and tax credits**

You cannot get employment and support allowance (ESA) if you are getting statutory sick pay (SSP) from an employer.[15] SSP runs out after 28 weeks, after which you can claim ESA.

You cannot get ESA if you are getting income support (IS) or jobseeker's allowance (JSA). You can claim contributory ESA if your partner is getting IS or JSA.[16] You are excluded if you get joint-claim JSA. You cannot get income-related ESA if your partner gets IS, income-based JSA or pension credit.

Income-related ESA passports you to full housing benefit and council tax benefit, Healthy Start food vouchers and vitamins if you are pregnant, free school meals and both discretionary and regulated social fund payments (see Chapter 17). ESA also passports you to other health benefits (see Chapter 11).

Notes

2. **Who is eligible**
1 s1 WRA 2007
2 Sch 1 paras 1-4 WRA 2007
3 DMG para 41063 vol 8
4 Reg 12 ESA Regs
5 Reg 9 ESA Regs
6 Sch 1 para 6 WRA 2007
7 Reg 18 ESA Regs
8 Regs 14-16 ESA Regs
9 Reg 131 ESA Regs

3. **Limited capability for work**
10 Reg 33(2) ESA Regs
11 para 4.5 Explanatory Memorandum to ESA Regs

4. **Amount of benefit**
12 s2 WRA 2007; reg 67(2) and (3) ESA Regs
13 s4 WRA 2007
14 Reg 67 and Sch 4 ESA Regs

7. **Other benefit and tax credits**
15 s20 WRA 2007
16 s1(3)(f) WRA 2007

Chapter 11
Health benefits

This chapter covers:
1. What are health benefits (below)
2. Who is eligible (p128)
3. Claiming health benefits and refunds (p134)
4. Challenging a decision (p136)
5. Overseas students (p136)

Basic facts
- People under 19 and in full-time education can get free prescriptions, sight tests, vouchers for glasses and dental treatment.
- Prescriptions are free in Wales. In addition, you can get a free dental examination if you are under 25, or are 60 or over.
- Prescriptions in Northern Ireland are also free.
- Other students can get help if they are on a low income or in certain other circumstances.

---

1. What are health benefits

Further information
This chapter gives an outline of the health benefit rules and focuses on issues relevant to students. For more detailed information on the rules, see CPAG's *Welfare Benefits and Tax Credits Handbook.*

Although most health treatment is free under the NHS for UK residents, there are fixed charges for some NHS services and treatments. These include:
- prescriptions;
- sight tests;
- glasses or contact lenses;
- dental treatment;
- wigs or fabric supports; *and*
- fares to hospital.

You are exempt from the charges in specified circumstances, or if your income is sufficiently low. As a student, you are not automatically exempt from paying these charges unless you fall into one of the categories listed on pp128–131. Otherwise, you can apply for a 'remission certificate' under the low income scheme (see p135). If you get a remission certificate, part or all of the charges are waived, depending on your income. For information about claims, see p134.

Note: you may also qualify for vouchers for Healthy Start food and for free vitamins. See p131 for further information.

2. **Who is eligible**

You are automatically exempt from NHS charges if:[1]
- you or a member of your family receive income support (IS), income-based jobseeker's allowance (JSA), income-related employment and support allowance (ESA) or the guarantee credit of pension credit (PC); *or*
- you or a member of your family receive:
  – child tax credit (CTC); *or*
  – CTC and working tax credit (WTC); *or*
  – WTC including a disability or severe disability element,
  and your gross annual income is £15,276 or less a year.

Note:
- There are other categories of people who are exempt – eg, if you are a permanent resident in a care home, a hospital inpatient, an asylum seeker (see p136), 16 or 17 and being financially maintained by a local authority, a war disablement pensioner and you need the item or service because of your war disability, or if you are in prison or a young offenders institution.
- You may also be exempt from some charges because of your age or a specific health condition – see the individual types of charge below.
- If you are not exempt on any of the grounds listed above or below, you may be entitled to a full or partial remission of charges on grounds of low income (see p132), but you have to apply for a 'remission certificate'.

If you are exempt because you receive tax credits

If you are exempt from NHS charges because you receive tax credits, you should be sent an NHS tax credits exemption certificate automatically. This could be up to six weeks after you are awarded tax credits. If you have an award of tax credits, but have not yet been sent your certificate, you can sign the relevant treatment forms to say you do not have to pay. You can use your award letter as evidence of this. If this is not accepted and you are charged, be sure to keep your receipts so you can claim a refund (see p135). If there is a delay in getting your exemption certificate you should seek advice.

If you are getting CTC but are exempt from charges because you are getting IS, income-based JSA, income-related ESA or the guarantee credit of PC, you do not get an NHS tax credits exemption certificate. However, if you stop getting IS, income-based JSA, income-related ESA or the guarantee credit of PC because of, for example, your student income, you need a certificate. You should let HM Revenue and Customs know about your change in circumstances as soon as possible. It notifies the NHS Business Services Authority in Newcastle upon Tyne, which issues you with a certificate.

Free prescriptions

The cost of a prescription in England is £7.20.[2] Prescriptions are free in Wales, if they are provided in Wales or if you have an entitlement card (ie, because you live in Wales, but your doctor is in England). Since 1 April 2010, they have also been free in Northern Ireland.

Otherwise, you qualify for free prescriptions if:[3]
- you are in one of the exempt groups listed on p128; *or*
- you are aged under 16, or under 19 and in full-time education (see below); *or*
- you are aged 60 or over; *or*
- you are pregnant or have given birth within the last 12 months (see p135); *or*
- you have one or more of the following specific medical conditions:
  - a continuing physical disability which prevents you from leaving home except with the help of another person;
  - epilepsy requiring continuous anticonvulsive therapy;
  - a permanent fistula, including caecostomy, ileostomy, laryngostomy or colostomy, needing continuous surgical dressing or an appliance;
  - one of the following conditions: diabetes mellitus (except where treatment is by diet alone), myxoedema, hypoparathyroidism, diabetes insipidus and other forms of hypopituitarism, forms of hypoadrenalism (including Addison's disease) for which specific substitution therapy is essential, myasthenia gravis; *or*
- your income is low enough (see p135).

'Full-time education' means full-time instruction at a recognised educational establishment – eg, a school, college or university. If you are studying elsewhere, or you have finished your A levels and are waiting to start college or university, check to see if you are exempt because you are on a low income.

Prepayment certificates

If you are likely to need a lot of prescriptions, but are not exempt from payment, you can reduce the cost by buying a prepayment certificate. A holder of a prepayment certificate does not have to pay any further charges for prescriptions for the duration of the certificate, regardless of how many are required.[4]

A three-month certificate saves money on more than four prescriptions, while a 12-month certificate saves money on more than 14 prescriptions. Applications can be made in England by post on Form FP95, available from chemists, some doctors' surgeries and relevant health bodies. This should be sent to the address on the form. Applications can also be made by telephone on 0845 850 0030 or online at www.nhsbsa.nhs.uk and at registered pharmacies.

Free sight tests

You qualify for a free NHS sight test if:[5]
- you are in one of the exempt groups listed on p128; *or*
- you are under 16, or under 19 and in full-time education (see p134); *or*
- you are aged 60 or over; *or*
- you are registered blind or partially sighted; *or*
- you have been prescribed complex or powerful lenses; *or*
- you have diabetes or glaucoma or are at risk of getting glaucoma; *or*
- you are 40 or over and are the parent, sibling or child of someone who has glaucoma; *or*
- you are a patient of the Hospital Eye Service; *or*
- your income is low enough.

Note: you may also qualify for a voucher towards the cost of buying or repairing glasses or contact lenses.[6]

Free dental treatment and dentures

If you live in Wales and are under 25 or are 60 or over, you qualify for free dental examinations.[7] Otherwise, you qualify for free dental treatment (including check-ups) and appliances (including dentures) if:[8]
- you are in one of the exempt groups listed on p128; *or*
- you are aged under 18, or are under 19 and in full-time education (see p134); *or*
- you are pregnant or have given birth within the last 12 months (see p135); *or*
- you are a patient of the Community Dental Service; *or*
- your income is low enough.

Note: you may also qualify for reduced-cost treatment and appliances on the grounds of low income.

Free wigs and fabric supports

You qualify for free wigs or fabric supports if:[9]
- you are in one of the exempt groups listed on p128; *or*
- you are under 16, or under 19 and in full-time education (see p134); *or*
- you are a hospital inpatient when the wig or fabric support is provided; *or*

- these are provided in Wales or you have an entitlement card; *or*
- your income is low enough.

Fares to hospital

You qualify for help with the costs of travel to hospital or any other establishment for NHS treatment or services if:[10]
- you are in one of the exempt groups listed on p128; *or*
- you live in the Isles of Scilly; *or*
- your income is low enough.

Note:
- You may also qualify for partial help with fares on the grounds of low income.
- In some cases, you can get help with the costs of travel to obtain NHS treatment abroad.

Healthy Start food and vitamins

You qualify for Healthy Start **food vouchers** if:[11]
- you are more than 10 weeks' pregnant and:
  - you are under 18; *or*
  - you are 18 or over and you (or a member of the family) are entitled to IS, income-based JSA, income-related ESA, or CTC, provided in the latter case that gross income for CTC purposes does not exceed £16,190 and there is no entitlement to WTC; *or*
- you are a mother aged 18 or over and have 'parental responsibility' for a child under one (or it is less than a year since her/his expected date of birth) and you (or a member of the family) are entitled to IS, income-based JSA or CTC, provided in the latter case that gross income for CTC purposes does not exceed £16,190 and there is no entitlement to WTC.
  If you qualify for vouchers for more than one child under this rule (eg, if you have twins), you get vouchers for each;
- you have a child under four and you (or a member of the family) are entitled to IS, income-based JSA or CTC, provided in the latter case that gross income for CTC purposes does not exceed £16,190 and there is no entitlement to WTC.

In practice, this means that each week you get one voucher for each of your children aged between one and four, two vouchers for each of your children under one (or within one year of their expected date of birth), plus one voucher if you are pregnant. Vouchers are worth £3.10 each and can be exchanged at registered food outlets for liquid cow's milk and cow's milk-based infant formula, fresh fruit and vegetables (including loose, pre-packed, whole, sliced, chopped or mixed fruit or vegetables, but not fruit or vegetables to which salt, sugar, herbs or other flavouring has been added).

You qualify for free **vitamins** if you qualify for Healthy Start food vouchers.[12]

Health in pregnancy grant

A health in pregnancy grant can be paid from the 25th week of pregnancy. This is a one-off lump sum of £190. To receive the grant, you must have received health advice on your pregnancy from a health professional. You can obtain the application from your midwife or GP and must return it to HM Revenue and Customs within 31 days of the health professional signing it.[13]

You must be present and ordinarily resident and have a right to reside in the United Kingdom. These terms are explained in CPAG's *Welfare Benefits and Tax Credits Handbook*.

Note: the Government plans to abolish the health in pregnancy grant from January 2011.[14]

The low income scheme

The NHS Business Services Authority has a means test to determine whether you qualify for either a full or partial remission certificate. The means test is roughly based on the applicable amounts for IS (see Chapter 14), but there are some differences.

Applications for help under the low income scheme should be made to the NHS Business Services Authority on Form HC1 (HC1W in Wales), available from Jobcentre Plus offices, NHS hospitals, some doctors' surgeries, some chemists, many students' union advice centres or at www.nhsbsa.nhs.uk.

Calculating entitlement

To qualify for help, you must have less than £16,000 capital, (£23,250 if you are in a care home in England, or £22,000 in Wales).[15]

If your income (see p133) does not exceed your requirements (see p133) by more than 50 per cent of the current cost of a prescription (at the time of writing this was £3.60), you receive a full remission certificate (an HC2 – or HC2W in Wales).[16] If your income exceeds your requirements by more than this amount, you receive a partial remission certificate (an HC3 – or HC3W in Wales), depending on the level of excess as follows:[17]

- a remission of dental charges and charges for wigs and fabric supports which are higher than three times your excess income;
- a voucher for glasses or lenses, reduced by an amount equal to twice your excess income;
- a reduction in the cost of a sight test to the amount of your excess income, if lower, plus the amount by which the cost exceeds the NHS sight test fee;
- a reduction by the amount of your excess income in the amount you can get for hospital fares.

If you qualify for a remission certificate, it is normally valid for 12 months. If you are a full-time student, your certificate is normally valid until the end of your course or the start of the next academic year. You should make a repeat claim shortly before the expiry date. Remember that if you qualify for IS or income-based JSA over the summer vacation, you are automatically exempt from NHS charges during that period (see p128).

Calculating income

Income is calculated in the same way as for IS, with some modifications.[18] The income that is taken into account is your own and that of your partner, where appropriate. Your parents' income is not taken into account. However, any money given to you by your parents may be taken into account when assessing eligibility. Information about how your income is calculated and how student income is treated is in Chapter 22.

Calculating requirements

Your requirements are based on those used for calculating the applicable amount for IS (see Chapter 14).[19]

This is an amount for basic weekly needs. Chapter 14 gives details of how to qualify for each premium. Your requirements are made up of:

- **personal allowances**
  - single person aged under 25 £51.85
  - single person under 25 entitled to an
    ESA component, or incapable of work for
    28 weeks since 27 October 2008 £65.45
  - single person aged 25 or over £65.45
  - single person aged 60 or over £132.60
  - lone parent aged under 60 £65.45
  - lone parent aged 60 or over £132.60
  - couple aged under 60 £102.75
  - couple aged 60 or over £202.40
- **premiums**
  - carer (as for IS);
  - disability (as for IS, except that you can include a disability premium after 28 weeks of incapacity for work, rather than 52 weeks). You can also get a disability premium if you or your partner are under 60 and get ESA with a work-related activity or support component, or have been getting ESA for at least 28 weeks, or have been incapable of work for at least 28 weeks and have had the incapacity since 27 October 2008. The amount of the disability premium goes up to £31.40 if you are single or a lone parent and *either* get ESA with the support component *or* get disability living allowance middle or highest rate care component and have been incapable of work for 28 weeks since 27 October 2008;
  - enhanced disability for an adult (as for IS);
  - severe disability (as for IS);

- **weekly rent** less any housing benefit (HB) and non-dependant deductions;
- **weekly council tax**, if you are liable, less any council tax benefit;
- **mortgage interest**, endowment payments and capital repayments on your home, as well as on loans to adapt a home for a disabled person, deducting any non-dependant deductions;
- **amounts for children**. If you have children you are likely to be exempt from charges through getting a qualifying benefit like IS, JSA or CTC. If you get CTC but are not exempt from charges, your children are not included in the low income assessment.

If your income is less than or no more than £3.60 (half the cost of a prescription in England) higher than your needs, you are entitled to health benefits. If your income is more than £3.60 higher than your needs, you will not get free prescriptions, but you might get partial help with other charges.

Example

Oliver is 21, and a third-year full-time undergraduate in Wales. His income is assessed to be £97.92 a week (see p133).

His requirements are calculated as his personal allowance (£51.85) plus his weekly rent (£85). This gives a total of £136.85. This is more than his income, so he receives full help with health costs. As a Welsh-domiciled student, however, Oliver does in any case qualify for free prescriptions and, as he is under 25, free dental examinations.

Deborah is 24, and a second-year full-time undergraduate in London. Her income is assessed to be £187.20 a week.

Her requirements are calculated as her personal allowance (£51.85) plus her weekly rent (£150). This gives a total of £201.85. This is £14.65 more than her income, so she receives full help with health costs.

3. **Claiming health benefits and refunds**

How and where you claim help with NHS charges depends on your circumstances. Some of these are shown below.

Under 19 and in full-time education

To claim the exemption from NHS **prescription charges**, you must sign the declaration form on the back of the prescription. To claim a free **sight test**, you must sign the optician's form before your test.

To claim free **dental treatment**, you must tell the dental receptionist before your treatment that you think you are exempt from charges. You should complete a form at this point. Remember, in Wales, if you are under 25 you qualify for free dental examinations.

Pregnant women and recent births

To claim free **dental treatment** and **prescriptions**, you must apply for a maternity exemption certificate on a form available from your midwife, health visitor or doctor.

You must claim **Healthy Start food and vitamins** in writing. You should complete the form in the Healthy Start application leaflet (HS01). This is available from maternity clinics and some doctor's surgeries or from 0845 607 6823. Information about Healthy Start and a downloadable claim form are also available at www.healthystart.nhs.uk. Your claim form must be countersigned by a health professional (eg, a midwife or health visitor) who certifies that you have been given appropriate advice about healthy eating and breastfeeding.

Prescribed condition

To claim free **prescriptions** because you have a prescribed condition, you must apply for an exemption certificate on a form available from your doctor, hospital or pharmacist.

The low income scheme

Applications for help under the low income scheme should be made to the NHS Business Services Authority on Form HC1, available from Jobcentre Plus offices, NHS hospitals, some doctors' surgeries, some chemists, many students' union advice centres or at www.nhsbsa.nhs.uk.

Refunds

If you pay for an item or service that you could have got free of charge or at a reduced cost, you can apply for a refund. You must apply within three months of payment, although the time limit can be extended if you can show good cause for applying late – eg, you were ill.[20]

For a refund of prescription charges use Form FP57, which you must get when you pay for the prescription at the pharmacy or dispensing chemist. A bilingual version (WP57) is available in Wales.

For other items and services use Form HC5, available from post offices, Jobcentre Plus offices, NHS hospitals and some doctors' surgeries.

If you wish to have your costs refunded on the basis of low income, but do not already have an HC2 or an HC3 remission certificate (see p132), you should send a completed HC1 form with the HC5 form.

4. Challenging a decision

If you think a decision about your health benefits is wrong:

- you can ask for a formal review. You should write to the Review Section, NHS Help with Health Costs, Sandyford House, Newcastle upon Tyne NE2 1BF. You can also request a review online at www.nhsbsa.nhs.uk;
- because decisions about health benefits are based on your circumstances at the time you apply for a certificate, you should consider making a fresh claim, or reporting the change in your circumstances, if you think you would now be entitled to more help with NHS charges.

If there are delays in obtaining a certificate, you can complain to the customer services manager. If necessary, you could pay for the treatment or items you need then try to obtain a refund (see p135).

5. Overseas students

Many overseas students can get free NHS treatment and help with NHS charges. Detailed information is available at www.ukcisa.org.uk.

Asylum seekers

If you are an asylum seeker or a dependant of an asylum seeker and receiving support from either the UK Border Agency or a local authority, you are eligible for full exemption from NHS charges. If you are getting asylum support, you should be sent an HC2 certificate with your first support payment. If you are not supported by the UK Border Agency or a local authority, you should apply using an HC1 form.

European Economic Area students and Swiss nationals

If you are a student from any part of the European Economic Area (EEA) or Switzerland you can get NHS treatment during a temporary stay in the UK on the same basis as UK residents, provided that you have a European health insurance card. You can also get help with NHS charges on the same basis as UK residents.

Other overseas students

If you are a non-EEA overseas student on a course lasting six months or longer, you qualify for NHS treatment and help with NHS charges on the same basis as UK residents. In addition, any immediate family members with you in the UK also qualify.

Health benefits (with the exception of health in pregnancy grants) are not classed as public funds and, therefore, do not affect your immigration status.

If you are an overseas student on a course lasting less than six months, you cannot usually get free NHS treatment or help with NHS charges. However, you can get emergency treatment, treatment for certain communicable diseases and compulsory psychiatric treatment free through the NHS, but other treatments and services incur a charge. You are, therefore, strongly advised to take out adequate medical insurance for the duration of your stay in the UK.

Notes

2. Who is eligible

1 Regs 3-5 NHS(TERC) Regs; regs 3-5 NHS(TERC)(W) Regs
2 Regs 3-6 NHS(CDA) Regs
3 Regs 4 and 5 NHS(TERC) Regs; NHS(CDA) Regs; NHS(FP&CDA)(W) Regs
4 Reg 9 NHS(CDA) Regs
5 Reg 13 NHS(GOS) Regs; reg 3 NHS(OCP) Regs
6 Regs 9 and 15 NHS(OCP) Regs
7 Reg 3 NHS(DC)(W) Regs
8 Regs 4 and 5 NHS(TERC) Regs; regs 4 and 5 NHS(TERC)(W) Regs; Sch 2 and 3 NHS(DC) Regs; reg 9 and Sch 5 NHS(DC)(W) Regs
9 Regs 4 and 5 NHS(TERC) Regs; NHS(CDA) Regs; NHS(FP&CDA)(W) Regs
10 Regs 3, 5 and 9 NHS(TERC) Regs; regs 3 and 5 NHS(TERC)(W) Regs
11 Reg 3 HSS&WF(A) Regs
12 Reg 3 HSS&WF(A) Regs
13 s131-138 HSCA 2008
14 para 2.45, Budget 2010, 22 June 2010
15 Sch 1 NHS(TERC) Regs; Sch 1 NHS(TERC)(W) Regs
16 Reg 5 NHS(TERC) Regs; reg 5 NHS(TERC)(W) Regs
17 Reg 6 NHS(TERC) Regs; reg 6 NHS(TERC)(W) Regs
18 Reg 16 and Sch 1 NHS(TERC) Regs; reg 15 and Sch 1 NHS(TERC)(W) Regs
19 Reg 17 and Sch 1 NHS(TERC) Regs; reg 16 and Sch 1 NHS(TERC)(W) Regs

3. Claiming health benefits and refunds

20 Reg 11 NHS(TERC) Regs; reg 10 NHS(TERC)(W) Regs; reg 10 NHS(CDA) Regs; Sch 1 para 1 NHS(FP&CDA)(W) Regs; regs 6 and 20 NHS(OCP) Regs; reg 10 NHS(DC) Regs; reg 10 NHS(DC)(W) Regs

12

Chapter 12

Housing benefit

This chapter covers:

Basic facts

- Housing benefit (HB) helps with the rent. In Northern Ireland, it also helps with rates.
- Full-time students aged under 19 are eligible if they are not on a higher education course.
- Full-time students aged 19 and 20 are usually eligible if they are finishing a non-advanced course that they were accepted on, enrolled on or started before they reached 19.
- Other full-time students can claim – eg, if they get income support, income-related employment and support allowance or income-based jobseeker's allowance, are a lone parent, have certain disabilities, or are over the qualifying age for pension credit.
- Student couples with a child can claim throughout the year.
- Students' partners are eligible to claim.
- There can be limits to the rent covered by HB.
- HB is a means-tested benefit. The amount you get is affected by your grant, loan or other income and your level of savings.
- Claims are administered by local authorities.

1. What is housing benefit

Further information

This chapter gives an outline of the housing benefit rules and focuses on issues relevant to students. For more detailed information on the rules, see CPAG's *Welfare Benefits and Tax Credits Handbook*.

Housing benefit (HB) helps with the rent. In Northern Ireland, it helps with both rent and rates. You can get help with rent in private, housing association or local authority accommodation, but not if you live with your parents. There are limits to the level of rent that HB will cover.

Most full-time students cannot claim HB, but part-time students can claim.

HB is means tested, so your loan and other income affect the amount you get.

2. Who is eligible

To qualify for housing benefit (HB), you must satisfy the basic rules (see below), your payments must be eligible for HB (see p141) and you must be a student who is eligible to claim (see p142).

Basic rules

As well as being a student who is eligible to claim HB (see p142), you must also meet all the following conditions to qualify.

- You or your partner are liable to pay rent (see below).
- You or your partner pay rent for the home in which you normally live (see p140).
- The payments you make (eg, your rent) are eligible for HB (see p141).
- You satisfy presence and residence conditions and are not a 'person subject to immigration control' for benefit purposes. You can get further advice from the UK Council for International Student Affairs (UKCISA – see Appendix 2).
- Your capital is no more than £16,000. There is no capital limit if you have reached the qualifying age for pension credit and are getting the pension credit guarantee credit.
- Your income is sufficiently low (see Chapter 20).

Liable for rent

You must be liable for rent. If you are jointly liable for the rent with others (eg, you have each signed the tenancy agreement), the amount of HB you get is based on your share of the rent (although, less commonly, it may not be an equal share if that seems reasonable to the local authority).

If you are a couple it does not matter whose name is on the rent agreement, either of you can claim. So if you are a student who is eligible for HB, you can claim for both of you. If you are not eligible for HB, your non-student partner can claim for both of you.

There are some circumstances in which a local authority has the discretion to treat you as liable for the rent even if you are not legally liable (eg, if you have taken over paying the rent from someone else), or to treat you as not liable for the rent when you are legally liable – eg, if your agreement to pay rent is not on a commercial basis.

Your normal home

Usually you can only get HB for one home, and that is the place where you normally live. There are rules that can help you if you are temporarily away from home, are liable for rent on more than one home, have just moved home and in some other situations. The rules that specifically help students are outlined below.

You are away from your term-time home

You cannot get HB for any weeks in the summer vacation when you are away from your term-time home, unless you would live there anyway even if you were not studying. To continue to get HB for weeks of absence, you must argue that your main purpose in living there is not simply to make it easier to attend the course – eg, you were settled there before the course, or you are independent of or estranged from your parents.[1] However, if your grant or loan covers the summer vacation, your HB does not stop for weeks of absence.[2] HB also does not stop if you have to go into hospital.

If you leave your home during the academic year (or any time if you live there not just to facilitate attendance on the course), you can continue to get HB as long as you intend to return, you do not sublet, and you are not likely to be away for more than 52 weeks.[3] You cannot use this provision if you can get HB under the 'two-homes rule' described below. The two-homes rule is more generous in any case because it is not time limited.

Examples

John flat-shares in Sheffield while attending university. He gets HB as a disabled student. During the summer vacation he goes home to his parents in Leicester for seven weeks. His HB stops for those seven weeks. He should give the local authority the dates he intends to be away.

Donna has always lived in Cardiff and is attending her local college. She is a lone parent and gets HB. She regularly visits family in Aberystwyth during vacations. Her HB continues during her absence.

You have two homes

Liable for rent on one home

If you are a single or lone-parent student who can claim HB and you live in one home so that you can attend your course and another home at other times but you are only liable to pay for one of these, you are treated as occupying the home for which you pay. You can get HB for that place even while you are not there. **Note:** you cannot get HB under this rule if you pay rent for both homes, or if you pay rent for one and a mortgage on the other.[4]

Example

Emily's usual home is in Bristol, where she lives with her 18-year-old daughter, who is at college. She has to pay rent for her Bristol home. Emily is studying at Leeds University and lives rent free with a cousin while in Leeds. Emily is eligible to claim HB for her Bristol home throughout the year. Whether any HB is payable, and at what times, depends on the amount of her student support.

Liable for rent on two homes

If you have to pay rent for two homes, there are some circumstances in which you can get HB paid for both.

- If you have moved into a new home before the tenancy has expired on the old one and you cannot reasonably avoid having to pay rent on your old home, you can get HB paid for both for up to four weeks.[5]
- If you qualify for HB on two homes because a move was delayed while you were adapting your new home for the needs of a disabled member of your family, you can get HB paid for both for up to four weeks.[6]
- If you have had to leave your home because of a fear of violence and are intending to return to your former home, you can get HB for up to 52 weeks.[7]
- If you are in a couple and one of you is a student eligible for HB, and you have to live in two separate homes, you can get HB on both homes indefinitely if the local authority decides it is reasonable.[8]

Eligible payments

You can get HB to help pay the rent – eg, to a private landlord, local authority, housing association or co-operative. You can also get HB for some other types of payment – eg, site rent for a caravan or mobile home, rent for a houseboat (including mooring charges), or payments for a licence or other permission to occupy your home. It is not essential to have a written agreement; it could be verbal. There are a number of situations in which you could be treated as not liable to pay rent. For example, you cannot get HB if:

- you live with, and pay rent to, your parents, a sister, brother, son or daughter (including in-laws, partners and step-relatives);

- you pay rent to someone, but your tenancy is not on a commercial basis. This rule often prevents students getting HB for accommodation owned by their parents. However, it is possible to get HB in these circumstances if you can prove that the tenancy is a commercial one. You need to provide evidence of regular rent payments or a tenancy agreement. Seek advice if you are in this position;
- your tenancy was contrived in order to try and get HB;
- you pay rent to an ex-partner with whom you used to share the home in which you now live, or your landlord is your child's parent.

The list above is not exhaustive.

Halls of residence

You can get HB for rent in university-owned accommodation such as halls of residence. Part-time students living in university-owned accommodation, however, can only get HB if, were they full time, they would be eligible to claim HB as a lone parent, a disabled student, someone with a child and a full-time student partner, or if they have reached the qualifying age for pension credit. If you get income support (IS), income-related employment and support allowance (ESA) or income-based jobseeker's allowance (JSA) as a part-time student, you can only get HB in a hall of residence if you also fall into one of these other full-time eligible groups.

Sometimes colleges manage accommodation that is owned by private companies, but which is intended to provide accommodation for students. This type of accommodation has always been eligible for HB.

During the summer vacation, you can get HB if it is necessary for you to remain in the hall of residence, providing your grant or loan covers the vacation period and you are expected to study throughout the year.

Students and housing benefit

Under 21

Even if you are studying full time, you can qualify for HB if:

- you are under 21 and not in higher education, and were under 19 when you were accepted on, enrolled on or started the course; *or*
- you are a child or 'qualifying young person' for child benefit purposes (see p100) – eg, you are under 20 and in full-time education or approved training. You must have been accepted on, enrolled on or started the course or training when you were under 19.[9]

You can claim HB whether or not you are entitled to IS or JSA as a full-time student. You must satisfy the basic HB rules outlined on p139. You can only get HB if you are living away from your parents. Your claim may be restricted to the 'single room rent' (see p147).[10]

> *Example*
> Robbie is 17 and studying electronics at NVQ Level 3. He shares a flat with friends. He can claim HB.

Bear in mind that you can get HB under this rule up until your 21st birthday but not beyond. If your course continues, check below to see if you are in one of the groups of students aged 21 or over who can claim HB. If not, ask your college if there is any discretionary financial assistance. Alternatively, you may be able to argue that HB should continue if you transfer to a part-time course.[11] (If you abandon or are dismissed from your full-time course, you stop being classed as a full-time student.) However, your student support is affected if you go part time, so get advice from your college if you are considering such a move.

Under 21 in full-time higher education

In this case you are treated exactly the same as a full-time student aged 21 or over. You are not eligible for HB unless you are in one of the groups listed on p144 who can claim HB.

'**Higher education**' includes teacher and youth worker training, foundation degree, first and postgraduate degree courses, higher national diploma (HND) and higher national certificate (HNC) courses, and courses at a higher level in preparation for a professional qualification.

Full-time students

If you are a full-time student 'attending or undertaking a full-time course of study', you cannot normally claim HB.[12] However, there are exceptions that allow some students to claim. If you are aged 21 or under, check to see if you come under the rules outlined above.

You count as a student from the first day you attend or undertake the course. You stop counting as a student after the last day of the final academic term in which you are enrolled, or from the day you finally abandon your course or are dismissed from it.[13]

Who counts as a full-time student

If you attend a **further education** college and your course is government funded, you will usually count as a part-time student as long as your course comprises 16 guided learning hours or less a week.[14] 'Guided learning hours' include all supervised study – eg, classes, lectures, tutorials and structured assessment periods. They do not include unstructured or unsupervised study time – eg, studying at home or in a library. A document called a 'learning agreement' is used to provide proof of course hours. It is important to use the official learning agreement. The hours on this document are calculated as an average figure and may differ from the hours on your timetable. Ask about your learning agreement at your college or check with your course tutor. The local authority uses your learning agreement to decide whether or not you are studying full time.

In Northern Ireland, the definition of a full-time course does not depend on the number of hours of guided learning, but on the institution's definition of 'full time'. A letter from the institution stating that your course is part time will be sufficient when applying for HB.

Students in **higher education** are counted as full-time students if the college or university says that the course is full time. Ask at your college, or check with the course tutor or the registry department for evidence of whether you are registered on a full- or part-time course.

If your course is only for a few hours each week, you should argue that it is not full time, but a course could be full time even if you only attend a few lectures a week. You may be asked for a 'learning agreement' to show whether you are registered as part time or full time. You are not required to provide this and your registration document should be sufficient evidence.

Guidance states that postgraduates stop being treated as full-time students for HB purposes when their course ends. If you go on to undertake further research or are writing up a thesis, whether or not you are regarded as full time depends on how much time this is taking, rather than on whether the course is full time and whether you are still registered on the course.

Who can claim housing benefit

You can claim HB as a full-time student if you are in one of the following groups.[15]

- **IS/JSA/ESA recipients.** If you are on IS, income-based JSA or income-related ESA, you receive maximum HB (see p146).
- **Lone parents.** If you are the lone parent of a child under 16 (or a qualifying young person – ie, under 20 and in full-time non-advanced education or approved training), you are eligible for HB. Prior to 25 October 2010 lone parents can only get IS until their youngest child's 10th birthday. On 25 October 2010 this will reduce to age seven before reducing again to age five in October 2011 (see p167). If your IS stops, make sure you notify the local authority to ensure your HB continues while your child stays on at school or college. **Note:** your entitlement to HB under this rule ends on your youngest child's 20th birthday or when you no longer have a child or qualifying young person living with you (eg, when s/he leaves school), even if you are part way through your course.
- **Under-21-year-olds** who are not in higher education, as long as they were under 19 when they started, accepted or enrolled on the course.
- **Children or 'qualifying young people'** for child benefit purposes (see p100) – eg, under-20-year-olds in full-time education or approved training who were accepted on, enrolled on or started the course or training when under 19.
- **Pensioners.** If you, or your partner, have reached the qualifying age for pension credit (PC), you are eligible for HB for the duration of your course.

Entitlement to PC for both men and women is linked to the minimum age at which a woman can receive state retirement pension. This will rise gradually from 60 to 65 between April 2010 and April 2020.

- **Disabled students.**
  - If you qualify for a disability premium or severe disability premium with your HB (eg, you get disability living allowance or long-term incapacity benefit (IB) or are registered blind), you are eligible for HB.
  - If you have had limited capability for work for the last 28 weeks, you should claim ESA (see p120) to have your limited capability for work acknowledged. You can add together the weeks of limited capability for work on either side of a gap of up to 12 weeks.
  - If you get a disabled students' allowance because of deafness, you are eligible for HB from the date you apply for the allowance.[16] However, if you are still waiting to receive confirmation about the allowance, the local authority may put off making a decision on your HB claim, but should then fully backdate your benefit.[17]
  - If you have been incapable of work for the last 28 weeks, this test may apply to you if you are already getting IB, or income support on the basis of disability. Otherwise, the limited capability for work test applies (see above).
- Student couples (of the same or opposite sex, where both members of the couple are students) with a child or qualifying young person. If you are a couple, your partner is also a full-time student and you have a dependent child or qualifying young person, you are eligible for HB. Unlike IS and JSA, where you can only claim in the summer vacation, you can claim HB throughout the year. If you are claiming IS or income-based JSA, remember that when those benefits stop at the end of the summer vacation, you need to notify the local authority. You then receive a new assessment based on your student support income.
- **Responsible for a boarded child.** If you are single and caring for a child boarded out with you by the local authority or a voluntary organisation, you are eligible for HB for the duration of your course, or as long as this responsibility lasts.
- **Students' partners.** If you are part of a couple and your partner is not a student, s/he is entitled to make a claim for both of you.

Studying part time

If you are a part-time student, you can claim HB throughout your studies. You must satisfy all the basic rules (see p139). You are a part-time student if you do not count as a full-time student under the definition on p143. If you are a part-time student living in university-owned accommodation, see p142 (halls of residence).

3. **Amount of benefit**

The amount of housing benefit (HB) you get depends on the maximum rent that the local authority is allowed to pay and on your income compared with the amount the law says you need to live on. To work out your HB go through the following steps.

Step 1: capital

If your capital is over £16,000 you cannot get HB unless you have reached the qualifying age for pension credit. People who have reached this age and get pension credit (PC) guarantee credit have all their capital ignored. Others who have reached the qualifying age, including those who get PC savings credit but not guarantee credit, are still excluded from HB if their capital is over £16,000. Some kinds of capital are ignored.

If your capital is over £6,000 (£10,000 if you live in a care home), £1 for every £250 or part of £250 over this amount is added to your income. If you have reached the qualifying age for pension credit, £1 for every £500 or part of £500 over this amount is added to your income.

You usually have to submit three months' bank statements to the local authority and details of any savings accounts you hold.

Some students believe that they are unable to claim HB or will receive reduced benefit when they receive their student support at the beginning of each term because this payment can in itself be over £6,000 (especially if childcare costs are included), or it can increase their original savings to above this amount. However, your student support payments count as income divided over the year, not as capital (see Chapter 20).

Examples

Paul makes a claim for HB. He has £7,300 in savings. His income is initially assessed as £71 a week but tariff income on the £1,300 over the capital limit generates a further £6 a week in income. Paul is treated as having £77 a week income for benefit purposes.

Paul receives arrears of disability living allowance of £4,500 after an appeal. This money is treated as capital and disregarded for 52 weeks. Paul continues to qualify for HB and be treated as having £77 a week income.

Claire receives her student support payment of £4,625 in her bank account in September. She has a separate savings account, containing £4,000. The only capital that is taken into account is the £4,000. This does not affect her HB.

Step 2: maximum housing benefit

Your maximum HB is your 'eligible rent' (see p147), minus any deductions made for your non-dependants (see Step 3). This might not be the actual amount of rent you are meant to pay – eg, if you pay service charges that cannot be covered by HB, or if the local authority decides your rent for HB purposes must be restricted. The latter might happen, for example, if your home is too big for the size of your family or too expensive, or you rent from a private landlord and your rent is higher than the 'local housing allowance'. See below for further information about rent restrictions, including the local housing allowance scheme.

Eligible rent

The amount of your rent that is eligible for HB might not be the same as the amount of rent you actually pay. HB does not cover some items included in rent, such as:

- water or sewerage charges;
- fuel charges – either the actual charge, if specified in the rental agreement, or a fixed rate is deducted;
- meal charges – if these are included in your rent, the local authority may deduct a fixed rate;
- service charges – some are included (eg, cleaning communal areas, provision of a laundry room, TV aerial and radio relay charges, including free-to-view TV but not an individual satellite dish or set-top box), and others are not – eg, sports facilities, TV rental.

In addition, unless you rent from a local authority, your eligible rent might be restricted if your rent is seen to be too high, or your accommodation is larger than is needed for a family of your size or, if the local housing allowance rules apply to you, your rent is higher than the 'local housing allowance'. See below for further information about the rent restriction rules.

If you rent from a local authority, your eligible rent is the same as the weekly rent actually due less any of the above ineligible charges. The same almost always applies if you rent from a housing association. If you pay rent monthly, convert it into weekly rent by multiplying by 12, dividing by 365 (or 366 in a leap year) and multiplying by 7.

Rent-free periods

If you have a regular rent-free period (eg, you get four weeks rent free every year), you get no HB during your rent-free period. Your applicable amount, weekly income, non-dependant deductions, the set deductions for meals and fuel charges and the minimum amount payable (but not your eligible rent) are all adjusted. **Note:** this does not apply if your landlord has temporarily waived the rent in return for your doing repairs.

Restrictions on rent

Your eligible rent might be restricted if you are a private or a housing association tenant. There are two main sets of rules that can apply:

- the local reference rent rules;
- the local housing allowance rules.

Note: some people are exempt from these rules and a third (more generous) set of rent restriction rules can apply. This is the case, for example, if you have been renting the same property and getting HB since 1 January 1996, or if you live in certain types of hostel or supported accommodation.

If you claimed or moved home before 7 April 2008, the **local reference rent** rules will normally apply to you, and the local authority normally will refer your case to a rent officer. The rent officer provides figures which the local authority must then use to decide your eligible rent for HB purposes. For details of these rules, see CPAG's *Welfare Benefits and Tax Credits Handbook*.

Most private sector tenants who claim HB or move home now will come under the **local housing allowance** rules. Under the rules, the following apply.

- Your eligible rent is based on a standard 'local housing allowance', set by the rent officer depending on the area in which you live and the size of your household. The local housing allowance that is appropriate when your claim is assessed is used. Your claim is then normally reassessed annually.
- If you are a single claimant under 25, the local housing allowance is based on accommodation in which a tenant has exclusive use of one bedroom only and all or some of the other facilities are shared. This does not apply if you get a severe disability premium, are a former care leaver aged under 22, or have a non-dependant living with you.
- If your rent is lower than the local housing allowance (and therefore your HB is higher than your rent), your eligible rent will be the lower of either the rent you are liable to pay plus £15 (in which case you can keep the difference between the rent and the eligible rent, although the Government intends to remove entitlement to this excess from April 2011) or the local housing allowance.

Note: more generous rules applied in the Pathfinder areas and if this applied to you, they may continue to apply for a transitional period.

Discretionary housing payments

If the local authority applies a rent reduction on your home and this is causing you hardship, it is worth applying to the local authority for discretionary housing payments. These are paid in exceptional circumstances to top up HB to the full amount of your rent. Discretionary housing payments are usually made for a temporary period and subject to regular review.

Step 3: non-dependants

Non-dependants are older sons and daughters or other adults living in your household. The Government expects these adults to contribute to your housing costs and a deduction is made from your eligible rent. The amount of the deduction depends on the income of the non-dependant. In Northern Ireland, there are non-dependant deductions for rates as well as rent.

No non-dependant deduction is made if either you or your partner are registered blind or have regained your eyesight in the last 28 weeks, or if you are receiving attendance allowance or the care component of disability living allowance (DLA), or equivalent benefits paid because of an injury at work or a war injury.

No deductions are made for someone who is:
- staying in the household but her/his normal home is elsewhere;
- a full-time student during the course of study;
- a full-time student during the summer vacation (but there is a deduction if they start to work more than 16 hours a week, unless their student support covers the summer vacation);
- a full-time student at any time if you or your partner are aged 65 or over;
- a joint occupier/tenant;
- a resident landlord;
- a subtenant;
- the claimant's partner, or dependent child under 20 as long as child benefit is still being paid;
- aged under 18;
- in hospital for over 52 weeks;
- in prison;
- under 25 and receiving income support (IS), income-based jobseeker's allowance (JSA), or income-related employment and support allowance (ESA) without a work-related activity component or support component (this usually applies only in the first 13 weeks of an ESA claim);
- receiving a training allowance in connection with a youth training scheme under specific provisions;
- a live-in paid carer from a voluntary organisation;
- receiving pension credit (PC).

If your non-dependant is working, you should give the local authority evidence of her/his gross income. If you do not, the local authority might make the highest deduction whatever her/his income. This can be particularly hard where older sons/daughters still living at home refuse to give their parents their income details.

If you or your partner are 65 or over, the deduction is not made (or changed) until 26 weeks after the non-dependant moves in with you (or there has been a change in respect of her/him).

Step 4: getting a means-tested benefit

If you get IS, income-based JSA, income-related ESA or PC guarantee credit, HB is the amount worked out at Step 2 (maximum HB) – ie, your eligible rent (and, in Northern Ireland, rates) less any amount for non-dependants. You do not need to continue with the rest of these steps.

Step 5: not getting a means-tested benefit

If you do not get IS, income-based JSA, income-related ESA or PC guarantee credit, you must compare your income with your weekly needs.

Step 6: work out your applicable amount

This is an amount for basic weekly needs. It is made up of:

- personal allowances; *and*
- premiums; *and*
- a work-related activity or support component, for those who have limited capability for work.

The applicable amount includes amounts for yourself and for your partner, if you have one. It also includes amounts for any dependent child(ren) or qualifying young people. The amounts for HB are the same as for IS (see pxvi), with the following differences.

- **Personal allowance:**
  - the child allowance is included in HB;
  - single people under 25 and lone parents under 18 who are entitled to main phase ESA get £65.45;
  - young couples get £102.75, unless both are under 18 and the claimant is not entitled to main phase ESA, in which case they get £78.30;
  - single people have a personal allowance of £132.60 if they have reached the qualifying age for pension credit but are under 65, or £153.15 if aged 65 or over;
  - couples get £202.40 if at least one has reached the qualifying age for pension credit and £229.50 if one or both is 65 or over.
- **Premiums:**
  - family premium, disabled child premium and enhanced disability premium for a child are included in HB. The family premium is increased by £10.50 if you have a child under one;
  - you do not get a disability premium if you have been assessed as having limited capability for work for ESA, and you (ie, not your partner) are the HB claimant.
- **Components:**
  - instead of a disability premium, add a work-related activity component of £25.95 if you have claimed ESA and have limited capability for work, or a

support component of £31.40 if you have limited capability for work-related activity (see p120).

Step 7: work out your weekly income

Chapter 20 explains how your loan or other income is taken into account and how to work out your weekly income. Income is generally calculated in the same way as for IS but with the following differences.

- Lone parents who are not claiming IS or income-based JSA receive a £25 earnings disregard.
- There is a 16/30 hours earnings disregard of £17.10 a week in certain circumstances.
- Claimants in receipt of widowed mother's/parent's allowance receive a £15 disregard.

Example

Caroline is a lone-parent student who earns £80.80 a week and receives £20 a week maintenance in addition to her student funds. She works 16 hours a week. She makes a claim for HB and has a total of £72.10 disregarded from her income (£10 for her student loan, plus £20 maintenance, £25 earnings and £17.10 for working 16 hours).

Step 8: calculate your housing benefit

If your income is *less than or the same as* your applicable amount, HB is the amount worked out at Step 2 (maximum HB) – ie, your eligible rent (and, in Northern Ireland, rates) less any amounts for non-dependants.

If your income is *more than* your applicable amount, work out 65 per cent of the difference between the two. Your HB is the amount worked out at Step 2 (maximum HB – ie, your eligible rent less any amounts for non-dependants) minus 65 per cent of the difference between your income and applicable amount.

In Northern Ireland, 65 per cent of the difference is applied to the eligible rent and 20 per cent of the difference is applied to the eligible rates. If your HB does not cover your full rates charges, you may qualify for extra help – called rate relief. Your rate relief is your remaining rates charges once your HB for rates has been deducted, minus 12 per cent of the difference between your income and your applicable amount.

Examples

Maria is 18 and studying full time for a national diploma in animal husbandry. She shares a private rented flat with a friend. They each pay £65 a week rent. Maria has an education maintenance allowance of £30 a week that she receives for 30 weeks. The rent officer uses the local housing allowance amount for a single room rent in Maria's area (£60 a week) to calculate her entitlement.

	£
Eligible rent	60.00
Applicable amount	51.85
Income:	0
Education maintenance allowance disregarded	
Weekly HB	**60.00**

Craig is a lone-parent father with two children aged three and six. He is a second-year student, covered by the 'current system' rules. He is also a joint tenant with his friend Karl, who is not a student. Craig's share of the rent is £80. His income is his student support, child tax credit (CTC) and child benefit. He makes a claim for HB at the start of the academic year. Craig's benefit entitlement from September 2010 is calculated as follows:

	£
Eligible rent	80.00
Applicable amount:	
Personal allowance	65.45
Allowances for two children	115.14
Family premium	17.40
Total applicable amount	**197.99**

	£
Income:	
Student loan	4,950
Less travel £303	
Less books £390	4,257
Divided by 42 weeks	
(6 September 2010 to 26 June 2011)	101.35
Less £10 disregard	91.35
Special support grant (disregarded in full)	
Parents' learning allowance (disregarded in full)	
CTC	98.94
Child benefit (£20.30 + £13.40)	33.70
Total income	**223.99**

Craig's HB is worked out as follows:

	£
Income	223.99
Less applicable amount (£197.99)	26.00
65% x £26.00	16.90
Eligible rent (£80.00) – £16.90	63.10

Craig is entitled to **£63.10 HB a week.**

Summer 2010

Craig's student loan is only treated as income between 6 September 2010 and 26 June 2011. If Craig has no other income at this point he is entitled to claim IS and receive full help with his rent – ie, **£80 HB a week**.

Northern Ireland

If Craig were living in Northern Ireland, his HB for rent would be calculated in exactly the same way. If, in addition to his rent, he were liable to pay rates of £15 a week, his HB for rates would be calculated as follows:

	£
Income less applicable amount	26.00
20% x £26.00	5.20
12% x £26.00	3.12

HB for rates:	
Maximum rates (£15.00) – £5.20	9.80
Rate relief:	
Maximum rates (£15.00) – £9.80	5.20
Remaining rate liability (£5.20) – £3.12	2.08

Craig would be entitled to **£63.10 HB** for rent and **£9.80** for rates, plus rate relief of **£2.08**.

4. **Claiming housing benefit**

Unless you are allowed to claim by telephone, all claims for housing benefit (HB) must be in writing on a properly completed claim form. You can get a claim form from your local authority HB office. When you return it, check that you have provided all the documents and information required and ask for a receipt.

You can sometimes claim HB by telephone if your local authority has published a telephone number for this purpose. **Note:** even if you cannot claim by telephone, if you telephone to ask for a claim form and return it within one month, your claim is backdated to the date of your phone call.

Providing you provide all the required information, the local authority should make a decision on your claim within 14 days (see p154). You should not delay your claim because you do not have all the evidence required, but you must provide this within one month. The local authority can allow you longer than one month if it thinks this is reasonable.

If you post the claim form, keep a copy and obtain proof of posting. Claim forms are often lost. If you need to fill in another one, the local authority can backdate your HB if you can show the date of the original claim and provide evidence that you claimed earlier.

When your housing benefit starts

Your HB usually starts from the Monday after you make your claim. It can be backdated for up to six months if you ask for this and you have continuous 'good cause' for not claiming throughout the whole period.

In deciding whether there is good cause to backdate a claim, a local authority must take account of how a reasonable person of your age, experience and state of health would have acted, or failed to act, in the circumstances.[18]

If you or your partner have reached the qualifying age for pension credit and are not getting income support, income-based jobseeker's allowance or income-related employment and support allowance, HB can be backdated for up to three months, whatever the reason for the delay.

Getting paid

HB is paid directly into your rent account if you are a local authority tenant, otherwise it is paid to you either by cheque, into your bank account or directly to your landlord. If the local housing allowance rules apply to you (see p148), your HB is usually paid to you and not to your landlord.

Unless budgeting is a problem for you, it is generally better to have HB paid to yourself. This is because of the lengthy delays and administrative problems that can occur during the processing of HB. In some instances a huge amount of credit can be owed to claimants by the time they receive payment of HB, which means they would have had to have paid most of their rent before the HB is paid to them to prevent possession proceedings. It can also be difficult and time consuming to get private landlords and housing associations to release the credit generated by a large back payment of HB.

By law, the local authority must make a decision on your claim, tell you what the decision is and pay you any HB to which you are entitled within 14 days of receiving your completed claim form with all the documentary evidence, or if that is not reasonably practicable, as soon as possible after that. However, in many areas there are long delays. If you are a private tenant, ask for an interim payment or payment on account, which is a standard amount paid at a reduced rate until your claim can be properly assessed. If the delay in HB is causing you to accrue rent arrears, it is worth getting advice on how much benefit you are entitled to so that you can budget for rent in the meantime. If your arrears build up and the landlord starts to take legal action and you qualify for free legal help, it may be worth asking a solicitor to issue a legal notice to the local authority to speed up the claim assessment. If you are a private or housing association tenant, local authorities are legally obliged to give you an interim payment of a reasonable amount unless it is obvious that you will not be entitled to HB or you have not supplied information requested.

5. **Overpayments**

If you are overpaid housing benefit (HB), you might have to repay it. An 'overpayment' is an amount of HB which has been paid, and to which the local authority later decides you were not entitled under the HB rules – eg, because of ignorance of, or a mistake about, the facts. Because it can take time to deal with a change in your circumstances, this can also lead to your being overpaid.

The local authority has discretion on whether or not to recover any amount of overpayment, no matter how it was caused, and to offset any overpayment with the HB to which you were entitled. However, an overpayment is not recoverable at all if you can show that it was caused by an 'official error', you did not cause the official error and you could not reasonably have been expected to realise you were being overpaid. If you have provided all the appropriate information for the local authority to determine your entitlement to HB, there is a good chance that you can argue that the overpayment was caused by official error and you could not have been expected to know you were being overpaid. It is important to keep a record of any information you give to the local authority and obtain a receipt when handing in any document so you can prove exactly what information you have given, should you need to at a later date.

Seek advice if you think the local authority's decision to recover an overpayment is wrong. You can appeal against the decision. While your appeal is being decided, local authority guidance advises staff to freeze the recovery of the overpayment until the outcome of the appeal is known, and this could help if you are facing hardship as a result of deductions from benefit. Even if the appeal is lost at a later date, the local authority has the discretion not to recover the money – eg, on grounds of hardship. See below for information about challenging a decision.

6. **Challenging a decision**

If you think a decision about your housing benefit (HB) is wrong (eg, because the decision maker got the facts or law wrong), there are a number of ways you can try to get the decision changed.

- You can seek a revision or a supersession of the decision. In some cases you have to show specific grounds. In others, you must apply within a strict time limit.
- You can appeal to an independent tribunal. There are strict time limits for appealing – usually one month from the date you are sent or given the decision. You can make a late appeal in limited circumstances.

If you are considering challenging a decision, you should seek advice as soon as possible.

Bear the following in mind.

- Students regularly receive incorrect HB assessments. This is because local authorities are often unfamiliar with the calculation of student income and take into account income that should be disregarded.
- If the college or university bursary is for course-related costs or tuition fees, it should be disregarded in full when calculating HB. This bursary may be called the special support bursary in some circumstances. You should produce evidence of what the bursary is for when you claim HB.
- The special support grant and special support bursary should be disregarded when working out entitlement to HB. If you receive the wrong grant initially (eg, a maintenance grant instead of a special support grant), this can reduce your benefit entitlement. In this case, you should request the correct grant from the local authority, then, if necessary, appeal the incorrect benefit decision (within the one-month time limit) requesting that the local HB office use its discretion to stockpile the appeal until the correct income is awarded. You need to give the new student support statement with the correct income to the HB department as soon as possible in order for benefit to be calculated correctly. Otherwise, it could be difficult to get the correct rate of benefit backdated, as there is no provision for student income to be applied retrospectively.
- If you have missed the appeal deadline, it might be worth complaining to the relevant Ombudsman if you have lost benefit as the result of an incorrect assessment of student support. It may be possible to receive compensation for the HB you have lost.
- If there has been a series of errors in the assessment of your benefit, you can complain to the local authority about the maladministration of the claim and then, in England, complain further to the local government Ombudsman. The Ombudsman scheme has been set up to look into complaints, try to put things right and award compensation, if appropriate. It is particularly useful if you are experiencing lengthy delays with local authority assessments and appeals. In Wales, the equivalent body is the Public Services Ombudsman for Wales, and in Northern Ireland, it is the Northern Ireland Ombudsman's Office. Contact details for all three organisations are in Appendix 2.

7. **Other benefits and tax credits**

If you are a full-time student and you get income support (IS), income-based jobseeker's allowance (JSA), income-related employment and support allowance (ESA) or pension credit (PC), you are also eligible for housing benefit (HB) if you pass the other conditions for HB. If your IS, income-based JSA or income-related ESA stops because you start full-time work or your earnings increase, you must reclaim HB directly from the local authority.

Child tax credit (CTC) and working tax credit (WTC) count in full as income when HB is worked out, unless you have reached the qualifying age for PC and are not on IS, income-based JSA or income-related ESA. It is the actual amount you are paid that counts. If your CTC or WTC award is reduced because an overpayment of tax credits is being recovered, it is the reduced amount that counts for HB. If you are underpaid CTC or WTC and get a lump-sum repayment, it is treated as capital for HB but can be ignored for 52 weeks. It therefore only affects your HB if it takes your savings above the capital limit after this time. In either case, your HB is only affected from the time your payments of CTC or WTC change; there is no retrospective reassessment of HB.

Bear in mind that you should tell the local authority about any changes in income when they occur, including benefit and tax credit changes. Do not assume that the Department for Work and Pensions or HM Revenue and Customs passes on the information for you.

Notes

2. **Who is eligible**
1   Reg 55 HB Regs
2   Regs 53(1) and 55 HB Regs
3   Reg 7(16)(c)(viii) HB Regs
4   Reg 7(3) HB Regs
5   Reg 7(6)(d) HB Regs
6   Reg 7(6)(e) HB Regs
7   Reg 7(6)(a) HB Regs
8   Reg 7(6)(b) HB Regs
9   Reg 56(2)(h) HB Regs
10   Reg 13(4) HB Regs
11   para 2.41-2.42 C2 GM
12   Regs 53(1) and 56(1) HB Regs
13   Reg 53(1) and (2)(b) HB Regs
14   Reg 53(1) HB Regs
15   Reg 56(2) HB Regs
16   Reg 56(2)(i) HB Regs
17   para 2.30 C2 GM

4. **Claiming housing benefit**
18   Reg 83(12) HB Regs; R(S) 2/63(T)

Chapter 13

Incapacity benefit

This chapter covers:
1. What is incapacity benefit (below)
2. Who is eligible (p159)
3. Amount of benefit (p161)
4. Claiming incapacity benefit (p161)
5. Challenging a decision (p162)
6. Other benefits and tax credits (p162)

Basic facts

- Incapacity benefit (IB) is an earnings-replacement benefit for people who are unable to work because of an incapacity or disability.
- It was abolished for most new claims from 27 October 2008 and replaced by employment and support allowance, although existing claimants continue to receive it.
- Existing claimants must be incapable of work according to a personal capability assessment.
- IB is not means tested, so most of the income you have does not affect the amount you receive.

1. **What is incapacity benefit**

Further information

This chapter gives an outline of the incapacity benefit rules and focuses on issues relevant to students. For more detailed information on the rules, see CPAG's *Welfare Benefits and Tax Credits Handbook*.

Incapacity benefit (IB) is an earnings-replacement benefit for people who are unable to work because of an incapacity.[1] Incapacity is assessed by the Department for Work and Pensions (DWP) (or the Department for Social Development in Northern Ireland) under the 'own occupation test' or the 'personal capability assessment' (see p160). IB is not means tested, so most income you have does not affect the amount you receive. Pension payments can, however, reduce the amount.

From 27 October 2008, you cannot usually make a new claim for IB. You must claim employment and support allowance instead (see Chapter 10).

It is expected that existing IB claimants will be transferred to the ESA system between 2011 and 2014.

2. **Who is eligible**

As incapacity benefit (IB) was abolished for most new claims from 27 October 2008, you cannot normally make a claim. If you received IB before 27 October 2008, you can continue to receive it. Otherwise, you can only make a new claim for incapacity benefit in the following circumstances:[2]

- You get income support (IS) on the basis of illness or disability and become eligible for IB as well. For example, you are getting IS as a disabled student but your IB had stopped because you were under 19 and in full-time education, and you have now turned 19.
- Your IB stopped within the last eight weeks because your period of incapacity for work ended and you are now in a new period of incapacity for work. For example, you started work, but this ended within eight weeks.
- Your IB stopped within the last two years and within a month of its stopping you began a training course for which you got a training allowance, or you started work. You must generally have been on IB for at least 28 weeks before it stopped. For full details of this linking rule, see CPAG's *Welfare Benefits and Tax Credits Handbook*.

These exceptions only apply up until 31 January 2011. After this, you must claim employment and support allowance (ESA).

If any of the three circumstances above apply, and you make your claim before 31 January 2011, you can claim IB (rather than ESA). In addition, you must:

- be incapable of work and not entitled to statutory sick pay; *and*
- be under pension age; *and either*
- satisfy the national insurance (NI) contributions conditions – if you already get IB on this basis there are no special rules for students, so starting a course does not affect your IB; *or*
- satisfy the 'incapacity in youth' conditions. There are special rules for students under 19 which mean you are not eligible if your course is full time,[3] unless the course itself or sufficient hours of tuition are discounted because they are designed for disabled people.[4] Part-time students under 19 and full-time students aged 19 or over are eligible (but you must be under a certain age to

make a claim). See p117 for details – the incapacity in youth rules are the same as the ESA in youth rules.

Examples

Carrie is 43 and has been getting IB for some years since she injured her back at work. She intends to begin a course leading to a qualification in accountancy. While on her course she can continue to get IB at the same rate as before, providing the Department for Work and Pensions (DWP) continues to treat her as incapable of work.

Adam is 17 and has cerebral palsy. He is on a full-time national diploma course in music, which is 21 hours of classes a week. He gets no special tuition because of his disability. His IB stopped when he started the course but he continues to get IS. When the course ends he can reclaim IB.

Bellavia is on a full-time course and gets IB. She starts working in the holidays and her IB stops. Her work ends after six weeks and she reclaims IB.

Incapacity benefit and studying

The test of incapacity is called the **'personal capability assessment'**. It assesses the extent to which a person's ill health or disability affects her/his ability to perform a range of activities. Unless you are exempt, you must pass this test to get IB. You are exempt if you are blind or get the disability living allowance highest rate care component, are paraplegic or tetraplegic, and in some other circumstances. Until the DWP (or Department for Social Development (DSD) in Northern Ireland) assesses you, your incapacity is accepted on the basis of a certificate from your doctor.

Studying part time or full time should not affect your entitlement to contribution-based IB (except for some full-time students under 19 – see p159). Beginning studies, however, may prompt the DWP to reassess your incapacity if you are not exempt, although this should not happen routinely. At the next assessment, your ability to perform set activities will be considered in the context of what you can do in a typical day, including your college or university routines. For example, you may be asked questions about:
- your ability to get around campus;
- your ability to get to and from lectures;
- how long you can sit comfortably to study;
- your ability to hold a pen to take notes or write essays;
- the support you need to produce assessed work and whether you need extra time.

The questions you are asked will depend on which of the set activities (walking, sitting, manual dexterity, vision) are relevant to your condition. Attending a full-time course is not the same as full-time work – the number of hours of attendance plus the nature of the course should be considered, as well as whether you are doing the course for therapeutic reasons to help cope with your illness. The support you require from the college, other students and members of staff should also be considered, as well as any specialist equipment required to do the course and entitlement to disabled students' allowance.

Example

Vicky is 29 and on IB. She starts a full-time course of study in August 2010. She continues to be eligible for IB, but is called for a medical reassessment. Her condition is still the same; she passes the assessment and her IB continues.

3. Amount of benefit

Weekly rate from April 2010

Short-term lower rate (first 28 weeks)	£68.95
Short-term higher rate (weeks 29 to 52)	£81.60
Long-term rate (after 52 weeks)	£91.40 + £15.00 if under 35 or £5.80 if under 45 at the start of your incapacity in some cases

If you have reached the qualifying age for pension credit, you may be entitled to higher rates; seek advice if this is the case.

You can also claim extra benefit for an adult dependant provided s/he does not earn too much. If you have a child, an adult dependant is someone who looks after her/him – eg, a spouse or civil partner, or unmarried/same-sex partner. If you do not have a child, an adult dependant is a spouse or civil partner aged 60 or over.

If your entitlement to IB started on or after 6 April 2001, it can be reduced if you receive certain kinds of pension income – eg, occupational pensions and certain health insurance policies. This does not apply if you are entitled to the highest rate disability living allowance care component.

4. Claiming incapacity benefit

You should normally start your claim by telephoning a Jobcentre Plus contact centre. Phone the national number on 0800 055 6688 (textphone 0800 023 4888).

The Department for Work and Pensions (DWP) then phones you to complete a full claim form.

If you are in Northern Ireland you should call 028 9033 6000 (textphone 028 9033 6206).

You will usually be interviewed after you claim. You need to send in medical certificates from your GP until you are assessed under the personal capability assessment. If you have to serve a 28-week qualifying period before you can get IB, ask your doctor for a backdated medical certificate and send this in with your claim. Ask for your claim to be backdated. Claims can normally only be backdated for three months, but you have less time to wait to qualify for benefit.

All new claimants are likely to be required to attend a work-focused interview after the first eight weeks of the claim. This is intended to ensure you maintain contact with the job market and eventually return to work.

IB is usually paid into your bank (or similar) account. Which account it goes into is up to you. If you do not want your benefit to go into an account that is already overdrawn, give the DWP details of an alternative account if you have access to, or can open, one.

If you are overpaid IB, you might have to repay it.

5. **Challenging a decision**

If you think a decision about your incapacity benefit (IB) is wrong (eg, because the decision maker got the facts or law wrong), there are a number of ways you can try to get the decision changed.
- You can seek a revision or a supersession of the decision. In some cases you have to show specific grounds. In others, you must apply within a strict time limit.
- You can appeal to an independent tribunal. There are strict time limits for appealing – usually one month from the date you are sent or given the decision. You can make a late appeal only in limited circumstances.

If you are considering challenging a decision, you should seek advice as soon as possible.

6. **Other benefits and tax credits**

If you get incapacity benefit (IB) and live with your parents, they cannot continue to get child benefit or child tax credit (CTC) for you. IB counts as income for means-tested benefits. The lower rate of short-term IB is ignored in the tax credits calculation if you get CTC or working tax credit, but other rates are taken into account.

Notes

1. **What is incapacity benefit**
   1 s30A SSCBA 1992

2. **Who is eligible**
   2 Reg 2 ESA(TP) Regs
   3 s30A(2A)(e) SSCBA 1992; reg 17 SS(IB) Regs
   4 Reg 17(3) SS(IB) Regs

Chapter 14

Income support

This chapter covers:
1. What is income support (p165)
2. Who is eligible (p165)
3. Amount of benefit (p177)
4. Claiming income support (p181)
5. Challenging a decision (p182)
6. Other benefits and tax credits (p183)

Basic facts

– Income support (IS) is basic financial support for people who are not required to be available for work.

– A full-time student under 20 (sometimes under 21) on a non-advanced course (known as 'relevant education') can claim if, for example, s/he is a parent, an orphan, has a disability, or is estranged or separated from her/his parents. Nineteen-year-olds must have been accepted on, or enrolled on, or started their courses before turning 19.

– Other full-time students can claim if they are a lone parent, and in some other circumstances.

– A part-time student can claim if s/he is a lone parent, a carer or pregnant, and in some other circumstances.

– IS was abolished for most new claims on the grounds of incapacity or disability from 27 October 2008, although existing claimants receiving IS on these grounds will continue to do so. People who are long-term sick or disabled should now claim income-related employment and support allowance instead.

– IS is a means-tested benefit. The amount you get is usually affected by your grant, loan and other income.

– IS can help with the cost of mortgage payments, loans for repairs and improvements, and some other housing costs.

– IS claims are administered by the Department for Work and Pensions via Jobcentre Plus, or the Department for Social Development in Northern Ireland.

1. What is income support

Further information

This chapter gives an outline of the income support rules and focuses on issues relevant to students. For more detailed information on the rules, see CPAG's *Welfare Benefits and Tax Credits Handbook*.

Income support (IS) is paid to people under the qualifying age for pension credit (PC) (see below) who are on a low income and are not required to be available for work – eg, because of childcare or other caring responsibilities. It is also paid to people in some other circumstances – eg, under-20-year-olds who are studying full time and who are estranged from their parents, or have no parents. Prior to 27 October 2008 disabled students could claim IS, but such students making a new claim must claim income-related employment and support allowance instead (see Chapter 10). You do not have to have paid national insurance contributions to qualify for IS. The amount you get is affected by your income, including some elements of student support. Even if you are entitled to IS, therefore, the amount may be reduced because of your student income. Chapter 20 explains how your income affects your benefit.

2. Who is eligible

To qualify for income support (IS), you must satisfy the basic rules of entitlement. If you are studying full time, you must also satisfy additional rules. For information on whether you can qualify while you are in 'relevant education' or a full-time student, see pp168 and 172.

Basic rules

You can qualify for IS if:[1]
- you fit into one of the groups of people who can claim IS (see p166);
- neither you nor your partner count as in full-time paid work. For you, this is working 16 hours or more a week. For your partner, this is working 24 hours or more a week;
- you are not entitled to contribution-based jobseeker's allowance (JSA) or contributory employment and support allowance (ESA), and neither you nor your partner are entitled to income-based JSA or income-related ESA;
- your partner is not entitled to pension credit (PC);
- you are aged at least 16;
- you have not reached the qualifying age for PC – if you have reached this age, you may be eligible for PC instead. Entitlement to PC for both men and

women is linked to the minimum age at which a woman can receive state retirement pension. This will rise gradually from 60 to 65 between April 2010 and April 2020. See CPAG's *Welfare Benefits and Tax Credits Handbook* for more details;

- your income is less than the amount the law says you need to live on (your 'applicable amount' – see p177);
- your savings and other capital are worth £16,000 or less;[2]
- you satisfy presence and residence conditions. You might be able to claim during a temporary absence abroad – for more detail see CPAG's *Welfare Benefits and Tax Credits Handbook*;
- you are not subject to immigration control for benefit purposes (although there are limited exceptions).

See Chapter 20 for how your income (including student income) and capital affect your benefit. **Note**: your student support payments count as income, *not* capital.

Groups of people who can claim income support

To qualify for IS, you must satisfy all the basic rules and fit into one of the groups of people who can claim. If you are a full-time student, see p172. If you are in 'relevant education', see p168.

If you are studying part time, you must be:[3]

- aged 16 to 24 and on a training course being provided by the Young People's Learning Agency or Skills Funding Agency for England or the National Assembly for Wales. This does not apply if you are a child or 'qualifying young person' for child benefit purposes (see Chapter 8);
- incapable of work (but only if you already receive incapacity benefit, or your IS claim links to a previous one – see p167). Note that unlike full-time students (see p172), part-time students can claim IS as soon as they are incapable of work – they do not need to wait for 28 weeks;
- registered blind (but only if you already receive incapacity benefit or your IS claim links to a previous one – see p167);
- you are entitled to statutory sick pay (SSP);
- a lone parent responsible for a child under 10 (seven, after October 2010 – see p167);
- someone who is:
  - fostering children under 16 or a child placed for adoption; *or*
  - on unpaid parental leave or paternity leave; *or*
  - looking after a child under 16 temporarily, while her/his partner is out of the UK or the child's parents (or the person who usually looks after her/him) are ill or temporarily away; *or*
  - looking after your partner or child (or qualifying young person) who is temporarily ill;

- pregnant, from 11 weeks before the birth (or earlier if incapable of work because of pregnancy), or you have had a baby not more than 15 weeks ago;
- a carer receiving carer's allowance, or you care for someone who gets (or who has claimed) attendance allowance or the middle or highest rate care component of disability living allowance;
- attending a court or tribunal as a justice of the peace (JP), juror, witness or party to the proceedings;
- remanded in custody pending trial or sentence (you can get IS for housing costs only);
- a refugee learning English in order to obtain employment, in your first year in Great Britain or Northern Ireland (see p168);
- subject to immigration control, but entitled to an urgent cases payment of IS;
- involved in a trade dispute, or you have recently returned to work following one.

If you do not fit into one of the above groups but your partner does, s/he might be able to claim IS instead of you.

Changes for disabled students

Since 27 October 2008, if you are incapable of work, disabled or registered blind, you cannot make a new claim for IS and must instead claim income-related ESA. See Chapter 10.

If you are already claiming IS as a disabled student, you can continue to do so – although there are plans to transfer all such claimants to the ESA system between 2011 and 2014 (see p159).

Changes for lone parents

From 25 October 2010, you can only make a new claim for IS as a lone parent if your youngest child is under age seven.

Prior to November 2008, the age limit was 16, and it has been lowered each year since then – to 12 on 24 November 2008, and then to 10 on 26 October 2009.

Note that the Government is planning to lower this limit again, to age five, from October 2011.

If you are on a course of education when the rules change, so that you are no longer eligible for IS as a lone parent, the rule change will not take effect until you have finished your course of education, unless your IS stops for another reason. This includes instances where relevant student income takes you above your 'applicable amount', even if your underlying eligibility for IS continues. You should seek advice if you are affected by the changes.

The changes do not affect foster parents.

If you are a lone parent, and your child is above the age at which you can count as a lone parent for IS, but is under 20 and a 'qualifying young person' (see p168), you can claim IS during the summer vacation.[4] You must be in one of the groups that is eligible for IS – eg, you are a carer (see p167). If you are not in one of these groups, you can claim JSA in the summer vacation instead (see Chapter 15).

Overseas students

Most overseas students cannot claim IS because they are subject to immigration control for benefit purposes. Even if you are entitled to IS, a successful claim for benefit could affect your right to stay in the UK, and it is best to get immigration advice before making a claim. If you are not eligible for benefit, but there are no restrictions on your partner, either as a student or as a 'person subject to immigration control', s/he may be able to claim instead. However, if s/he receives benefit and you are a 'person subject to immigration control', this may affect your right to remain in the UK under the immigration rules. You should get advice from the UK Council for International Student Affairs (UKCISA – see Appendix 2).

In certain exceptional circumstances, it may be possible for an overseas student to claim IS for up to six weeks (see p170).

Studying and claiming income support

The general rule is that you cannot qualify for IS if you are studying full time. If you are already claiming IS, your entitlement may be affected if you start full-time study. There are, however, exceptions to the rules. If you are:

- under 20 and in 'relevant education', see below;
- a 'full-time student', see p172.

To see if you can claim IS while studying part time, see p175.

Under 20 and in relevant education

You cannot usually qualify for IS if you are in **'relevant education'**.[5] You count as being in relevant education if you are a 'qualifying young person' for child benefit purposes – ie, you are under 20 and in full-time non-advanced education or approved training (see p100).[6] You must have been enrolled on, accepted on or started the education or training before you were 19.

Note:

- You can continue to count as being in relevant education for a period after your education or training ends (see p171).
- There is not a 'relevant education' rule for housing benefit (HB) or council tax benefit (CTB) purposes, so you might be able to claim HB and CTB even if you cannot claim IS (see Chapters 12 and 23).

Definitions

'Non-advanced education' is usually study at Level 3 or below[7] – eg, NVQs up to Level 3, GNVQs up to intermediate level, and GCSE, AS and A levels. In effect, this definition covers any course that is not 'a course of advanced education'. See p172 for what counts as advanced education.

A course is **'full time'** if you attend for more than 12 hours a week.[8] This includes time spent during term time receiving tuition, undertaking supervised study, examinations or practical work. Meal breaks and unsupervised study on or off the premises are ignored.

If you are in advanced education (see p172 for a definition), you may be able to claim IS as a 'full-time student' (see p172).

Who can claim income support

If you are in relevant education, you qualify for IS if:[9]
- you are a parent of a child for whom you are treated as responsible and who lives in the same household as you; *or*
- you are disabled (but only if you already receive incapacity benefit or IS, or your IS claim links to a previous one – see p167) – ie,
  - you qualify for the IS disability premium or severe disability premium as part of your applicable amount (see p177); *or*
  - you have been treated as incapable of work for a continuous period of at least 28 weeks (two or more periods of incapacity separated by a break of no more than eight weeks count as one continuous period); *or*
- you have no parent and no one acting as your parent – eg, a foster parent; *or*
- you have to live away from your parents (or someone acting in their place) because:
  - you are 'estranged'; *or*
  - you are in physical or moral danger. The danger does not have to be caused by your parents. Therefore, a young person who is a refugee and cannot rejoin her/his parents can claim IS while at school;[10] *or*
  - there is a serious risk to your physical or mental health.

Estrangement implies emotional disharmony, where you have no desire to have any prolonged contact with your parents or they feel similarly towards you.[11] It is possible to be estranged even if your parents are providing you with some financial support or you still have some contact with them. If you are in care, it is possible to be estranged from your local authority. If so, you could qualify for IS if you live away from the accommodation provided by the local authority;[12] *or*
- you live apart from your parents (or anyone acting as your parent) and they cannot support you financially because they are:
  - in prison; *or*
  - prohibited from coming to Great Britain because they do not have leave to enter under UK immigration laws; *or*
  - chronically sick, or mentally or physically disabled. This covers people who are substantially and permanently disabled or who could qualify for an IS disability premium or higher pensioner premium, or have an armed forces grant for car costs because of disability;[13] *or*

- you have left local authority care and are living away from your parents (or anyone acting as your parent) by necessity (but see below); *or*
- you are a person from abroad with limited leave to remain in the UK without recourse to public funds and your funds from abroad are temporarily disrupted, but are likely to resume. You can get IS for a maximum of six weeks. Note that this provision is rarely used, so seek advice if your claim is refused; *or*
- you are a refugee who is learning English in order to obtain employment. You must be on a course of more than 15 hours a week and, at the time the course started, you must have been in Great Britain for a year or less. You can get IS for a maximum of nine months.

Note: a person acting in place of your parents includes a local authority or voluntary organisation if you are being cared for by them, or foster parents, but only until you leave care. It does not include a person who is your sponsor under the immigration laws.[15] If you are not in any of the above groups, you cannot get IS. Instead:

- you may have to rely on any statutory support to which you are entitled and any discretionary support your college or school may offer you (see Chapter 1 for more details);
- your parents (or a person acting in their place) may be able to claim child benefit and child tax credit (CTC) for you.

In some circumstances, you may count as both a person who can claim IS while in relevant education and as a person for whom someone else can claim child benefit and CTC. You should seek advice about how you would be better off financially.

Example

Clara is 17. She has been living with her mother and stepfather. Her mother is in hospital as a result of domestic violence from Clara's stepfather. Clara has moved out of her family home because she is at risk of physical harm. She is able to claim IS.

Ahmed is 18 and studying full time for A-levels. He is a refugee whose parents live in Somalia. It would be dangerous for him to return home. Ahmed is eligible for IS.

Care leavers

Since 1 October 2001 (in England and Wales) and 22 November 2002 (in Northern Ireland), some 16- and 17-year-olds who were formerly looked after by a local authority receive financial and other support from the local authority and cannot qualify for IS. You cannot usually qualify for IS if:[16]

- you were looked after by a local authority for at least 13 weeks after the age of 14, ending after you turned 16; *or*

- you are not subject to a care order, but you were in hospital or detained in a remand centre, or a young offenders or similar institution, when you turned 16, and immediately before that you were looked after by a local authority for at least 13 weeks since your 14th birthday.

There are exceptions to the rules if you are a lone parent.

The local authority is responsible for providing funding for accommodation, practical life skills, education and training, employment, financial support, specific support needs and contingency plans for support if independent living breaks down.

Care leavers aged 18 and over are treated like any other claimant and you may be able to make a claim for IS. The local authority still has a duty to assist you with your expenses associated with education and training until you have completed the agreed programme of education and training, set out in a 'Pathway Plan'.[17]

Example

Brandon is 17 and lives in England. In May 2003, when he was 10, he was taken into foster care after his mother died. He has now left foster care and lives in a housing association flat. He cannot claim IS because, since October 2001, he has been looked after by a local authority for over 13 weeks. It is his local authority's responsibility to provide for his living and housing costs to a level equivalent to what he would receive if he were claiming IS or HB.

When you turn 20

If you turn 20, you no longer count as being in relevant education, even if you are still studying. However, you may then count as a full-time student. You can only receive IS if you are in one of the categories of full-time students who can claim (see p174). This may mean you cannot qualify for IS from your 20th birthday even if you qualify up to that date. However, your IS may be able to continue if you are under 21 on a non-advanced course you started when you were under 19, and you are without parental support (p169).

When relevant education ends

When your course or training ends, you continue to count as being in relevant education:

- if you are enrolled on another course; *or*
- until the latest of the following:
  - the 31 August after your 16th birthday;
  - if you are under 18, the end of your 'extension period' (see p102);
  - the first Sunday on or after your 'terminal date' (see p102); *or*
- until you turn 20, if this is earlier than any of the above.

Once you have left relevant education (or you turn 20), you might be able to qualify for IS or JSA if you satisfy the rules for getting these benefits (see p165 and Chapter 15).

Full-time students

If you are a full-time student you cannot usually qualify for IS for the duration of your course, including vacations.[18] See p174 for exceptions to this rule. See p175 if you are studying part time and p176 if you give up or change your course. See Chapter 25 if you take time out from studies.

In general, students are expected to receive student support (eg, student loans and supplementary grants) to support them while in full-time education. See Chapters 1 to 6 for details of student support.

Who counts as a full-time student

You count as a full-time student if you are not a 'qualifying young person' for child benefit purposes (see p100) and:[19]

- you are under 19 and on a full-time course of advanced education (see below); or
- you are 19 or over but under the qualifying age for pension credit (PC – see p165) and on a full-time course of study. If your course is full time, you are treated as a full-time student regardless of the level of the course, unless you are aged under 20 and can still be treated as in 'relevant education' (see p168). See p173 for what counts as a full-time course; or
- you are on a sandwich course (see p173).

You are treated as a student until either the last day of your course or until you abandon or are dismissed from it.[20] The 'last day of the course' is the date on which the last day of the final academic year is officially scheduled to fall according to the term dates fixed by the college.[21] If you are unsure when your course is scheduled to end, ask the college or university for a copy of its official term dates.

Note: if you are 19 and in relevant education, you do not count as a full-time student. Instead, the rules on p168 apply.

• •

Definitions

A **'course of advanced education'** means:[22]

- a course leading to a postgraduate degree or comparable qualification, a first degree or comparable qualification, a diploma of higher education, a higher national diploma or higher national certificate of either the Business and Technology Education Council (BTEC) or any other courses above advanced GNVQs or equivalent, national diplomas or A-levels, or a teaching qualification; or any other courses above advanced GNVQs or equivalent, OND or A-levels, or a teaching qualification; *or*

- any other full-time course which is a course of a standard above advanced GNVQ or equivalent, ordinary national diploma, a national diploma or national certificate of either the Business and Technology Education Council (BTEC) or any other courses above advanced GNVQs or equivalent, national diplomas or A-levels, or a General Certificate of Education (advanced level).

A 'sandwich course'[23] (excluding a course of initial teacher training) is one that consists of alternate periods of study at your educational institution and periods of industrial, professional or commercial placement, or work experience. Taking the course as a whole, you must attend periods of study at your institution for an average of not less than 18 weeks a year. If your periods of full-time study and work experience alternate within any week of your course, the days of study are aggregated with any weeks of full-time study to determine the number of weeks of full-time study in each year. If your course includes the study of one or more modern languages for at least half of your study time, any period during which you are working while living in the country whose language is part of your course is counted as a period of work experience.

Full-time courses

Whether your course is full time depends on the country in which you are studying and on who is funding your education. Your course counts as full time if:

- it is funded by the Young People's Learning Agency (YPLA) or Skills Funding Agency (SFA) in England or the National Assembly for Wales and involves more than 16 'guided learning hours' a week.[24]

  Courses include academic and vocational qualifications, basic literacy, numeracy and information and communication technology (ICT) skills, English as a second language programmes, access to higher education courses and courses developing independent living skills for people with learning difficulties.

  'Guided learning hours' include all supervised study – eg, classes, lectures, tutorials and structured assessment periods. They do not include unstructured or unsupervised study time – eg, studying at home or in a library. You should be given a 'learning agreement' by your education provider stating the number of guided learning hours you are undertaking. This is used to provide proof of your course hours. On this document the hours are calculated as an average figure and may differ from those on your timetable. The Jobcentre Plus office uses your learning agreement to decide whether you are studying full time; *or*

- it is *not* funded by the YPLA, SFA or the Welsh Assembly and it is a 'full-time course of study' (see below) – eg, you are on a full-time course of higher education.

There is no definition of a **'full-time course of study'** in the IS rules. Whether your course counts as full time depends on how it is defined by the college or university. A course could be full time even if you only have to attend for a few hours a week. Definitions are often based on local custom and practice within education institutions, or determined by the demands of course validating bodies, or by the fact that full-time courses can attract more resources. The education establishment's definition is not final, but if you want to challenge it, you have to produce a good argument showing why it should not be accepted.[25] If your course is only for a few hours each week, you should argue that it is not full time. However, a course could be full time even though you only have to attend a few lectures a week. You should check how your course is described by the educational institution and how you are registered on it.

Full-time students who can claim income support

Even if you are a full-time student, you can qualify for IS if you are:[26]

- a **lone parent** who is responsible for a child under 10 (seven, from 25 October 2010 – see p167) who lives in your household. Once your only or youngest child turns 10 (seven, from October 2010), you cannot claim IS unless you fit into one of the other groups of full-time students who can claim (see p166). Check to see if you can qualify for JSA instead (see Chapter 15). Note that transitional rules apply for full-time students who started a course before the age limit changes on 25 October 2009 (see p166);
- **fostering** a child under 16 through a local authority or voluntary organisation and are not a member of a couple;
- a **disabled student** (but see p167 – disabled students making a new claim must usually claim ESA) – ie,
    - you qualify for the IS disability premium or severe disability premium as part of your 'applicable amount' (see p177); *or*
    - you qualify for a disabled students' allowance because you are deaf; *or*
    - you have been treated as incapable of work for a continuous period of at least 28 weeks. Two or more periods of incapacity separated by a break of no more than eight weeks count as one continuous period. See Chapter 13 for further information about incapacity for work;
- a **person from abroad** with limited leave to remain in the UK without recourse to public funds and your funds from abroad are temporarily disrupted, but are likely to resume. You can get IS for a maximum of six weeks. For example, you could claim IS if you are an international student who is funded by a government scholarship and those funds cannot be paid because of a natural disaster – eg, an earthquake. Note that this provision is rarely used, so seek advice if your claim is refused;
- a **refugee** who is learning English in order to obtain employment. You must be on a course of more than 15 hours a week and, at the time the course started, you must have been in Great Britain for a year or less. You can get IS for a maximum of nine months;

- a member of a **couple who are both full-time students**, and you or your partner are responsible for a child or 'qualifying young person'. You can only claim IS under this rule during the summer vacation. You must fit into one of the groups of people who can claim IS as a part-time student (see below). If you cannot qualify for IS, check whether you qualify for JSA instead;
- you are on a non-advanced course, are under 21, and started or were accepted on or enrolled on the course when you were under 19, and you are:
  - an orphan, and no one is acting in place of your parents; *or*
  - living away from your parents because you are estranged from them; *or*
  - living away from your parents because you are at serious risk of harm; *or*
  - living away from your parents, they cannot support you financially, and they are sick or disabled, in prison or not allowed to enter Britain.

If you are a full-time student who cannot claim IS, check to see if you can claim JSA, ESA or PC instead. If you have a partner who is not a full-time student, s/he might be able to claim IS, JSA or PC for you. Remember that your student support income is taken into account in working out how much IS, JSA or PC s/he can get.

Part-time students

You count as a part-time student if you are studying, but are not in 'relevant education' (see p168) or a full-time student (see p172). In the latter case, you should check with the educational institution to see how you are registered and whether your course counts as part time. You can qualify for IS while a part-time student if you satisfy all the basic rules of entitlement (see p165) and you fit into one of the groups of people who can claim IS (see p166).

What counts as part time

Generally, it is your college or university that determines whether you count as a part-time or full-time student, rather than the actual number of hours that you study or attend lectures. However, if your course is funded or partly funded by the SFA/YPLA or the Welsh Assembly, you count as being on a part-time course if it involves up to 16 guided learning hours a week. This should be set out in a 'learning agreement' provided by your college (see p173).

If you are currently studying part time on a course you previously attended full time, or if you are attending a modular or similar course (see p176) on a part-time basis, the Department for Work and Pensions may say that you are attending a full-time course and should, therefore, be treated as a full-time student. It may be possible to challenge this interpretation.[27] You should seek specialist advice if you are in this situation.

Health-related courses

If you attend a health-related course for which you are entitled to receive an NHS bursary (see p67), you are treated as attending a full-time course.

Modular courses

A '**modular course**' is one that is made up of two or more modules and the institution requires you to do a certain number successfully to complete the course.[28] If you are attending or undertaking part of a modular course that is full time, you are treated as a full-time student for the duration of the modules, from the day those modules begin until the last day of registration on those modules (or earlier if you abandon the course or are dismissed from it).[29] This includes all vacations during the modules on which you are registered and, except for the final module, the vacation immediately following the modules. It also includes periods when you are attending the course to do re-sits of any modules you have undertaken on a full-time basis. This is the case even if you are registered part time with the institution while you are doing these re-sits. You should seek advice from your students' union or institution's student services about the student support to which you might be entitled while you are re-sitting.

Because the rules provide no definition of a full-time course (unless it is funded by the YPLA/SFA or the Welsh Assembly – see p173) you may be able to argue that you are not attending a full-time course.[30] If you are in any doubt, you should seek advice.

If the modular course allows you to undertake some modules on a part-time basis, you are not excluded from IS while you are studying part time. Remember, however, that you must not be studying any modules that you have previously done on a full-time basis.

See the example on p195 for further details.

Giving up or changing your course

If you are in any of the circumstances below, your entitlement to any student support you receive might be affected and you should seek specialist advice.

- If you abandon your course or are dismissed from it, you can claim IS from the day after that date provided you satisfy the other rules of entitlement.
- If you complete one course and start a different one, you are not treated as a student during any period between the courses.[31]
- If you are on a sandwich course (see p173), or your course includes a compulsory or optional period on placement, you count as a full-time student during the sandwich or placement period even if you have been unable to find a placement or your placement comes to an end prematurely.[32]
- If you attend a course at an educational institution which provides training or instruction to enable you to take examinations set and marked by an entirely different and unconnected body (ie, a professional institution) and you abandon or take time out from it because you fail the examinations set by the other body (or you finish the course at the educational institution but fail the exams), you may be able to argue that you are not a student from the date you left the course at your educational institution, even if you intend to re-sit the examinations set by the other body at a later date.[33]

If you are taking time out of your course for any other reason, see Chapter 25.

You may also retain entitlement to some student support on a statutory or discretionary basis – eg, through student loans or hardship funds. You should seek specialist advice.

Changing from full-time to part-time attendance

If you have to change from full-time to part-time attendance on a full-time course for personal reasons, you may be able to argue that you have abandoned your full-time course and are registered on a part-time course and, therefore, you are not a full-time student.[34] If, because of exam failure or any other reason, you change to a different course, or your college requires you to change the level of course (eg, from A level to GCSE) and this involves a change from full-time to part-time study, you should argue that you are a part-time student (see p175).[35] However, changing your attendance may affect your entitlement to any student support you may be receiving. You should seek advice on this before acting.

3. **Amount of benefit**

Income support (IS) is a means-tested benefit that tops up your income to a level that is set by the Government. The amount you get depends on your basic weekly needs (your 'applicable amount' – see below) and on how much income and capital you have (see Chapter 20). Some students may find, therefore, that they can only receive IS for part of any year – eg, during the summer vacation.

The amount of IS you get depends on your circumstances and the circumstances of your partner. The following steps show how to work out the amount of IS to which you are entitled.

Note: benefit rates are increased in April each year, but it is usually possible to find out what the new rates will be from the beginning of December. Check the Department for Work and Pensions (DWP) (or the Department for Social Development in Northern Ireland) website.

Step 1: capital

If your capital is over £16,000, you cannot get IS. Some kinds of capital are ignored. Note that student support grants and loans count as income, not as capital.

Step 2: work out your applicable amount

This is an amount for your basic weekly needs. It is made up of:
* a personal allowance;
* premiums for any special needs – eg, if you have been incapable of work for a period, are disabled or are caring for a disabled person;

- housing costs (see p179), principally for mortgage interest payments.

See pxv for the current rates.

Allowance and premiums for children

If you claim IS and are getting child tax credit (CTC), IS does not include allowances and premiums for your children. CTC does not count as income for IS, nor does child benefit.

If you were getting IS on 5 April 2004 and this included allowances and premiums for your children but you were not yet entitled to CTC, you will be transferred onto CTC sometime in the future. Until then, you continue to get allowances and premiums for your children as part of your IS. A change of circumstances, such as starting a full-time course, may trigger the transfer. You should seek advice about whether you might be better off financially if you claim CTC now rather than wait until you are transferred.

Step 3: work out your weekly income

Chapter 19 explains how your loan, grant or other income is taken into account and how to work out your weekly income.

Step 4: deduct weekly income from applicable amount

If your income is *less than* your applicable amount, IS equals the difference between the two.

If your income is *the same as or more than* your applicable amount, you cannot get IS. You can claim again if your income drops – eg, during the summer vacation when your student loan and adult dependants' grant are no longer treated as income.

Example

Karen is aged 35, a full-time first-year undergraduate student and a lone parent of Penny, aged two. She gets a full loan to pay for her tuition fees of £3,290, a full special support grant of £2,906 per year, a full student loan of £4,950 per year, a parents' learning allowance of £1,508 per year and £60 a week childcare grant. Her only other income is £20.30 a week child benefit and £54.67 a week CTC.

During the academic year September 2010 to June 2011

Step 1	Karen has no savings or capital.	
Step 2	Her applicable amount is:	
	Personal allowance for herself	£65.45
Step 3	Her weekly income during the period of study is:	
	Student loan	
	(The loan for tuition fees, special support grant, parents' learning allowance, childcare grant, CTC and child benefit are disregarded. Her loan, less certain disregards, is divided over the 43 weeks of the academic year. See Chapter 20)	£89.00

Step 4   Karen's income is above her applicable amount so she cannot get IS.

During the summer vacation June 2011 to September 2011

Step 2   Karen's applicable amount will be based on the same elements
            as above, but note that the rates usually increase in April.
            Based on April 2010 rates, her applicable amount is:
            Personal allowance for herself   £65.45

Step 3   Her weekly student income from the end of June 2011 to the beginning
            of September 2011 is nil. This is because her loan for living costs only
            counts as income during the academic year.
            Child benefit and CTC continue to be disregarded.

Step 4   Based on April 2010 rates, her weekly IS is £65.45. Karen should reclaim IS at
            the end of June.

Housing costs

If you own or are buying your home, your IS applicable amount can include help
with a variety of housing costs.[36] Normally, help only starts once you have been
getting IS for a period of 13 weeks (sometimes up to 39 weeks), although there are
some exceptions. For help with rent, you need to claim housing benefit (HB – see
Chapter 12). This is only a brief outline of some of the rules – see CPAG's *Welfare
Benefits and Tax Credits Handbook* for further details.

Your applicable amount can include help with:

- mortgages and other loans for house purchase;
- loans used to pay for specified types of repairs and improvements or to meet a
  service charge for these; *and*
- other housing costs – eg, ground rent, payments under co-ownership schemes
  and service charges.

IS does *not* include amounts for insurance or any endowment premiums.

The amount you get for loans is based on a standard interest rate, so it could be
higher or lower than what you actually pay. If you have a 'non-dependant' living
with you (eg, an adult child or a parent) a deduction is usually made because s/he
is assumed to be making a contribution towards your housing costs. Payment is
usually made directly to your mortgage lender. It is important to note that:

- if your loans amount to more than £200,000 (if the 13-week notice period
  applies) or £100,000 (if the 39-week notice period applies), your housing costs
  might not be met in full;
- the amount you are paid might be restricted if:
  - the DWP (or the Housing Executive in Northern Ireland) decides that your
    costs are excessive – eg, if your home is bigger than you need; *or*
  - you took out or increased your loan while on IS, jobseeker's allowance (JSA)
    or pension credit (PC), or during a period between claims (see p180).

Buying a house while on benefit

You cannot usually get IS to help you pay the cost of a loan to buy a home if you became liable for it, or increased it, while on IS, JSA or PC, or during a period of up to 26 weeks between claims. There are exceptions to the rules. These include where:

- you are replacing one mortgage with another. However, you cannot usually get help with any increase (but see below);
- you took out or increased the loan to buy a home more suitable for the needs of a disabled person, or to provide separate bedrooms for a son and daughter aged 10 or over;
- you buy a home and immediately beforehand you were in rented accommodation and getting HB. You can only get IS for housing costs up to the amount of HB you were entitled to, plus any other housing costs you were already getting.

The waiting periods

Your income (eg, your student income) may mean that you cannot qualify for IS until housing costs are included in your applicable amount because your income is higher than your personal allowances and premiums. In this case, there are special rules that allow you to be treated as entitled to IS during your waiting period.[37]

If you are a lone parent or a carer, you must make a claim for IS first, get refused, then claim again once your waiting period is over. You can also be treated as entitled to IS during periods when you are getting incapacity benefit, statutory sick pay, or national insurance credits for unemployment or incapacity.

The rules are complicated and you should seek specialist advice if you are in this situation.

Living away from home

Housing costs are usually only paid for the home in which you live. There are a number of exceptions, including some specifically for full-time students – eg, if you have moved somewhere to study, but your normal home is elsewhere.

If you have to live away from your normal home because you are a full-time student or are on a training course, you can get housing costs for:

- both homes indefinitely if you are one of a couple and it is unavoidable for you to live in two separate homes.[38] It must be reasonable for you to get housing costs for both; *or*
- the home for which you pay if you are a single person or lone parent and have to pay for either your normal home or your term-time accommodation, but not both.[39]

Otherwise, in some circumstances you can get housing costs for your normal home for up to 52 weeks if you are away temporarily and are unlikely to be away for longer than this (or in exceptional circumstances, substantially longer than this). This applies if you are a full-time student living away from your partner who cannot get housing costs for both of your homes, or a single claimant or lone parent who is liable to pay housing costs on both a term-time and a home address.[40] It also applies in other situations, including if you are in hospital, a care home or prison.

4. **Claiming income support**

If you think you might be entitled to income support (IS), you should claim as soon as you can. There are only very limited situations where backdating is allowed.

You can make initial contact about claiming by telephone or letter. You may also be able to start a claim online at www.dwp.gov.uk/eservice. The date of your initial contact is important because it usually determines the date from which you can be paid IS.

Normally, you must start your claim by telephoning the national number – 0800 055 6688. During this phone conversation, the date of a work-focused interview is set, unless it is agreed you do not need to attend one. You are then sent a statement recording the information you gave over the telephone, which you are asked to sign, and details of the evidence and information you should bring with you to the interview (or forward to the Department for Work and Pensions (DWP), or the Department for Social Development (DSD) in Northern Ireland). The signed statement comprises your official claim.

It is best to start your claim in this way if you can. However, if you cannot, or do not want to, use the telephone to start your claim, the Jobcentre Plus office can still deal with your claim in other ways. You might, for example, be invited for a face-to-face interview or, in some cases, an old-style claim form can be accepted.

You should request an old-style claim form if you need one to make your claim – eg, if you are a disabled student and need the help of an adviser. Old-style claim forms are available from Jobcentre Plus offices and online at www.direct.gov.uk. In Northern Ireland you can get the form from the NI Direct website at www.nidirect.gov.uk. They might be available at your student services department or at local advice centres. If you obtain a claim form, it is still important to telephone the DWP (or DSD) or Jobcentre Plus office to let them know that you want to claim IS. If you do not, you could lose benefit. You should complete the form and send or take it to the DWP (or DSD) or Jobcentre Plus office within one month of your initial contact.

Whenever you call the DWP (or DSD), you need to provide your national insurance number. You also need this number, as well as that of your partner, when you claim, as well as any other information required on the claim form. If you are a member of a couple, either of you can make the claim, but whoever claims must be eligible in her/his own right.

Getting paid

Payment is usually made directly into your bank (or similar) account. Which account it goes into is up to you. If you do not want your benefit to go into an account that is overdrawn, give the DWP or DSD details of an alternative account if you have access to, or can open, one.

If you are overpaid IS, you might have to repay it.

5. **Challenging a decision**

If you think a decision about your income support (IS) is wrong (eg, because the decision maker got the facts or law wrong), there are a number of ways you can try to get the decision changed.

- You can seek a revision or a supersession of the decision. In some cases, you have to show specific grounds. In others, you must apply within a strict time limit.
- You can appeal to an independent tribunal. There are strict time limits for appealing – usually one month from the date you are sent or given the decision. You can make a late appeal in limited circumstances.

If you are considering challenging a decision, you should seek advice as soon as possible.

If your claim for IS is unsuccessful, consider whether you can challenge the decision. You should bear the following in mind.

- As student claims are not necessarily commonplace and the rules about how student income is treated are complex, it is always worth checking a decision with a student adviser in your students' union or institution.
- If the decision maker says you are a full-time student, but you disagree, you should get advice to see if there are grounds for challenging the decision.
- Claims for IS are sometimes refused because the Department for Work and Pensions (or Department for Social Development in Northern Ireland) miscalculates student income or takes the wrong types of student income into account.
- You might not currently be entitled to IS, but would be once you or a member of your family become entitled to a 'qualifying benefit' – eg, disability living allowance or carer's allowance. In this case, you need to claim. Your initial claim will be refused. However, if you claim again once the qualifying benefit is awarded, your IS will be backdated to the date of your original claim, or the date on which the qualifying benefit was first payable (if later). Alternatively,

you might be entitled to a higher rate of IS once the 'qualifying benefit' is awarded. In this case, you need to ask for a revision or a supersession of your IS award. Your IS should then be increased from the date the qualifying benefit was first payable.

Note: you may find that you can qualify for IS in the summer vacation (even if you cannot qualify during term time) because of the way your grant and loan are divided throughout the year. In this case, you need to claim again as soon as you think you might qualify.

6. **Other benefits and tax credits**

Income support (IS) tops up any other income you have to the level of your basic requirements (your applicable amount), so most other benefits are taken into account as income when working out the amount of your IS. This means they reduce your IS pound for pound. Disability living allowance, attendance allowance, guardian's allowance, housing benefit (HB) and council tax benefit (CTB) are, however, always disregarded as income.

If you get IS, and you have rent (and, in Northern Ireland, rates) or council tax to pay, you are eligible as a student for HB and CTB.

Child tax credit (CTC) is ignored as income when assessing IS. Child benefit is ignored unless you still have amounts for children in your IS and you do not get CTC. In this case, £10.50 a week of your child benefit is disregarded if you have a child under one.

Even though getting a benefit may reduce your IS, it can still be worth claiming. Getting another benefit may, for instance, mean you qualify for premiums, and therefore a higher rate of IS. For example, getting carer's allowance means you qualify for a carer premium – so you may be better off overall.

You cannot claim employment and support allowance and IS at the same time.

Passported benefits

If you are entitled to IS, you are also entitled to:
- free prescriptions;
- free dental treatment;
- free sight tests;
- vouchers for glasses;
- Healthy Start food and vitamins;
- education benefits, such as free school lunches.

See Chapter 11 for information about health benefits. You may also qualify for social fund payments (see Chapter 17).

Notes

2. Who is eligible

1 s124 SSCBA 1992
2 Regs 45 and 53 IS Regs
3 Reg 4ZA and Sch 1B IS Regs
4 Social Security (Lone Parents and Miscellaneous Amendments) Regulations 2008 No.3051
5 s124(1)(d) SSCBA 1992
6 s142 SSCBA 1992; regs 2-7 CB Regs; reg 12 IS Regs
7 Reg 1(3) CB Regs, definition of 'advanced education'
8 Reg 1(3) CB Regs, definition of 'full-time education'
9 Reg 13(2)(a)-(e) IS Regs
10 R(IS) 9/94
11 R(SB) 2/87
12 CIS/11441/1995
13 Reg 13(3)(b) IS Regs
14 CIS/11766/1996
15 R(IS) 9/94
16 C(LC)A 2000; C(LC)(E) Regs; C(LC)(W) Regs; C(LC)A(NI) 2002
17 ss23C, 24, 24A or 24B CA 1989
18 Reg 4ZA(2) IS Regs
19 Reg 61(1) IS Regs, definition of 'full-time student'
20 Regs 2(1) and 61(1) IS Regs, definition of 'period of study'
21 Reg 61(1) IS Regs, definition of 'last day of the course'
22 Reg 61(1) IS Regs
23 Reg 61(1) IS Regs
24 Reg 61(1) IS Regs
25 R(SB) 40/83; R(SB) 41/83
26 Reg 4ZA(3) and Sch 1B IS Regs
27 CIS/152/1994; R(IS) 15/98; CJSA/836/1998; R(IS) 1/00
28 Reg 61(4) IS Regs
29 Reg 61(2)(a) and (3) IS Regs
30 R(IS) 15/98; R(IS) 7/99; CJSA/836/1998; R(IS) 1/00
31 R(IS) 1/96
32 CIS/368/1992; R(IS) 6/97
33 R(JSA) 2/02
34 paras 30230-33 DMG
35 CIS/152/1994; R(IS) 15/98

3. Amount of benefit

36 Sch 3 IS Regs
37 Sch 3 para 14 IS Regs
38 Sch 3 para 3(6)(b) IS Regs
39 Sch 3 para 3(3) IS Regs
40 Sch 3 para 3(11)(viii) and (12) IS Regs

Chapter 15

Jobseeker's allowance

This chapter covers:
1. What is jobseeker's allowance (below)
2. Who is eligible (p186)
3. Amount of benefit (p196)
4. Claiming jobseeker's allowance (p198)
5. Challenging a decision (p199)
6. Other benefits and tax credits (p200)

Basic facts

– Jobseeker's allowance (JSA) is basic financial support for people who are required to be available for, and looking for, work.
– Full-time students cannot normally claim.
– Student couples with children can claim in the summer vacation.
– Lone parents can claim in the long vacation.
– Part-time students can claim if they are available for, and actively seeking, work.
– There are two main types of JSA. Contribution-based JSA is paid if you have sufficient national insurance contributions; income-based JSA is means tested, so the amount you get is usually affected by your grant, loan and other income.
– JSA claims are administered by Jobcentre Plus.

1. What is jobseeker's allowance

Further information

This chapter gives an outline of the jobseeker's allowance rules and focuses on issues relevant to students. For more detailed information on the rules, see CPAG's *Welfare Benefits and Tax Credits Handbook*.

Jobseeker's allowance (JSA) is a benefit for people of working age (under 65 for men, and under the retirement age for women, which is rising from 60 to 65 between 2010 and 2020) who are not in full-time paid work and who are expected to 'sign on' as available for and actively seeking work.

Full-time students cannot normally qualify for JSA, but there are exceptions. Part-time students can claim if they satisfy the rules for entitlement.

There are two main types of JSA. You can qualify for **contribution-based JSA** if you have paid (or been credited with) sufficient national insurance contributions. It is paid for 26 weeks and in addition to any student income or other income you might have, although certain pension payments of more than £50 a week reduce the amount you get. You can qualify for **income-based JSA** if you satisfy the means test. The amount you get is affected by your income, including some elements of student support. So even if you are entitled to income-based JSA, the amount may be reduced. Chapter 20 explains how your income affects your benefit.

A third type of JSA, **joint-claim JSA**, is very similar to income-based JSA. It is paid to some couples who have to make a joint-claim for JSA (see p199). In this *Handbook*, references to income-based JSA include references to joint-claim JSA unless otherwise stated.

2. **Who is eligible**

To qualify for jobseeker's allowance (JSA), you must satisfy the basic rules of entitlement. If you are studying full time, you must also satisfy additional rules. For information on whether you can qualify while you are in 'relevant education' or a full-time student, see p188.

Basic rules

You can qualify for JSA if:[1]

- you do not count as in full-time paid work and, if you are claiming income-based JSA, nor does your partner. For you, this is 16 hours or more a week. For your partner, this is 24 hours a week;
- you are capable of work. However, you can continue to get JSA for up to two weeks if you are sick;
- you satisfy what are known as the 'labour market conditions' – ie, you:
  – are available for work. You must be willing and able to take up work immediately (although some people are allowed some notice). You must be prepared to work at least 40 hours a week. People with caring responsibilities (including for a child under 16) and disabled people can restrict their hours to less than 40 a week;
  – are actively seeking work;
  – have a current jobseeker's agreement. This sets out the hours you have agreed to work, the type of work you are looking for and any restrictions on, for example, hours, travel and pay;
- you are under pension age (rising from 60 for women from April 2010, 65 for men);

- you are not getting income support (IS);
- you are present in Great Britain (although JSA can be paid in other countries in some circumstances); *and*
- you meet the conditions for either contribution-based JSA or income-based JSA, or both (see below). If you meet the conditions for both, you can get contribution-based JSA topped up by income-based JSA.

Overseas students

Most overseas students cannot claim JSA because they are subject to immigration control for benefit purposes. Even if you are entitled, a successful claim for benefit could affect your right to stay in the UK and it is best to get immigration advice before making a claim. If you are not eligible for benefit, but there are no restrictions on your partner, either as a student or as a 'person subject to immigration control', s/he may be able to claim instead of you. However, if s/he receives benefit and you are a 'person subject to immigration control', this may affect your right to remain in the UK under the immigration rules. You should get advice from the UK Council for International Student Affairs (UKCISA – see Appendix 2).

Contribution-based jobseeker's allowance

As well as satisfying all the basic rules above, to qualify for contribution-based JSA, you must:[2]
- have paid (or been credited with) sufficient national insurance contributions; *and*
- not have earnings above a specified amount. The specified amount is your rate of contribution-based JSA, plus one penny.

You need to have paid contributions of 25 times the lower earnings limit in one of the two complete tax years (6 April to 5 April) before the start of the benefit year (which runs from the first Sunday in January) in which you claim. You also need to have paid or been credited with contributions on earnings of 50 times the lower earnings limit in these years. See Chapter 24 for more information on national insurance.

Income-based jobseeker's allowance

As well as satisfying all the basic rules above, to qualify for income-based JSA:[3]
- you must be aged 18 or over. You can still get income-based JSA if you are aged 16 or 17, but there are extra rules (see p196);
- neither you nor your partner are getting IS, income-related employment and support allowance (ESA) or pension credit (PC);
- you must satisfy residence conditions;
- you must not be subject to immigration control for benefit purposes (although there are some limited exceptions);

- you must have income of less than your 'applicable amount' (see p197);
- you must have savings and capital worth £16,000 or less.

See Chapter 20 for how income (including student income) and capital affect your benefit. **Note:** your student support payments count as income, *not* capital.

Studying and claiming jobseeker's allowance

The general rule is that you cannot qualify for JSA if you are studying full time. If you are already claiming JSA, your entitlement might be affected if you start studying full time. There are exceptions to the rules. If you are:

- under 20 and in 'relevant education', see below;
- a full-time student, see below.

To see if you can claim JSA while studying part time, see p192.

Under 20 in relevant education

You cannot qualify for JSA if you are in what is known as 'relevant education'.[4] You count as in relevant education if you are a child or 'qualifying young person' for child benefit purposes (see p100). The rules are the same as for IS (see p165). However, unlike for IS, so long as you do not count as a full-time student (see p189), you are *not* treated as being in relevant education if:[5]

- you are on the full-time education and training option of the New Deal; *or*
- you are on a non-advanced course, which does not count as a full-time course under the rules for full-time students (see p173); *and*
  - you got JSA, incapacity benefit (IB), ESA, or IS on the grounds that you were incapable of work, or were on a modern apprenticeship scheme or other similar training:
  - for at least three months before the start of the course; *or*
  - for three out of the last six months before the start of the course, if you were working the rest of the time.

If you cannot get JSA, you may have to rely on any statutory support to which you are entitled and any discretionary support your college or school may offer you (see Chapter 1 for more details). You may be able to claim IS if you fit into one of the groups who can claim while in relevant education (see p168). Alternatively, your parents (or a person acting in their place) may be able to claim child benefit and child tax credit for you.

Full-time students

If you are a full-time student, you cannot usually qualify for JSA for the duration of your course, including vacations, because you are treated as unavailable for work, even if you are available.[6] See p190 for exceptions to this rule. See p192 if you are studying part time and p195 if you give up or change your course. See Chapter 25 if you take time out from studies.

In general, students are expected to receive student support (eg, student loans and supplementary grants) to support them while in full-time education. See Chapters 1 to 6 for details of student support.

Who counts as a full-time student

You count as a full-time student if you are not a 'qualifying young person' for child benefit purposes (see p100) and you are:[7]

- under 19 and on a full-time course of advanced education; *or*
- 19 or over but under pension age (rising from 60 for women from April 2010, 65 for men) and on a full-time course of study. If your course is full time, you are treated as a full-time student regardless of the level of the course, unless you are aged under 20 and can still be treated as in 'relevant education' (see p188).

You may also count as a full-time student while you are on a sandwich course (see p173).

For what counts as a course of advanced education, see p172, and as a full-time course of study, see p173. The rules are the same as for IS.

Note: if you are 19 and in relevant education, you do not count as a full-time student. Instead, the rules on p188 apply.

When you count as a full-time student

You count as a full-time student during your **'period of study'**. This is the whole of your course from the first day you attend or undertake the course until either the last day of your course, including short and long vacations, or until you abandon or are dismissed from it.[8] It includes a period of study in connection with the course after you have stopped doing the course itself. The Department for Work and Pensions (DWP) says it does not include freshers' week unless your course actually starts that week.[9]

You do not count as a student between courses. For example, you can claim JSA in the summer between completing an undergraduate degree and starting a postgraduate course.

If you are a postgraduate writing up your thesis at the end of your course, you may have difficulty getting JSA if this is regarded as 'a period of study undertaken by the student in connection with the course'.[10] However, the DWP says you are *not* a full-time student during the period after the end of the course when you are expected to complete any course work.[11] If you do claim, remember that to qualify for JSA you must be both available for and actively seeking work. If you say you are not prepared to fit your thesis around a job should one come up, the Jobcentre Plus office may decide that you are not available for work.

Full-time students who can claim jobseeker's allowance

Even if you are a full-time student, you can qualify for JSA if you are:

- one of a couple, both of you are full-time students and either or both of you are responsible for a child aged under 16 (or a 'qualifying young person' aged under 20 – see p100). This exception only applies during the summer vacation. The person who claims must be available for work and meet all the other basic rules for JSA;[12] *or*
- a lone parent with a dependent child aged under 16 (or a 'qualifying young person' aged under 20 – see p100). You must be available for work and meet the other basic rules for JSA. You can get JSA during the summer vacation only. You may be able to claim IS instead, depending on the age of your youngest child (see p167);[13] *or*
- aged 25 or over and on a full-time 'qualifying course', approved in advance by an employment officer at the Jobcentre Plus office. See p191 for further information; *or*
- a full-time student on an employment-related course approved in advance by an employment officer at the Jobcentre Plus office (for one period of up to two weeks in any 12 months);[14] *or*
- attending a compulsory residential course as part of an Open University course (for up to one week for each course);[15] *or*
- attending a residential training programme run by the Venture Trust (for one programme only for a maximum of four weeks in any 12-month period);[16] *or*
- a full-time student who has suspended your studies because of illness or caring responsibilities, and you have either recovered from your illness or ceased caring and are waiting to return to your course.[17] You can qualify for JSA for up to a year. See Chapter 25 for further information.

If you are a full-time student who cannot claim JSA, check to see if you can claim IS, ESA or PC instead. If you have a partner who is not a full-time student, s/he may be able to claim IS, ESA JSA or PC for you. Remember that your student support income is taken into account when working out how much IS, ESA, JSA or PC s/he can get.

Examples

Kiera and Mike are a couple and are both studying full time on degree courses. They have a seven-year-old son. Kiera signs on for JSA during the summer vacation, claiming benefit for herself and Mike. They also get housing benefit (HB), child tax credit (CTC) and child benefit throughout the year.

Marvin is unemployed and looking for work. His partner, Claudette, is studying full time for a degree. They have two children so get CTC and child benefit. Marvin can claim JSA, but the amount he receives is affected by Claudette's student loan for living costs and maintenance grant. Her parents' learning allowance is ignored. Marvin may also receive HB and council tax benefit.

In some situations, you can take a full-time **'qualifying course'** and continue to get JSA. While you are on the course, you are treated as available for and actively seeking work. You can get JSA while attending a 'qualifying course' if you:[18]

- are aged 25 or over; *and*
- have been 'receiving benefit' (see below) for at least two years at the time the course starts; *and*
- have been given approval to attend the course by an employment officer at the Jobcentre Plus office; *and*
- satisfy the conditions for being treated as available for and actively seeking work (see below).

Definitions

A **'qualifying course'** is a course of further or higher education which is employment related and lasts no more than 12 consecutive months.[19] A higher level course can also be a qualifying course if your employment officer agrees.

'Receiving benefit' means getting JSA or IS as an unemployed person, or national insurance credits for unemployment or because you are 60 or over.[20] It also means getting IS as an asylum seeker, but only if you have been accepted as having refugee status or have been granted exceptional leave to remain in the UK, and you were getting IS as an asylum seeker, or were subsequently paid backdated IS, at some time in the 12 weeks before you were first entitled to JSA, which includes the date that your course starts.

While on a qualifying course, you are treated as being available for work in any week:[21]

- that falls entirely or partly in term time, so long as you provide written evidence within five days of it being requested confirming that you are attending and making satisfactory progress on the course. This must be signed by you and by the college or educational establishment; *or*
- in which you are taking exams relating to the course; *or*
- that falls entirely in a vacation if you are willing and able to take up any 'casual employment' immediately. 'Casual employment' means employment you can leave without giving notice or, if you must give notice, which you can leave before the end of the vacation.

While on a qualifying course, if you are treated as being available for work, you are also treated as actively seeking work.[22] If this is in any week which falls entirely in a vacation, you must take such steps as can reasonably be expected in order to have the best prospects of getting casual employment.

Studying part time

You count as a part-time student if you are studying, but you are not in 'relevant education' (see p188) or a full-time student (see p188). In the latter case, you should check with the education institution to see how you are registered and whether your course counts as part time. See p175 for further information about what counts as part time. The rules are the same as for IS.

You can qualify for JSA while studying part time if you meet the labour market conditions – ie, you are available for work, actively seeking work and you have a valid jobseeker's agreement. If you have agreed restrictions with the DWP on the hours that you are available for work, there are special rules that can help you claim JSA and study part time (see p193).

> *Examples*
>
> Tina is attending a further education college and studying for A levels funded by the Skills Funding Agency. She has 15 hours a week of classes. She is a part-time student.
>
> Parminda is studying for a degree in social science at a university in Wales. The university describes the course as part time and, therefore, the course is counted as part time for JSA purposes.

Studying and availability for work

When you claim JSA you may have agreed which hours of the day and which days of the week you are available for work. This 'pattern of availability' is set out in your jobseeker's agreement. You are allowed to do this so long as the hours you choose still give you a reasonable chance of getting work and do not considerably reduce your prospects of getting work.

If the hours you study are completely different to the hours you have agreed to be available for work, you should have no problem. But if there is some overlap, or if you have agreed to be available for work at any time of day and on any day of the week, the Jobcentre Plus office must be satisfied that you are available for work despite your course. It expects you to:[23]

- arrange the hours of the course to fit round a job;
- be prepared to give up the course if a job comes up;
- be ready to take time off the course to attend a job interview; *and*
- be ready to start work immediately.

Deciding if you are available for and actively seeking work

Guidance tells Jobcentre Plus office decision makers to look at various factors when deciding whether you are genuinely available for work while studying part time. These are:[24]

- what you are doing to look for work;
- whether your course will help you get work. Bear in mind that if you say the course is necessary to get the kind of job you want, the Jobcentre Plus office may assume you are not prepared to give it up to do another kind of job and decide that you are not available for work. It is important that you stress how the course will improve your general employability skills, such as communication, IT, team work or organisational skills;
- whether you can be contacted about a possible job if you are studying away from home. Some colleges offer a central phone number you can give. You should check this with student services;
- whether you gave up work or training to do the course;
- your hours of attendance on the course;
- whether it is possible to change the hours if necessary;
- whether, if you missed some attendance, you could still complete the course;
- how much you paid for the course and whether any fee could be refunded if you gave up the course. The Jobcentre Plus office is likely to assume that you would not be prepared to give up the course to take a job if you have paid a significant amount in course fees;
- whether any grant would need to be repaid if you gave up your course.

The guidance for decision makers states that where a number of claimants are following the same course, some may be able to show that they are available, but others may not.[25] The decision maker should not operate a blanket policy of treating all students on the same course as not being available. Equally, you cannot assume that you will be treated as available just because other people on your course are getting JSA. Each claim should be considered individually. The decision maker assumes that you may be less willing to leave a course if you are near the end of the course, or as the chance of obtaining a qualification approaches.[26] When you claim JSA, you are given a student questionnaire (Form ES567S, *Attending a Training or Education Course*) to complete, asking about such factors.

Once you have qualified for JSA, you must continue to be available for and actively seeking work. When you 'sign on' you must show what steps you have taken to look for work – eg, checking job advertisements or applying for jobs. If you do not look for work each week, or you turn down a job or an interview, you could lose your JSA under a sanction, which could be for up to 26 weeks. If this happens, you can appeal. You might be able to get the sanction period reduced or have it overturned. You should seek advice and ask for a hardship payment in the meantime.

If you have restricted your availability for work

Special rules allow your course of study to be ignored when deciding whether you are available for work. These apply if you are a part-time student, and:[27]

- you have been allowed to restrict the total hours you are available for work:
  - because of your physical or mental condition, caring responsibilities or because you are working short time; *or*
  - to at least 40 hours a week; *and*
- the hours of your course are within your 'pattern of availability' (see above) and you are willing and able to rearrange these to take up a job at times that fall within this pattern; *and*
- you got JSA, incapacity benefit (IB) or IS on the grounds that you were incapable of work, or were on a training course under specific provisions:
  - for at least three months before the start of the course; *or*
  - for three out of the last six months before the start of the course, if you were working the rest of the time.

The three-month and six-month periods can only begin after you have reached your 'terminal date' (see p102).

Note: you still have to be available for and actively seeking work during the rest of the week when you are not on your course.

Health-related courses

If you attend a health-related course for which you are entitled to receive an NHS bursary (see p67), you are treated as attending a full-time course.

Modular courses

A **'modular course'** is one made up of two or more modules and the institution requires you to do a certain number successfully to complete the course.[28] If you are attending or undertaking part of a modular course that is full time according to the rules described above, you are treated as a full-time student for the duration of the modules from the day those modules begin until the last day of registration on those modules (or earlier if you abandon the course or are dismissed from it).[29] This includes all vacations during the modules on which you are registered and, except for the final module, the vacation immediately following the modules. It also includes periods when you are attending the course to do re-sits of any modules you have undertaken on a full-time basis. This is the case even if you are registered part time with the institution while you are doing these re-sits. You should seek advice from your students' union or institution's student services about the student support to which you may be entitled while you are re-sitting.

Because the rules provide no definition of a full-time course (unless it is funded by the Young People's Learning Agency (YPLA) or Skills Funding Agency in England, or the Welsh Assembly – see p173), you may be able to argue that you are not attending a full-time course.[30] If you are in any doubt, you should seek advice.

If the modular course allows you to undertake some modules on a part-time basis, you are not excluded from JSA while you are studying part time. Remember, however, that you must not be studying any modules that you have previously studied on a full-time basis.

> **Example**
> Carlton is 42 and single. He started a BSc undergraduate degree in October 2010. He registers for six modules in year one on a full-time basis. For this academic year, until 31 August 2011, Carlton is treated as a full-time student for JSA and cannot claim.
> At the end of year one, he fails a module. For year two, he registers on a part-time basis to retake his failed module and to take two new modules. Although he is registered with the university on a part-time basis, for JSA purposes from 1 September 2011 to 31 August 2012 he is still classed as a full-time student because he is undertaking a module he has previously done on a full-time basis. He cannot claim JSA during this period.
> During year three, he registers with his university on a part-time basis to study three new modules. From 1 September 2012 to 31 August 2013 he will be counted as a part-time student for JSA. As long as he meets the conditions for receiving JSA (eg, being available for and actively seeking work), he may claim.

Giving up or changing your course

If you are in any of the circumstances below, your entitlement to any student support you may receive might be affected and you should seek specialist advice.

- If you abandon your course or are dismissed from it, you can claim JSA from the day after that date so long as you satisfy the other rules of entitlement.
- If you complete one course and start a different one, you are not treated as a student during any period between the courses.[31]
- If you are on a sandwich course (see p173), or your course includes a compulsory or optional period on placement, you count as a full-time student during the sandwich or placement period even if you have been unable to find a placement, or your placement comes to an end prematurely.[32]
- If you attend a course at an educational institution which provides training or instruction to enable you to take examinations set and marked by an entirely different and unconnected body (ie, a professional institution) and you abandon or take time out from it because you fail the examinations set by the other body (or you finish the course at the educational institution but fail the exams), you may be able to argue that you are not a student from the date you left the course at your educational institution, even if you intend to re-sit the examinations set by the other body at a later date.[33]

If you are taking time out of your course for any other reason, see Chapter 25.

You may also retain entitlement to some student support on a statutory or discretionary basis – eg, through student loans or hardship funds. You should seek specialist advice.

Changing from full-time to part-time attendance

If you have to change from full-time to part-time attendance on a full-time course for personal reasons, you may be able to argue that you have abandoned your full-time course and are registered on a part-time course and, therefore, that you are not a full-time student.[34] If, because of exam failure or any other reason, you change to a different course, or your college requires you to change the level of course (eg, from A level to GCSE) and this involves a change from full-time to part-time study, you should argue that you are a part-time student (see p192).[35] However, changing your attendance may affect your entitlement to any student support you may be receiving. You should seek advice on this before acting.

16/17-year-olds

You can usually only get JSA if you are aged 18 or over. If you are under 18 you can get income-based JSA in some circumstances, provided you meet all the other rules of entitlement. The situations in which you can qualify for JSA include the following.

- You are in severe hardship. All your circumstances should be considered. Payments are discretionary and usually for just eight weeks at a time.
- You come within one of the groups of people who can claim IS (see p166). In this case, you may be able to choose whether to claim JSA or IS.
- You are a part of a couple with a child.
- You are married (or in a civil partnership) and your partner is aged 18 or over. JSA is paid for a limited period after you leave education or training.
- You are married (or in a civil partnership) and your partner is under 18 and:
  – registered for work or training; *or*
  – long-term sick or disabled; *or*
  – a student who can claim IS; *or*
  – a carer who can claim IS.
  JSA can be paid for a limited period after you leave education or training.

3. **Amount of benefit**

The amount of jobseeker's allowance (JSA) you get depends on whether you are claiming contribution-based JSA or income-based JSA.

Contribution-based jobseeker's allowance

Contribution-based JSA is paid at different weekly rates, depending on your age.

You may get less money if you have part-time earnings or an occupational or personal pension, but the amount is not affected by a student loan or grant. Contribution-based JSA is only paid for up to 26 weeks. You can claim income-based JSA to top up your contribution-based JSA or after your contribution-based JSA runs out, if you satisfy the means test.

Income-based jobseeker's allowance

Income-based JSA is a means-tested benefit that tops up your income to a level set by the Government. The amount you get depends on your basic weekly needs and those of your partner (your 'applicable amount') and on how much income and capital you have (see Chapter 20). Some students may find, therefore, that they can only receive JSA for part of any year – eg, during the summer vacation.

Your applicable amount is made up of:
- a personal allowance;
- premiums for any special needs – eg, if you are disabled or are caring for a disabled person;
- housing costs (see p179), principally for mortgage interest payments.

The total of these is called your 'applicable amount'. If you have no other income (the student loan and some grants count as income), you are paid your full applicable amount. Otherwise, any income you do have is topped up with income-based JSA to the level of your applicable amount. If your weekly income is above your applicable amount, you are not entitled to income-based JSA. See Chapter 20 for how to work out your weekly income. The rules are the same as for IS, except for some couples, when the following applies.
- If only one of you is under 18, you get the higher £102.75 personal allowance if the younger partner is responsible for a child or is eligible for income-based JSA, severe hardship payments, income support (IS) (or would be if not a member of a couple) or income-related employment and support allowance (ESA).
- If both of you are under 18, you get the higher £78.30 personal allowance if:
  – you or your partner are responsible for a child; *or*
  – if you were both single, both of you would be eligible for income-based JSA or your partner would be eligible for IS or income-related ESA; *or*
  – you are both eligible for severe hardship payments, or one of you is and the other is eligible for income-based JSA, IS or income-related ESA; *or*
  – you are married or civil partners and one of you is registered with the Careers Service, or both of you are eligible for income-based JSA.
- Joint-claim couples can get a disability premium (at the couple rate) if one has had limited capability for work for 364 days (196 days if terminally ill). You need to claim ESA to establish limited capability for work even if you might not get it.
- Claimants who are entitled to housing costs after 13 weeks will only have housing costs included in their applicable amount for two years.

The current levels of personal allowances and premiums for JSA can be found on pxv of this handbook.

4. **Claiming jobseeker's allowance**

If you think you might be entitled to jobseeker's allowance (JSA), you should claim as soon as you can. There are only very limited situations where backdating is allowed.

You can make initial contact about claiming by telephone or letter. You may also be able to start a claim online at www.dwp.gov.uk/eservice. The date of your initial contact is important because it usually determines the date from when you can be paid JSA.

You must usually start your claim by telephoning the national claim centre on 0800 055 6688, who will then take information from you and arrange an interview. You will be sent a statement recording the information you gave over the telephone, which you are asked to sign, and details of the evidence and information you should bring with you to the interview. The signed statement comprises your official claim.

It is best for you to start your claim in this way if you can. However, if you cannot, or you do not want to, use the telephone to start your claim, the Jobcentre Plus office can still deal with your claim in other ways. You might, for example, be invited for a face-to-face interview or, in some cases, an old-style claim form can be accepted. JSA claim forms are only available from Jobcentre Plus offices.

Whenever you call the Department for Work and Pensions (DWP) (Department for Social Development (DSD) in Northern Ireland), you need to provide your national insurance number. You also need this number, as well as that of your partner, when you claim, as well as other information required on the claim form.

Showing you are available for and actively seeking work

When you claim JSA, you may be given a form to complete about the work for which you are available and how you are actively seeking work. The information you give forms the basis of your jobseeker's agreement. You may also be asked to fill in a student questionnaire. When completing the forms, remember that even though you are a student, you are expected to be available for and actively seeking work. In your answers you should make sure that you do not cast doubt on your willingness to work. If you are a part-time student, you may be asked to get a learning agreement (see p173) from your college to show that you are studying part time.

Couples

If you are a full-time student but your partner is not, s/he can claim JSA for both of you if s/he is eligible for JSA. In some cases, you both need to claim JSA (known as 'joint-claim JSA'), but only your partner may need to continue to 'sign on' and look for work. Similarly, your partner can get JSA for both of you if you are not yet a full-time student, but you have applied for, or been accepted on a course. You *must* make a joint claim if:

- neither of you has dependent children; *and*
- at least one of you is 18 or over; *and*
- at least one of you was born after 28 October 1947.

Getting paid

Jobseeker's allowance is usually paid directly into your bank (or similar) account. Which account it goes into is up to you. If you do not want your benefit to go into an account that is overdrawn, give the DWP (or DSD) details of an alternative account if you have access to, or can open, one.

If you are overpaid JSA, you might have to repay it.

5. **Challenging a decision**

If you think a decision about your jobseeker's allowance (JSA) is wrong (eg, because the decision maker got the facts or law wrong), there are a number of ways you can try to get the decision changed.

- You can seek a revision or a supersession of the decision. In some cases you have to show specific grounds. In others, you must apply within a strict time limit.
- You can appeal to an independent tribunal. There are strict time limits for appealing – usually one month from the date you are sent or given the decision. You can make a late appeal in limited circumstances.

If you are considering challenging a decision, you should seek advice as soon as possible.

If your claim for JSA is unsuccessful, consider whether you can challenge the decision. You should bear the following in mind.

- As student claims are not necessarily commonplace and the rules about how student income is treated are complex, it is always worth checking a decision with a student adviser in your students' union or institution.
- If the decision maker says you are a full-time student, but you disagree, you should get advice to see if there are grounds for challenging the decision.

- Claims for JSA are sometimes refused because the Department for Work and Pensions (or Department for Social Development) miscalculates student income or takes the wrong types of student income into account.
- If your JSA is not paid because you are sanctioned (eg, if the decision maker says you gave up a job voluntarily or were dismissed for misconduct), it is always worth getting advice about challenging the decision. Even if a tribunal agrees that a sanction should be applied, it can reduce the length of the sanction period. However, getting advice is important because a tribunal can also *increase* the period of a sanction.
- You might not currently be entitled to JSA, but would be once you or a member of your family become entitled to a 'qualifying benefit' – eg, disability living allowance or carer's allowance. In this case, you need to claim. Your initial claim will be refused. However, if you claim again once the qualifying benefit is awarded, your JSA will be backdated to the date of your original claim, or the date on which the qualifying benefit was first payable (if later). Alternatively, you might be entitled to a higher rate of JSA once the 'qualifying benefit' is awarded. In this case, you need to ask for a revision or a supersession of your JSA award. Your JSA should then be increased from the date the qualifying benefit was first payable.

6. **Other benefits and tax credits**

You cannot get income support (IS) and jobseeker's allowance (JSA) at the same time. If you are eligible for both, you need to choose which to claim. In general, the amounts of income-based JSA and IS are the same, but you are not expected to be available for work to qualify for IS.

Income-based JSA tops up any other income you have to the level of your basic requirements (your applicable amount), so most other benefits are taken into account as income when working out the amount. This means they reduce your JSA pound for pound. Disability living allowance, attendance allowance, guardian's allowance, housing benefit (HB) and council tax benefit (CTB) are, however, always disregarded as income.

If you get income-based JSA, you are also eligible for HB and CTB if you meet the other qualifying criteria for these benefits.

Child tax credit (CTC) is ignored as income when assessing JSA. Child benefit is ignored unless you still have amounts for children in your income-based JSA and you do not get CTC. In this case, £10.50 a week of your child benefit is disregarded if you have a child under one.

Even though getting a benefit may reduce your income-based JSA, it can still be worth claiming. Getting another benefit may, for instance, mean you qualify for premiums and, therefore, a higher rate. For example, if your partner gets carer's allowance, you qualify for a carer premium – so you may be better off overall.

Passported benefits

If you are entitled to income-based JSA, you are also entitled to:
- free prescriptions;
- free dental treatment;
- free sight tests;
- vouchers for glasses;
- Healthy Start food and vitamins;
- education benefits, such as free school lunches.

See Chapter 11 for information about health benefits. You may also qualify for social fund payments (see Chapter 17).

Contribution-based JSA does not give you automatic access to these benefits, but you may qualify for health benefits on low-income grounds (see Chapter 11).

Notes

2. Who is eligible
1 s1 JSA 1995
2 s2 JSA 1995
3 ss3 and 13 JSA 1995
4 s1(2)(g) JSA 1995; reg 54 JSA Regs
5 Reg 54(3) JSA Regs
6 Reg 15(1)(a) JSA Regs
7 Reg 1(3) JSA Regs, definition of 'full-time student'
8 Regs 1(3A) and 4 JSA Regs
9 para 30221 Vol 6 DMG
10 Reg 4(b) JSA Regs
11 para 30238 DMG
12 Reg 15(3)(a) JSA Regs
13 Reg 15(3)(b) JSA Regs
14 Reg 14(1)(a) JSA Regs
15 Reg 14(1)(f) JSA Regs
16 Reg 14(1)(k) JSA Regs
17 Reg 1(3D) and (3E) JSA Regs
18 Reg 17A(2), (3) and (5) JSA Regs
19 Reg 17A(7) and (8) JSA Regs
20 Reg 17A(7), (7A) and (7B) JSA Regs
21 Reg 17A(3) and (7) JSA Regs
22 Reg 21A JSA Regs

23 paras 21239-41 DMG
24 para 21242 Vol 4 DMG
25 para 21243 DMG
26 para 21244 DMG
27 Reg 11 JSA Regs
28 Reg 1(3C) JSA Regs
29 Reg 1(3A)(a) and (3B) JSA Regs
30 R(IS) 15/98; R(IS) 7/99; CJSA/836/1998; R(IS) 1/00
31 R(IS) 1/96
32 CIS/368/1992; R(IS) 6/97
33 R(JSA) 2/02
34 paras 30230-33 DMG
35 CIS/152/1994; R(IS) 15/98

Chapter 16

Maternity, paternity and adoption benefits

This chapter looks at:

1. What are maternity, paternity and adoption benefits (below)
2. Who is eligible (p203)
3. Amount of benefit (p205)
4. Claiming maternity, paternity and adoption benefits (p205)
5. Challenging a decision (p206)
6. Other benefits and tax credits (p206)

Basic facts

– Women having a baby can claim statutory maternity pay if they have an employer, or maternity allowance if they have recently worked or been self-employed.
– The mother's (or adopter's) partner can claim statutory paternity pay.
– Someone adopting a child can claim statutory adoption pay or statutory paternity pay.
– Part-time and full-time students are eligible for these benefits.
– Statutory maternity, paternity and adoption pay are administered by employers. Claims for maternity allowance are administered by the Department for Work and Pensions (or the Department for Social Development in Northern Ireland).

1. What are maternity, paternity and adoption benefits

Further information

This chapter gives an outline of the rules for maternity, paternity and adoption benefits and focuses on issues relevant to students. For more detailed information on the rules, see CPAG's *Welfare Benefits and Tax Credits Handbook*.

Statutory maternity pay

You can get statutory maternity pay (SMP) if you are pregnant and within the 11 weeks before your expected week of childbirth, or if you have just had a baby. You must have an employer and earn at least £97 a week on average. SMP is paid for 39 weeks.

Maternity allowance

Maternity allowance (MA) is a benefit for women who have recently worked, either in an employed or self-employed capacity. It is paid for up to 39 weeks.

Statutory paternity pay

Statutory paternity pay (SPP) is a benefit for people whose partners are having a baby or adopting a child. It is payable for two weeks if you are taking leave from work to care for your partner or for the child. Unmarried and same-sex partners can claim SPP.

Statutory adoption pay

Statutory adoption pay (SAP) is a benefit for people who are adopting a child and earning an average of at least £97 a week from employment. It is paid for a maximum of 39 weeks. If a couple (including same-sex couples) are adopting a child, one can claim SAP and the other can claim SPP for two weeks.

2. Who is eligible

Students are eligible for maternity, paternity and adoption benefits if they meet the basic conditions. What follows is a brief outline of the qualifying conditions.

Statutory maternity pay

You can get statutory maternity pay (SMP) if:
- you are pregnant (and are within the 11 weeks before your expected week of childbirth) or have recently had a baby;[1] *and*
- you have worked for the same employer for 26 weeks ending with the 15th week before your expected week of childbirth;[2] *and*
- you have ceased work for the employer who pays you SMP; *and*
- your average gross earnings are at least £97 a week;[3] *and*
- you give your employer the correct notice (at least 28 days before you expect a payment to start or, if this is not practicable, as soon as practicable after that date).

You must provide evidence of the expected date of birth – eg, by providing a Form MAT B1, within three weeks after the start of the maternity pay period.

Maternity allowance

You can get maternity allowance if you cannot get SMP and:

- you are pregnant (and within the 11 weeks before your expected week of childbirth) or have recently had a baby;[4]
- you have worked, in either an employed or self-employed capacity, for at least 26 weeks out of the 66 weeks before your expected week of childbirth;[5] *and*
- your average earnings are at least £30 a week.[6]

Statutory paternity pay

You can get statutory paternity pay (SPP) if:[7]

- in either the 15th week before the expected week of childbirth or the week in which the adopter is told of being matched with a child, you have been employed by the same employer for at least 26 weeks, and you continue in that job up to the day the baby is born or the day the child is placed for adoption (in other words, 41 weeks in total); *and*
- your average gross earnings are at least £97 a week; *and*
- you give your employer the correct notice and information (at least 28 days before your pay period is due to start, or if this is not practicable, as soon as practicable after that date); *and*
- you are not working for the employer who pays you SPP; *and*
- you do not work for any other employer.

In addition, for claims based on birth:

- you are the child's father or partner of the child's mother and you will be caring for the child or supporting the mother; *and*
- you are the child's father and you will have responsibility for his/her upbringing *or* your partner is the child's mother and, apart from the mother's responsibility, you will have the main responsibility for the child's upbringing.

In addition, for claims based on adoption:

- your partner or you and your partner are adopting a child; *and*
- the person adopting the child is doing so under UK law; *and*
- you have (or expect to have) the main responsibility for the upbringing of the child (along with the other adopter); *and*
- you intend to care for the child or to support the person adopting the child; *and*
- you have not elected to receive statutory adoption pay (SAP).

You can use Form SC3 (for claims based on birth) or SC4 (for claims based on adoption) to provide the necessary information to your employer. You can obtain these from your employer or from HM Revenue and Customs.

You cannot get both SPP (adoption) and SAP at the same time, although one member of a couple can claim SAP while the other claims SPP (adoption).

Statutory adoption pay

You can get SAP if:[8]
* you are adopting a child; *and*
* the child has been placed with both you and your co-adopter and your co-adopter is not claiming SAP; *and*
* you have not elected to receive SPP; *and*
* you have worked for the same employer for 26 weeks, ending with the week in which you are told you have been matched with a child for adoption; *and*
* your average gross earnings are at least £97 a week (April 2010 rates); *and*
* you have ceased work for the employer who pays you SAP; *and*
* you give your employer the correct notice and information at least 28 days before you expect a payment to start, or if this is not practicable, as soon as possible after that date.

3. Amount of benefit

Rates from April 2010

Statutory maternity pay	First six weeks: 90% of average weekly earnings
	Following 33 weeks: £124.88 (or 90% of earnings if less)[9]
Maternity allowance	For 39 weeks: £124.88 (or 90% of earnings if less)
Statutory paternity pay	For two weeks: £124.88 (or 90% of earnings if less)
Statutory adoption pay	For 39 weeks: £124.88 (or 90% of earnings if less)[10]

4. Claiming maternity, paternity and adoption benefits

You claim statutory maternity pay (SMP), statutory paternity pay (SPP) and statutory adoption pay (SAP) from your employer. You must provide appropriate notice and information. For SMP you must provide evidence of the expected date of birth. You can use Form MAT B1, issued by your doctor or midwife. For SPP you can use Form SC3 for SPP (birth) and Form SC4 for SPP (adoption) to give the required information to your employer. These forms are produced by HM Revenue and Customs and are available from www.hmrc.gov.uk.

You claim maternity allowance (MA) from your local Jobcentre Plus office on Form MA1.

Getting paid

Your employer usually pays SMP, SPP or SAP in the same way as your normal wages or salary.

MA is usually paid directly into your bank (or similar) account. Which account it goes into is up to you. If you do not want your benefit to go into an account that is overdrawn, give the Department for Work and Pensions (or Department for Social Development in Northern Ireland) details of an alternative account if you have access to, or can open, one.

If you are overpaid MA, you might have to repay it. If your employer attempts to recover SMP, SPP or SAP it says you were not entitled to, you should seek advice.

5. Challenging a decision

If you think a decision about your maternity allowance is wrong (eg, because the decision maker got the facts or law wrong), there are a number of ways that you can try to get the decision changed.

- You can seek a revision or supersession of the decision. In some cases you have to show specific grounds. In others you must apply within a strict time limit.
- You can appeal to an independent tribunal. There are strict time limits for appealing – usually one month from the date you are sent or given the decision. You can make a late appeal in limited circumstances.

If you are considering challenging a decision, you should seek advice as soon as possible.

If you disagree with your employer's decision on your entitlement to statutory maternity pay, statutory paternity pay or statutory adoption pay, or your employer fails to make a decision, you can ask HM Revenue and Customs (the Revenue) to make a formal decision on your entitlement.

If either you or your employer is unhappy with the decision, you can appeal to the First-tier Tribunal (Tax). Your appeal should reach the Revenue within 30 days of the date the decision was issued.

6. Other benefits and tax credits

There are a number of other benefits you may be able to get when you have a baby, including the following:

- When the baby is born, you can get child benefit (see Chapter 8).
- You can also claim child tax credit (CTC) or increase your existing award. Tell HM Revenue and Customs (the Revenue) within three months of the birth. See Chapter 18 for further details.
- If you are under 19 (or under age 20 if you were accepted on, enrolled on or started the course before your 19th birthday) and in full-time non-advanced education, you count as in relevant education and you are eligible for income support (IS) as a parent (father or mother). See Chapter 14 for further details.
- If you are a lone parent, you are eligible for IS and housing benefit (HB) whether or not you are a full-time student (see pp144 and 174). If your baby has not yet been born (or your child has not yet been placed with you for adoption), you may still qualify for IS and HB on another ground. See Chapter 12 for further details.
- If you get a qualifying benefit (including IS and CTC at a rate above the family element), you can claim a Sure Start maternity grant from the social fund within three months of the birth (see p209). If you are waiting for a decision on your qualifying benefit, make sure you still claim the maternity grant within three months of the birth. If you are refused the grant, rather than your claim being held until your benefit or tax credit is awarded, make another claim within three months of being awarded the benefit or tax credit. See Chapter 17 for more details.
- You can claim a health in pregnancy grant after the 25th week of pregnancy. Claim via your midwife and get the form to the Revenue within 31 days of the date the midwife's having signed it. Note: the Government has announced that the health in pregnancy grant will be abolished from January 2011.

Notes

2. Who is eligible
1 s164(2)(c) SSCBA 1992
2 s164(2)(a) SSCBA 1992
3 s164(2)(b) SSCBA 1992
4 s35 SSCBA 1992
5 s35(1)(b) SSCBA 1992
6 ss35(1)(c) and 35A(4) SSCBA 1992
7 ss171ZA(2) and (3), 171ZB(2) and (3), 171ZC, and 171ZE(4) and (7) SSCBA 1992; regs 4 and 11 SPPSAP(G) Regs; reg 4(2)(b) and (c) PAL Regs
8 s171ZL(2)-(4) and (6) SSCBA 1992; regs 3 and 24 SPPSAP(G) Regs

3. Amount of benefit
9 s166 SS CBA 1992
10 Regs 2 and 3 SPPSAP(WR) Regs

Chapter 17

The social fund

This chapter looks at:

1. What is the social fund (p209)
2. Sure Start maternity grants (p209)
3. Funeral payments (p210)
4. Cold weather payments (p211)
5. Winter fuel payments (p211)
6. Community care grants (p212)
7. Budgeting loans (p213)
8. Crisis loans (p214)
9. Challenging a decision (p214)

Basic facts

– To get help from the social fund (except crisis loans) you must receive a qualifying benefit – eg, income support or child tax credit at a rate higher than the family element.

– Both part-time and full-time students can qualify if they satisfy the rules of entitlement.

– If you are in receipt of a qualifying benefit, it does not matter how much student support income you get – this has already been taken into account in working out your qualifying benefit.

– Full-time students under 20 who are on a non-advanced course or are in approved training cannot get a crisis loan unless they are eligible for income support, pension credit or income-based jobseeker's allowance.

– Other full-time students can claim a crisis loan, but if they do not get income support, pension credit or income-based jobseeker's allowance they can only claim for expenses arising out of a disaster.

– The social fund has two parts, comprising regulated and discretionary payments.

– The social fund is administered by local Jobcentre Plus offices.

1. **What is the social fund**

Further information
This chapter gives an outline of the social fund rules and focuses on issues relevant to students. For more detailed information on the rules, see CPAG's *Welfare Benefits and Tax Credits Handbook*.

The social fund comprises two types of payments.[1]
- **Regulated social fund** payments, made up of:
  - Sure Start maternity grants;
  - funeral payments;
  - cold weather payments;
  - winter fuel payments.
- **Discretionary social fund** payments, made up of:
  - community care grants;
  - budgeting loans;
  - crisis loans.

You are entitled to regulated social fund payments if you satisfy the qualifying conditions.

The discretionary part of the social fund has a fixed budget.[2] There is no legal entitlement to a payment and no right of appeal to an independent tribunal if you are refused. Even though you might meet all the criteria for a payment, you may not get one. If you are turned down, you should ask for a review. If you are refused again, you can ask for a further review by social fund inspectors.[3]

2. **Sure Start maternity grants**

A Sure Start maternity grant is a grant of £500 to help with the costs of a new baby (from April 2011 the Government plans to make this available for a first child only).[4]

To qualify you or your partner must:[5]
- have been awarded:
  - income support; *or*
  - income-based jobseeker's allowance; *or*
  - child tax credit at a rate above the family element (£1,090 a year when you have a child under one, otherwise £545); *or*
  - income-related employment and support allowance; *or*
  - working tax credit including a disability or severe disability element; *or*
  - pension credit (guarantee or savings credit); *and*

- have received health and welfare advice from a health professional.

In addition:
- you or a member of your family must be pregnant or have given birth in the last three months (including where the baby was stillborn); *or*
- you or your partner must have adopted a child aged under 12 months.

Note: you can also qualify if you and your spouse have been granted a parental order allowing you to have a child by a surrogate mother.

You claim on Form SF100, which you can get from the local Jobcentre Plus office or from www.direct.gov.uk. You must make your claim up to 11 weeks before the birth or within three months after the birth (or adoption, residence order or parental order).[6]

If you are waiting to hear about a claim for one of the qualifying benefits, the Department for Work and Pensions may defer making a decision until the claim for the qualifying benefit is decided. If your maternity grant application is refused in these circumstances, you must reclaim within three months of the decision awarding the qualifying benefit. If you claim before your baby is born, you must submit a maternity certificate (MAT B1) or another medical note showing your expected date of childbirth. If you claim after the child is born, you must show a maternity, birth or adoption certificate.

3. Funeral payments

A funeral payment can be made to help with burial or cremation costs. To qualify you must accept responsibility for the funeral expenses[7] and must have been awarded:[8]
- income support; *or*
- income-based jobseeker's allowance; *or*
- child tax credit at a rate above the family element (£1,090 a year when you have a child under one, otherwise £545); *or*
- income-related employment and support allowance; *or*
- working tax credit including a disability or severe disability element; *or*
- pension credit (guarantee or savings credit); *or*
- housing benefit; *or*
- council tax benefit; *or*
- second adult rebate where you are the second adult.

You qualify for a payment if you were the partner of the deceased, or the deceased was a child for whom you were responsible. You may also qualify if you were the parent, son or daughter of the deceased, or a close relative or friend of hers/his. In this case you must show that it is reasonable for you to accept responsibility for the funeral expenses. The rules on this are complicated and there are exceptions, so you should seek advice if you are refused a payment.[9]

You must claim on Form SF200 (which you can get from your local Jobcentre Plus office or download from the Department for Work and Pensions (DWP) website) at the local DWP office. You must claim within three months of the funeral.[10] If you are waiting to hear about a claim for one of the qualifying benefits, the DWP may defer making a decision on your claim until the claim for the qualifying benefit is decided. If your funeral payment application is refused in these circumstances, you must reclaim within three months of the decision awarding the qualifying benefit.

4. **Cold weather payments**

Cold weather payments are made to help you with heating costs during periods of cold weather.

A period of cold weather is a period of seven consecutive days during which the average daily temperature is equal to or below 0 degrees Celsius. A payment of £8.50 is made for each week of cold weather. There is no need to apply as the Department for Work and Pensions (DWP) or, in Northern Ireland, the Department for Social Development, should automatically select those people who are eligible and send out payments.[11]

To qualify for a cold weather payment, you must have been awarded income support (IS), income-based jobseeker's allowance (JSA) or pension credit (PC) guarantee or savings credit for at least one day in the period of cold weather. Unless you are entitled to PC:[12]

- your IS or income-based JSA must include a disability, severe disability, enhanced disability, disabled child, pensioner or higher pensioner premium; *or*
- you must be responsible for a child under five; *or*
- you must get child tax credit which includes a disability or severe disability element.

There are no time limits for claiming a cold weather payment as you do not have to submit a claim. If, however, you think you have missed out on a payment you should have received, contact your local Jobcentre Plus office.

5. **Winter fuel payments**

Winter fuel payments are made to people who have reached the qualifying age for pension credit (PC), are ordinarily resident in Great Britain and who reached the qualifying age for PC by the third Monday in September (the qualifying week). You cannot get a payment if you are receiving pension credit or income-based jobseeker's allowance and have been in residential care for 12 weeks or more. There are other situations when you might not get a payment or where you might get a reduced payment. Seek advice if you think you have been wrongly refused a winter fuel payment or if you have been paid less than the amount to which you think you are entitled.

Rates from September 2010

Aged 60–79 (in the qualifying week)	£250
Aged 80 or over (in the qualifying week)	£400

Note that these rates represent a temporary increase for winter 2010/11, and may reduce for winter 2011/12. Payments should be made automatically without having to make a claim, if you are in receipt of certain social security benefits or if you received a payment in the previous year. Otherwise, you should contact the Winter Fuel Helpline on 0845 915 1515 or textphone 0845 601 5613 to make a claim.

6. **Community care grants**

Community care grants (CCGs) are non-repayable grants intended to help you live independently in the community. There is no ceiling on the amount for which you can apply. You can claim for items such as:
- removal expenses, furniture and household equipment;
- redecoration and refurbishment;
- bedding, clothing and footwear;
- domestic appliances, such as heaters and washing machines;
- items needed because of a disability;
- expenses for setting up home if, for example, you have been homeless or living in temporary accommodation.

You must need the CCG for a specific purpose – eg, to ease or prevent exceptional pressure on you and your family, to assist with continued independent living in the community, or to help with certain travel expenses (eg, to visit someone who is ill or attend a relative's funeral).[13]

In order to qualify for a CCG, you must usually be in receipt of a qualifying benefit when your application is treated as made.[14] The qualifying benefits are:
- income support;
- income-related employment and support allowance;
- income-based jobseeker's allowance; *or*

• pension credit (guarantee or savings credit).

You should apply to the Jobcentre Plus office on Form SF300. If you are moving out of care or temporary accommodation, you need to apply to the office covering the area to which you are moving.

7. Budgeting loans

You can get a budgeting loan (BL) to help you pay for certain items that are difficult to budget for when on benefits for a long period. These are:[15]
• furniture and household equipment;
• clothing and footwear;
• removal expenses;
• rent in advance;
• home improvements, maintenance and security;
• travelling expenses;
• jobseeking expenses or expenses on starting work;
• repaying hire purchase loans and other debts for any of the above expenses.

Budgeting loans are interest-free loans of between £100 and £1,500. You must be able to afford to repay the loan.[16] The amount you can get depends on the size of your family and the amount of outstanding BL debt you may already have. To qualify, you must have been getting one of these benefits for at least 26 weeks before your application is decided:[17]
• income support;
• income-related employment and support allowance;
• income-based jobseeker's allowance;
• pension credit (guarantee or savings credit).

You should apply to the local Jobcentre Plus office on Form SF500. You should always apply for a community care grant (CCG) first, if you are eligible, rather than a BL because you do not have to repay a CCG. Your application for a BL will not be normally considered as an application for a CCG even though both benefits can pay for the same items. If you are refused a CCG, you can always apply for a BL at a later date.

You can reapply for a BL at any time for the same or different items.

You should always consider the repayment terms of the BL before taking up the loan because set amounts are deducted from weekly benefit and these could cause you hardship. You can ask for repayments to be reduced if this is the case. You are not charged interest on a BL, so it may be preferable to other types of loans.

8. **Crisis loans**

Crisis loans are intended to help with expenses in an emergency or after a disaster. They are interest-free loans paid only if you have no other money to meet your immediate needs. If your college has a hardship fund to which you can apply, you should apply to this first. You are likely to be refused a crisis loan if the hardship fund could help instead.

You may get a crisis loan, for example, if you have lost money that you needed to live on, if your regular income has not been paid and you are in hardship, if there has been a disaster like a fire or flood that has caused damage, or if you need to pay fuel reconnection charges. A crisis loan has to be the only way of preventing serious damage or risk to your health and safety, or that of a member of your family.

You are encouraged to apply by telephone, but an application can be made in writing on Form SF401 at your local Jobcentre Plus office.

Under 20 in non-advanced education or approved training

If you are under 20 and in full-time non-advanced education or approved training (see pp101 and 272) and you began your course before your 19th birthday, you can claim a crisis loan if you are eligible for income support (IS), income-related employment and support allowance (ESA) or income-based jobseeker's allowance (JSA).[18] If you are not eligible for these benefits, you cannot get a crisis loan.

Other full-time students

If you are under 19 and in full-time advanced education (see p172) or you are older and in full-time education (advanced or non-advanced) and you are eligible for IS, income-based JSA, income-related ESA or pension credit, you can claim a crisis loan as normal. If you are not eligible for one of these benefits, you can only get a crisis loan to alleviate the consequences of a disaster, not in any other circumstances.[19]

9. **Challenging a decision**

Regulated social fund decisions are made on behalf of the Secretary of State and can be challenged by revision, supersession and appeal, the rules of which are the same as for most other benefits. See CPAG's *Welfare Benefits and Tax Credits Handbook* for information about challenging a decision.

Discretionary social fund decisions cannot be appealed, but you can apply for a review within 28 days of the date the decision was issued to you.[20] A decision must be reviewed if it is based on a mistake of the law or material fact, or (in the case of community care grants and crisis loans) if there has been a change of circumstances since the decision was issued, or (in the case of budgeting loans) there has been a change in the district budget.[21]

Challenging repayment terms

You cannot request a review of repayment terms or the decision to recover a loan, but you can ask the Department for Work and Pensions or Department for Social Development to reschedule the loan by lowering weekly repayments, if the repayment terms are causing you hardship or if there has been a change in your financial circumstances.[22]

Notes

1. What is the social fund
  1 s138 SSCBA 1992
  2 s168 SSAA 1992
  3 s38 SSA 1998; SF Dirs 31-39; s66 SSAA 1992

2. Sure Start maternity grants
  4 Reg 5(2) SFM&FE Regs
  5 Reg 5(1)(a) and (b) SFM&FE Regs
  6 Reg 19 and Sch 4 para 8 SS(C&P) Regs

3. Funeral payments
  7 Reg 7(7) SFM&FE Regs
  8 Reg 7(3) and (4) SFM&FE Regs
  9 Regs 7(8) and 8 SFM&FE Regs
  10 Sch 4 para 9 SS(C&P) Regs

4. Cold weather payments
  11 Regs 1(2), 1A and 2(1) and (2), and Schs 1 and 2 SFCWP(G) Regs
  12 Regs 1, 1A and 2 and Schs 1 and 2 SFCWP(G) Regs

5. Community care grants
  13 SF Dir 4
  14 SF Dir 25

7. Budgeting loans
  15 SF Dir 2
  16 SF Dirs 10, 11 and 50-53
  17 SF Dir 8(1)(a)

8. Crisis loans
  18 SF Dir 15
  19 SF Dir 16(a)

9. Challenging a decision
  20 Reg 2(1)(a) and (2)(a) SF(AR) Regs
  21 SF Dir 31
  22 s38(13) SSA 1998

Chapter 18

Child tax credit

This chapter covers:

1. What is child tax credit (below)
2. Who is eligible (p217)
3. Amount of child tax credit (p218)
4. Claiming child tax credit (p221)
5. Challenging a decision (p222)
6. Other benefits and tax credits (p223)

Basic facts

– Child tax credit is paid to families with children.
– Both part-time and full-time students with a child can qualify if they satisfy the rules of entitlement.
– The amount of child tax credit you get is affected by your income, but most student support is ignored when working this out.
– Tax credit claims are administered by HM Revenue and Customs.

1. What is child tax credit

Further information

This chapter gives an outline of the child tax credit rules and focuses on issues relevant to students. For more detailed information on the rules, see CPAG's *Welfare Benefits and Tax Credits Handbook*.

Child tax credit (CTC) is paid to people on low incomes with children. It is paid whether or not you are working. CTC is administered by HM Revenue and Customs (the Revenue). Claims are assessed on an annual basis, usually based on your income and that of your partner (of either sex) over the previous tax year.

Being a student does not affect your entitlement to CTC. You can qualify for CTC so long as you satisfy the rules of entitlement.

More information about tax credits is available on the Revenue's website. A tax credit calculator is available at www.hmrc.gov.uk/taxcredits/calculator.htm and the Revenue also runs a helpline on 0845 300 3900 (textphone 0845 300 3909).

Proposed changes

The Government plans a number of changes to tax credits from April 2011.[1]
- The extra CTC for a child under one, the baby element (£545 a year), will be removed from CTC.
- Families with income over £40,000, instead of the current £50,000, will lose the maximum family element (£545 a year) which will be reduced at the rate of 41 per cent of the excess income instead of the current 6.67 per cent.
- Families with income over £16,190 a year (or £6,420 if eligible for working tax credit) will get less tax credits because the maximum award will be reduced at the rate of 41 per cent of the excess income instead of the current 39 per cent.
- The level of in-year rises of income that will be disregarded from calculations of tax credit entitlement will decrease from £25,000 to £10,000.

More changes are planned for future years.

Changes to social security benefits

If you claim income support (IS) or income-based jobseeker's allowance (JSA) and are getting CTC, IS and income-based JSA, do not include allowances and premiums for your children. Instead, you get financial support for your children in your CTC. You can get CTC in addition to IS and JSA, and in addition to child benefit.

However, if you were getting IS or income-based JSA on 5 April 2004 and this included allowances and premiums for your children but you were not yet entitled to CTC, you will be transferred to CTC sometime in the future. Until then, you continue to get allowances and premiums for your children in your IS or income-based JSA. A change of circumstances, such as starting a full-time course, may trigger the transfer.

2. Who is eligible

You can qualify for child tax credit (CTC) if:[2]
- you (and your partner) are 16 or over; *and*
- you are a lone parent and have at least one child or qualifying young person for whom you are responsible (see p218); *and*
- you satisfy presence and residence conditions; *and*

- you are not subject to immigration control for tax credit purposes. You can get further advice from the UK Council for International Student Affairs (UKCISA – see Appendix 2); *and*
- you have a low income (see p220).

You count as responsible for a child or qualifying young person if:
- s/he normally lives with you; *or*
- you have the main responsibility for her/him. This only applies if you and another person (eg, your child's other parent) make competing claims for the same child.

Someone counts as a child until 1 September following her/his 16th birthday, whether or not s/he is in education.[3] Someone counts as a 'qualifying young person' if s/he is:[4]
- under 20 and in full-time non-advanced education or approved training, or has been enrolled or accepted to undertake it. This does not apply if s/he is undertaking the education or training because of her/his employment. The education or training must have begun (or s/he must have been enrolled or accepted to undertake it) before s/he reached 19; *or*
- under 18, has ceased full-time education or approved training and it is not more than 20 weeks since s/he did so. For this rule to apply, s/he must notify HM Revenue and Customs that s/he has registered for work or training with the Careers Wales or Connexions service.

Students and child tax credit

You are not excluded from claiming CTC simply because you are a student. Indeed, the student support system was changed so that financial support for your dependent child(ren) would be provided via CTC.

Students funded through the NHS student support system in England and Wales are still able to claim both dependants' grant and CTC, but this arrangement remains under review and may change in future years.

When calculating how much CTC you can get, student loans and most other student income is disregarded. See Chapter 21 for how income affects tax credits.

3. **Amount of child tax credit**

The amount of child tax credit (CTC) you get depends on:
- your maximum CTC. This is made up of a combination of 'elements' (see p219);
- how much income you have. If you have a partner, your joint income is taken into account. See p220 and Chapter 21 for further information; *and*

- the threshold that applies to you (see below).

The elements and threshold can be increased every April.

Maximum child tax credit

Your maximum CTC is calculated by adding together all the elements that apply to you.[5] The elements and rates for 2010/11 are shown in the table below. Note that HM Revenue and Customs (the Revenue) works out your entitlement by using daily rates of the elements for which you qualify.

	Maximum annual amount	Daily rates
Family element (one per family)	£545	£1.50
Baby element (one per child under one year old)	£545	£1.50
Child element (one per child)	£2,300	£6.30
Disabled child element (one per child in receipt of disability living allowance or registered blind)	£2,715	£7.44
Severely disabled child element (one per child in receipt of the highest rate care component of disability living allowance)	£1,095	£3.00

Calculating child tax credit

You automatically qualify for maximum CTC if you are on income support, income-based jobseeker's allowance or pension credit. In all other cases, to work out the amount of your CTC, the Revenue compares your income with your threshold. If you qualify for CTC on its own, the threshold is £16,190. However, if you qualify for CTC and working tax credit (WTC), the threshold is £6,420.

If your income is the same as or lower than the threshold, you get maximum CTC. If your income is higher than the threshold, maximum CTC is reduced by 39 per cent of the excess.[6]

If you qualify for WTC (see Chapter 19) as well as CTC, the elements are tapered away in the following order:
- WTC elements (other than the childcare element); *then*
- WTC childcare element; *then*
- CTC child elements (other than the family element – including the baby element if relevant).

The family element of CTC (including the baby element) is not reduced unless your annual income is higher than £50,000. At this point, the family element is tapered away at a rate of £1 for every £15 of income you have over £50,000 (6.67 per cent).

Note, however, the Government proposes to reduce the income threshold to £40,000 from April 2011.

Examples

Mhairi has two children, James aged two and Meena aged four. Meena has asthma and gets the lowest rate care component of disability living allowance. Mhairi's maximum CTC for the tax year April 2010 to April 2011 includes two child elements, a family element and a disabled child element (for Meena). Whether she gets the maximum CTC or a reduced amount depends on her income.

Agnes applies for CTC in May 2010. She has a four-year-old daughter, Lizzie. Agnes' income for tax credits purposes in the tax year 2009/10 was £17,190, £1,000 over the threshold. Her income in 2010/11 will be only slightly higher, so the previous year's income is used to estimate her tax credits.

Agnes' estimated entitlement to CTC for the tax year 6 April 2010 to 5 April 2011 is calculated as follows:

	£
Maximum CTC	
Child element	2,300
Family element	545
Total	**2,845**

Compare income to threshold: £17,190 – £16,190 = £1,000.
Apply 39 per cent to the excess: 39 per cent x £1,000 = £390.
Deduct excess from maximum CTC: £2,845 – £390 = £2,455.
Agnes will receive £2,455 over the year.

Treatment of income

How income affects tax credits is covered in Chapter 21. It is important to remember that:

- most student income is fully disregarded when calculating entitlement to tax credits;
- income is calculated annually over a complete tax year (from 6 April to 5 April);
- the amount of income used to calculate CTC is worked out by comparing income in the current tax year with that in the previous tax year. Then, if income has:[7]
  - gone down, CTC is calculated using current-year income;
  - stayed the same or has increased by £25,000 or less, CTC is calculated using the previous year's income;
  - increased by more than £25,000, CTC is calculated using the current year's income, but deducting £25,000.

Examples

Antonio is a mature student. He is a lone parent with one child, Eva. In the tax year 2009/10 he was working full time and got a good salary. He starts university in September 2010 and now his only income apart from child benefit is his student loan, special support grant, parents' learning allowance and childcare grant. He claims and is awarded CTC. The amount he is awarded is equivalent to the family element (pro rata from three months before his claim) based on his earnings in 2009/10. Antonio phones the Tax Credit Helpline and gives details of his student support. The Revenue reassesses his CTC. Because his current year's income is less than that in the previous year, and is below the threshold, he is awarded maximum CTC.

Dosh is a lone parent and has a daughter, Sylvie, who is one. Dosh was getting income support (IS) before she became a student. She now gets a student loan, a special support grant, a parents' learning allowance and has part-time earnings of £5,000. She claims CTC and is awarded maximum CTC based on the IS she was getting in 2009/10. As regards her income for 2010/11, her student support is disregarded for the tax credit calculation, but her part-time earnings are taken into account. However, although her actual income in 2010/11 has gone up since the previous year, the increase is less than £25,000. Her CTC award is therefore still based on the previous year's income and Dosh is still entitled to maximum CTC.

4. **Claiming child tax credit**

Your first claim for tax credits must be made in writing on Form TC600. You use the same form for both child tax credit (CTC) and working tax credit (WTC). If you are a member of a couple, you must make a joint claim with your partner. It is very important to claim in time. A claim for tax credits can be backdated for a maximum of three months.[8] Unlike for means-tested benefits, you do not have to show any reasons for your delay.

Forms are available directly from the Tax Credit Office and from HM Revenue and Customs (the Revenue) enquiry centres, Jobcentre Plus offices, some money advice centres, Citizens Advice Bureaux, or institutions' finance offices or student services departments.

There is no section on the claim form to list student income, so it should be included in 'other'. You should only enter that part of student income that is taken into account for tax credits; disregarded income should not be listed on the form. Thus, only dependants' allowances paid by local authorities, certain bursaries or grants, or any professional and career development loan paid for living costs should be entered as income. All other student income, including loans, grants, bursaries, childcare grants, travel, books and equipment grants, and all discretionary funds, should be ignored and not entered. See Chapter 21 for a list of what student income is disregarded. If you are unsure of what to include, you should contact your students' union or association, or your institution's student adviser.

You should send the completed form to the Tax Credit Office. It can also be sent if necessary to any Jobcentre Plus office, Department for Work and Pensions office or Revenue enquiry centre.[9] You might be able to claim online on the Revenue website. However, at the time of writing, this service had been suspended.

Renewal awards

At the end of the tax year in which you claimed CTC, you (and your partner if you are a member of a couple), receive a 'final notice' from the Revenue asking you to confirm that your income and/or your household circumstances are as stated for the tax year just passed. The deadline is 31 July. The Revenue then makes a final decision, based on your actual income during the tax year. It decides whether you were entitled to CTC and, if so, the amount of your award. This is known as the 'end of year review'. The Revenue uses this information to renew your award for the next tax year.

Getting paid

CTC is usually paid directly into the bank account (or similar account) of whoever is deemed to be the main carer of your child(ren). Which account it goes into is up to you. If you do not want your benefit to go into an account that is overdrawn, give the Revenue details of an alternative account if you have access to, or can open, one.

If you are overpaid CTC, you might have to repay it. See below if you want to challenge a decision.

5. **Challenging a decision**

If you think a decision about your child tax credit, is wrong (eg, because the decision maker got the facts or law wrong), there are a number of ways you can try to get the decision changed.

- You can seek a revision of the decision if your circumstances have changed or HM Revenue and Customs (the Revenue) has reasonable grounds for believing you are entitled to tax credits at a different rate or there has been an official error.
- You can appeal to an independent tribunal. There are strict time limits for appealing – normally 30 days from the date on the decision letter. You can make a late appeal in limited circumstances.

If you are considering challenging a decision, you should seek advice as soon as possible.

Disputing recovery of an overpayment

A big source of difficulty is tax credit overpayments. All tax credit overpayments are recoverable and there is no right of appeal against a decision to recover an overpayment. However, the Revenue should use its discretion when deciding whether to recover the overpayment. Factors such as hardship and official error must be taken into account. It is always worth disputing whether an overpayment should be recovered, as the Revenue suspends recovery while it considers the situation. You should do this on Form TC846.

If an overpayment is recovered, this is usually done by reducing ongoing tax credit payments. There are maximum amounts by which payments can be reduced. These are:

- 10 per cent, if you get a maximum award;
- 100 per cent, if you only get the family element of child tax credit;
- 25 per cent, in all other cases.

Note: there is a right of appeal against the decision about entitlement to tax credits – ie, whether you have been overpaid.

---

6. **Other benefits and tax credits**

Child tax credit (CTC) does not count as income when calculating your entitlement to income support (IS), jobseeker's allowance (JSA) and pension credit (PC), but working tax credit (WTC) does. CTC (unless you are on IS or income-based JSA or are 60 or over) and WTC are taken into account as income for housing benefit and council tax benefit. If you get arrears of CTC, these count as capital and can be disregarded for a year for means-tested benefit purposes. This is also the case for arrears of WTC, except for PC purposes.

If you are entitled to CTC, you may also qualify for:

- health benefits (see Chapter 11). You do not have to satisfy the income test for these if your gross annual income is £15,276 or less;
- education benefits, such as free school lunches. You do not have to satisfy the income test if you are getting CTC (but not WTC) and your gross annual income is £16,190 or less.

You may also be entitled to a Sure Start maternity grant and a social fund funeral expenses payment if you are awarded CTC at a rate which exceeds the family element.

Notes

1. What is child tax credit
1 Budget 2010, 22 June 2010, para 2.37-
2.42

2. Who is eligible
2 ss3(3) and (7), 8 and 42 TCA 2002; regs
3-5 CTC Regs; reg 3 TC(R) Regs; reg 3
TC(I) Regs
3 s8(3) TCA 2002; regs 2 and 4 CTC Regs
4 s8(4) TCA 2002; regs 2 and 5 CTC Regs

3. Amount of child tax credit
5 s9 TCA 2002; reg 7 CTC Regs
6 Reg 8 TC(ITDR) Regs
7 s7(3) TCA 2002

4. Claiming child tax credit
8 Reg 7 TC(CN) Regs
9 Regs 2 and 5 TC(CN) Regs

Chapter 19

Working tax credit

This chapter covers:
1. What is working tax credit (below)
2. Who is eligible (p226)
3. Amount of working tax credit (p227)
4. Claiming working tax credit (p230)
5. Challenging a decision (p231)
6. Tax credits and benefits (p231)

Basic facts
– Working tax credit (WTC) is paid to top up low wages.
– Both part-time and full-time students can qualify if they satisfy the rules of entitlement.
– WTC includes an amount to help you with childcare costs.
– The amount you get is affected by your income, but most student support is ignored when working this out.
– Tax credit claims are administered by HM Revenue and Customs.

1. What is working tax credit

Further information
This chapter gives an outline of the working tax credit rules and focuses on issues relevant to students. For more detailed information on the rules, see CPAG's *Welfare Benefits and Tax Credits Handbook*.

Working tax credit (WTC) is paid to people in low-paid work to top up wages and help with expenses, including childcare costs, associated with being in work. WTC is administered by HM Revenue and Customs (the Revenue). Claims are assessed on an annual basis, usually based on your income and that of your partner (of either sex) over the previous tax year.

Being a student does not affect your entitlement to WTC. You can qualify for WTC so long as you satisfy the rules of entitlement. Note, however, that you cannot receive both the higher education childcare grant (or NHS childcare allowance) and the WTC childcare element (see p228).

More information about tax credits is available on the Revenue's website. A tax credit calculator is available at www.hmrc.gov.uk/taxcredits/calculator.htm. The Revenue also runs a helpline on 0845 300 3900; textphone 0845 300 3909.

Proposed changes

The Government plans a number of changes to tax credits from April 2011. These are outlined on p217.

In addition, for WTC it is proposed that from April 2011 people aged over 60 will qualify for working tax credit (WTC) if they work at least 16 hours a week, rather than 30 hours as is currently the case.[1]

2. **Who is eligible**

You qualify for working tax credit (WTC) if:[2]
- you (and your partner) are 16 or over; *and*
- you (or your partner) are in full-time paid work, that is:
  - you (or your partner) are responsible for a child or qualifying young person and you work at least 16 hours a week; *or*
  - you have a disability which puts you at a disadvantage in getting a job, you qualify for a WTC disability element and work at least 16 hours a week. You qualify for a disability element if you get or have been getting specific benefits; *or*
  - you are 25 or over and work 30 hours a week; *or*
  - you (or your partner) are 50 or over, have been claiming a qualifying benefit (eg, income support, jobseeker's allowance or incapacity benefit) for at least six months and now work more than 16 hours a week; *and*
- you satisfy presence and residence tests; *and*
- you are not subject to immigration control for tax credit purposes. Further advice is available from the UK Council for International Student Affairs (UKCISA – see Appendix 2); *and*
- you are not claiming employment and support allowance; *and*
- you have a low income (see p229).

You must be actually working, or have accepted an offer of work which is expected to start within seven days. The work must be expected to last for at least four weeks.

Note: in some cases you can be treated as if you are in full-time paid work when you are not, or as if you are not in full-time paid work even if you are. In particular, you are treated as in full-time paid work for the four weeks immediately after you stop working at least 16 hours a week, so long as you counted as being in full-time paid work before stopping. If you are unsure whether you count as being in full-time paid work, seek advice.

Students and working tax credit

You are not excluded from claiming WTC simply because you are a student. However, you must count as being in full-time paid work. So if, for example, you do sufficient hours of paid work (16 or 30 as the case may be) in addition to your studies or during the holidays, you can qualify for WTC. Remember that the work must be expected to last for four weeks.

Any work you do in studying for a degree or other qualification does not count as full-time paid work – any grant or loan you receive is for your maintenance and not paid in return for work done on the course. You are also not in full-time paid work if you are a student nurse because the NHS bursary and other grants or loans you get are not payments for work done on the course and do not count as income for tax credit purposes.[3] However, if you are paid in return for the work you do (eg, you are paid by an employer during a work placement), and you work sufficient hours, you could argue that you are in full-time paid work. There are a number of situations when you do not count as in full-time paid work even if you are – eg, if you are on a government training scheme being paid a training allowance.

When calculating how much WTC you can get, student loans and most other student income are disregarded. See Chapter 21 for how income affects tax credits.

Examples
Sian is aged 26. She does not work during the academic year but in the summer vacation she gets a job for 30 hours a week and expects to work for nine weeks. Sian qualifies for WTC. Whether any WTC is payable depends on the level of her wages and other income.

Katherine and Spencer have a four-year-old child at nursery school. Katherine is a student and Spencer works 20 hours a week. Katherine works 16 hours a week during the summer only. They qualify for WTC throughout the year. During the summer they can get a 30-hour element included in their WTC and they can also get a childcare element (for help with nursery charges), but only if Katherine is not in receipt of the childcare grant.

3. **Amount of working tax credit**

The amount of working tax credit (WTC) you get depends on:
- your maximum WTC. This is made up of a combination of 'elements' (see p228);

- how much income you have. If you have a partner, your joint income is taken into account. See p229 and Chapter 21 for further information; *and*
- the threshold that applies to you (see p229).

The elements and threshold can be increased every April.

Maximum working tax credit

Your maximum WTC is calculated by adding together all the elements that apply to you.[4] The elements and rates for 2010/11 are shown in the table below. Note that HM Revenue and Customs (the Revenue) works out your entitlement by using daily rates of the elements for which you qualify.

	Maximum annual amount	Daily rates
Basic element	£1,920	£5.26
Lone parent or couple element	£1,890	£5.22
30-hour element	£790	£2.17
Disability element	£2,570	£7.05
Severe disability element	£1,095	£3.00
50+ return to work element (16–29 hours)	£1,320	£3.62
50+ return to work element (30+ hours)	£1,965	£5.39
Childcare element (one child)	Max £140.00	
Childcare element (two or more children)	Max £240.00	

Childcare costs

The childcare element of WTC is 80 per cent of the weekly 'relevant childcare charges' you pay for your child(ren). The maximum weekly amount payable is 80 per cent of £175 (£140 a week) if you have one child, or 80 per cent of £300 (£240 a week) if you have two or more children.[5]

You qualify for a childcare element if you incur 'relevant childcare charges' and:[6]

- you are a lone parent and in full-time paid work (see p226); *or*
- you are a member of a couple and:
  – you are both in full-time paid work (see p226); *or*
  – one of you is in full-time paid work (see p226) and the other is incapacitated, in hospital or in prison.

You can only get a childcare element to help meet the cost of 'relevant childcare charges'. This means the childcare must be provided by, for example, a registered childminder, a nursery, an after-school club or a local authority daycare service.

Note: you cannot get a higher education (HE) childcare grant or NHS childcare allowance if you have chosen to get a WTC childcare element. The HE childcare grant and NHS childcare allowance pay a higher percentage of childcare costs (85 per cent) and it can be paid year-round, so it is usually better to apply for this.[7]

Calculating working tax credit

To work out the amount of your WTC, the Revenue compares your income to your threshold. If you qualify for WTC, either on its own or with child tax credit (CTC), the threshold is £6,420. See p219 for information about how the threshold is applied if you also qualify for CTC.

If your income is the same as, or lower than, the threshold, you get maximum WTC. If your income is higher than the threshold, maximum WTC is reduced by 39 per cent of the excess.[8]

Note: you automatically qualify for maximum WTC if you are on income support (IS), income-based jobseeker's allowance (JSA) or pension credit. In practice, however, there are not many situations when you can claim IS or income-based JSA at the same time as WTC.

Example
Steph is 37. She is a part-time student, but also works 31 hours a week. She qualifies for WTC. Steph's maximum WTC includes a basic element and a 30-hour element.

Treatment of income

The way that income affects tax credits is covered in Chapter 21. It is important to remember that:

- most student income is fully disregarded when calculating entitlement to tax credits;
- income is calculated annually over a complete tax year (from 6 April to 5 April);
- the amount of income used to calculate WTC is worked out by comparing income in the current tax year with that in the previous tax year. If income has:[9]
  - gone down, WTC is calculated using the current year's income;
  - stayed the same or has increased by £25,000 or less, WTC is calculated using the previous year's income;
  - increased by more than £25,000, WTC is calculated using the current year's income but deducting £25,000.

Examples
Chrystal is a student. Her partner, Jerome, is working 35 hours a week. In the tax year 2009/10 Jerome was working part time and earned £9,000. In 2010/11, he will earn £22,000. Their only other income (both in the previous and current year) is Chrystal's student support. They claim and are awarded WTC. The Revenue calculates their award

based on Jerome's earnings in 2009/10. This is because, although their income has gone up, the increase is less than £25,000.

Note that if their circumstances do not change, they are unlikely to qualify for WTC in 2011/12. This is because the calculation will then be based on their income in 2010/11.

Naveed is 36 and is the lone parent of one child aged 15. He is a part-time student. He also works 21 hours a week. He qualifies for both CTC and WTC. His income for tax credit purposes in the tax year 2009/10 was £18,000. His income in 2010/11 will be about £18,700 so the previous year's income is used to estimate his tax credits, as this is not more than £25,000 higher than last year.

Naveed's estimated entitlement to CTC and WTC for the tax year 6 April 2010 to 5 April 2011 is calculated as follows.

	£
CTC family element	545
CTC child element	2,300
WTC basic element	1,920
WTC lone parent element	1,890
Total	**6,655**

Compare income to threshold: £18,000–£6,420 = £11,580
Apply 39 per cent to the excess: 39% x £11,580 = £4,516.20
Deduct excess from maximum WTC: £6,655–£4,516.20 = £2,138.80

Naveed receives tax credits of £2,138.80 over the year.

4. **Claiming working tax credit**

For further information about claiming working tax credit (WTC) and about renewal awards, see p221. The rules are the same as for child tax credit.

Getting paid

WTC (other than the childcare element) is usually paid directly into your bank (or similar) account. WTC childcare element is paid into the account of whomever is deemed to be the main carer of your child(ren). Which account it goes into is up to you. If you do not want your benefit to go into an account that is overdrawn, give HM Revenue and Customs details of an alternative account if you have access to, or can open, one.

If you are overpaid WTC, you might have to repay it. See p231 if you want to challenge a decision.

5. Challenging a decision

If you think a decision about your working tax credit, is wrong (eg, because the decision maker got the facts or law wrong), there are a number of ways you can try to get the decision changed.

- You can seek a revision of the decision if your circumstances have changed or HM Revenue and Customs has reasonable grounds for believing you are entitled to tax credits at a different rate or there has been an official error.
- You can appeal to an independent tribunal. There are strict time limits for appealing – normally 30 days from the date you are sent or given the decision. You can make a late appeal in limited circumstances.

If you are considering challenging a decision, you should seek advice as soon as possible.

A big source of difficulty is tax credit overpayments. See p223 for information. The issues are the same as for child tax credit.

6. Tax credits and benefits

See p223 for information. The issues are the same as for child tax credit (CTC).

If you are entitled to working tax credit (WTC), you may also qualify for health benefits (see Chapter 11). You do not have to satisfy the income test for these if your gross annual income is £15,276 or less and your WTC includes a disability or a severe disability element, or you get CTC as well as WTC.

You may also be entitled to a Sure Start maternity grant and a social fund funeral expenses payment if your WTC award includes the disability or severe disability element.

Notes

1. What is working tax credit
 1 Budget 2010, 22 June 2010, para 2.121

2. Who is eligible
 2 ss3(3) and (7), 10 and 42 TCA 2002 and regs 4-8 WTC(EMR) Regs; reg 3 TC(R) Regs; reg 3 TC(I) Regs
 3 R(FIS) 1/83; R(FIS) 1/86; para 02403 TCTM, 'Student nurses'

3. Amount of working tax credit
 4 s11 TCA 2002; regs 3 and 20 and Sch 2 WTC(EMR) Regs
 5 Reg 20(3) WTC(EMR) Regs
 6 Regs 13 and 14 WTC(EMR) Regs
 7 Reg 45(3) E(SS) Regs
 8 Reg 7 TC(ITDR) Regs
 9 s7(3) TCA 2002

Part 3

Treatment of student income

Chapter 20

....

How income affects means-tested benefits

This chapter covers:
1. Working out your income (p236)
2. Loans and grants (p237)
3. Dividing income throughout the year (p242)
4. Hardship funds and other payments (p249)
5. Earnings (p250)
6. Benefits and tax credits (p251)
7. Maintenance (p252)
8. Savings and capital (p252)

This chapter explains how your weekly income affects your entitlement to means-tested benefits – income support (IS), income-related employment and support allowance (ESA), income-based jobseeker's allowance (JSA), housing benefit (HB) and council tax benefit (CTB). It explains how much of your student support is taken into account and how much can be disregarded, and considers how other types of income, such as earnings, are treated. It applies to both full- and part-time students.

If you, or your partner if you have one, have reached the qualifying age for pension credit (PC) (see p165) and are not getting IS or income-based JSA, your student support is ignored as income for HB and CTB.

The way your income is assessed for tax credits and health benefits is different (see Chapters 21 and 22).

....

Basic facts
– Student loans for living costs are normally divided over 42 or 43 weeks from the beginning of September to the end of June (for students starting their course in the autumn) and taken into account as income for means-tested benefits during that period. If your income is too high, you will not get IS, ESA or income-based JSA over those weeks, and your HB or CTB will be reduced.
– Student loans for living costs are normally *not* taken into account as income for means-tested benefits from around the end of June until the beginning of September. You may

be able to get IS or more HB during these months even if your income was too high during the academic year.
– Some student support does not affect the amount of ESA/IS/JSA or HB/CTB you receive.

1. Working out your income

The way that student income is taken into account for income support (IS), employment and support allowance (ESA), income-based jobseeker's allowance, housing benefit (HB) and council tax benefit is essentially the same. Chapters 10, 14 and 12 take you through the ESA, IS and HB assessments step by step. This chapter explains how much weekly income counts in those assessments.

Calculating income for means-tested benefits

Step 1   **Add together annual income from grants and loans.**
Add together the annual amount of any student grants and/or loans for living costs, ignoring elements that are wholly disregarded.

Step 2   **Apply annual disregards.**
From the total annual grants and loans for living costs, deduct disregarded amounts for books, equipment and travel.

Step 3   **Divide income into weekly amount.**
Divide the annual amount of grants and loans for living costs by the number of benefit weeks in the period over which the grant and loan are counted as income for benefit purposes.

Step 4   **Deduct any weekly disregard.**
If you have a student loan for living costs, deduct £10 a week – this is the weekly disregard. If you have a regular hardship fund payment for living costs, deduct £20 a week, or £10 a week if you are also eligible to receive a student loan for living costs.

Step 5   **Add other income to weekly amount of grant and loan for living costs.**
Add together any other weekly income – eg, from hardship funds (p252), professional and career development loans (p250), earnings (p250), tariff income from capital (p252), benefits and tax credits (p251) – ignoring any amount that is disregarded. This total, added to the weekly grant and loan total in Step 4, is the amount of income used in the benefit assessment.

If you want to work out benefit entitlement during the long vacation, p242 explains when the long vacation starts and finishes for benefit purposes – ie, when your student loan or grant counts as nil income. You should then total up on a weekly basis any other income that you have over the vacation.

2. **Loans and grants**

Student loan for fees

Loans for fees are disregarded.[1]

Student loan for living costs

You should include in the student loan:
- the maximum loan for which you are eligible. This is taken into account as your income whether or not you apply for it.[2] This means that students cannot choose to apply for maximum income support (IS) rather than applying for a loan. You will simply be treated as though you had taken out the full loan and your benefit will be reduced accordingly;
- the assessed contribution from a parent or partner, whether or not you receive it. For IS, however, if you are a lone parent or a disabled student, you should only include contributions that are actually paid;[3]
- any payments for extra weeks' attendance.

You should deduct from the annual student loan the following disregarded amounts:[4]
- £390 for books and equipment;
- £303 for travel.

There is a further disregard of £10 a week that applies once the student loan has been divided into the relevant weekly amount (see p242).

Professional and career development loans

How professional and career development loans are treated depends on what they are paid for. Disregard any amounts paid for:
- tuition fees;
- course costs.

Any amounts paid for living costs are treated as income. This amount should be divided over the period for which the loan is paid.[5]

Professional studies loans

Loans paid to postgraduate students by banks for vocational study are treated in the same way as professional and career development loans (see above).

Grants

In general, grants intended for living costs are taken into account as income, and grants for other costs (such as books, travel, equipment, childcare or course-related support for disabilities) are disregarded. For the way that hardship funds are treated, see p249.

If you are a full-time undergraduate assessed for support in England, Wales or Northern Ireland and receive a special support grant (eg, if you are a lone parent – see Chapter 2), this is disregarded as it is paid for course-related costs.[6] If you receive a maintenance grant (eg, if you are the partner of a jobseeker's allowance (JSA) or IS claimant), this is taken into account in full as it is paid for living costs.

If you are *not* eligible for a student loan, deduct from your grant the following disregarded amounts:

- £390 for books and equipment;
- £303 for travel.

Grants in higher education

The following higher education (HE) grants are completely **disregarded**:

- grant for tuition fees;[7]
- HE grant for full-time undergraduate students under the 'old system' in England and Wales;[8]
- special support grant for full-time undergraduate students in England, Wales and Northern Ireland;[9]
- childcare grant;
- disabled students' allowance;[10]
- Welsh Assembly learning grant for 'old system' students;
- Welsh individual learning account payments;[11]
- parents' learning allowance;
- travel expenses;[12]
- course costs grant for part-time undergraduate students;[13]
- institutional bursaries paid for anything other than living costs.[14]

The following grants are **taken into account**:

- maintenance grant for full-time undergraduate students assessed in England and Northern Ireland;
- Assembly learning grant for 'current system' students in Wales;
- maintenance bursary for full-time 'old system' undergraduate students assessed in Northern Ireland;
- adult dependants' grant;
- institutional bursaries paid for living costs.

Healthcare student allowances

Take into account the following:

- means-tested NHS bursary for degree-level healthcare courses in England and Wales;
- means-tested Department of Health, Social Services and Public Safety (DHSSPS) bursary for degree-level healthcare courses in Northern Ireland;

- non-means-tested NHS bursary for nursing, midwifery or operation department practitioner students in England and degree-level nursing courses in Wales;
- non-means tested DHSSPS bursary for nursing and midwifery students in Northern Ireland;
- dependant's grants for healthcare students (for housing benefit (HB) and council tax benefit (CTB), and some existing ESA, IS and JSA claimants with no child tax credit (CTC) award);[15]
- single parent's allowance or addition.

Disregard the following grants:
- childcare allowances;
- disabled students' allowance;[16]
- parents' learning allowance;
- travel expenses.[17]

Other grants for vocational courses

Take into account the following:
- NHS social work student bursary in England;[18]
- Care Council for Wales (CCW) social work student bursary in Wales;
- initial teacher training incentive bursaries.[19]

Disregard the following grants:
- DHSSPS social work incentive bursary in Northern Ireland;
- travel expenses.

Postgraduate grants

Postgraduate maintenance grants and dependants' grants awarded by a research council, or for postgraduate social work students, are taken into account in the same way as for undergraduates (see p238). You should **ignore** the following:
- disabled students' allowance;
- grants for tuition fees;
- grants for residential study away from your normal home;
- grants intended to meet the costs of books and equipment.

Grants in further education

The following further education (FE) grants are **disregarded**:
- education maintenance allowance;[20]
- Care to Learn grants paid for childcare costs;
- childcare bursaries paid through the discretionary support funds;

- residential bursaries paid through the discretionary support funds (ESA/IS/JSA only);
- Welsh Assembly learning grant for further education;
- the Northern Irish FE grant;

- additional grant allowances for disabled students;
- the first £693 per year (equivalent to the travel, books and equipment disregard) of the adult learning grant, which may be disregarded for HB and CTB at the discretion of the local authority.[21] **Note:** you cannot receive both an adult learning grant and JSA.[22]

The following grants are **taken into account** in full:

- the adult learning grant, subject to the standard disregard for travel, books and equipment;
- the maintenance element only of FE and advanced FE awards in Northern Ireland, subject to the standard disregard for travel, books and equipment.

Discretionary funds

Discretionary funds paid by colleges and universities for course or living costs may be called hardship funds, the Access to Learning Fund, Financial Contingency Fund or other discretionary support funds. If these funds are paid for course costs, they should be disregarded. If they are paid for living costs, they should be treated as capital if paid in a lump sum,[23] or as income if paid regularly.[24] Your university should be able to give you a letter for the relevant benefit office explaining the purpose of the payment.

Grants and loans checklist

Student support	Treatment
Further education income	
Adult learning grant	Disregarded are:
	– £390 a year books and equipment;
	– £303 a year travel
	Note: you cannot receive both an adult learning grant and JSA.
Care to Learn grants	Disregarded
Education maintenance allowance	Disregarded
Discretionary support funds/ Financial Contingency Fund/ hardship funds	Taken into account if paid for basic living costs regularly, disregarded if paid for other items
Northern Ireland FE bursaries	Disregarded are:
	– £390 a year books and equipment;
	– £303 a year travel
Welsh Assembly learning grant for further education	Disregarded

Undergraduate income

Access to Learning Fund grant	Taken into account if paid for basic living costs (as capital if not regular payments), disregarded if paid for other items
Adult dependant's grant	Taken into account in full
Care leavers' vacation grant (Northern Ireland)	Taken into account in full
Childcare grant	Disregarded
Disabled students' allowance	Disregarded
Financial Contingency Fund grant	Taken into account if paid for basic living costs (as capital if not regular payments), disregarded if paid for other items
HE grant (full-time undergraduates in 'old system')	Disregarded
HE special support grant (full-time undergraduates in 'current system')	Disregarded
HE maintenance grant (full-time undergraduates in 'current system')	Taken into account in full
Course costs grant (part-time undergraduates)	Usually disregarded (as it is less than the general books/equipment and travel disregards)
Hardship funds	Taken into account if paid for basic living costs (as capital if not regular payments), disregarded if paid for other items
NHS bursary/nursing and midwifery bursary	Taken in account, except: – £390 a year books and equipment; – £303 a year travel
NHS dependant's grant	Taken into account
Parents' learning allowance	Disregarded
Social work bursary in England and Wales	Disregard any element for non-living costs such as travel or tuition fee costs; take into account the remainder in full
Social work bursary in Northern Ireland	Disregarded
Student loan for fees	Disregarded
Student loan for living costs	Disregarded are: – £390 a year books and equipment; – £303 a year travel; – £10 a week; – amount of student's contribution to loan disregarded as non-loan income; – partner's contribution disregarded from her/his income

Travelling expenses	Disregarded
Welsh Assembly learning grant (full-time undergraduates in 'old system')	Disregarded
Welsh Assembly learning grant (full-time undergraduates in 'current system')	Taken into account in full

Postgraduate income

Research council tuition fees	Disregarded
Research council maintenance grant	Disregarded are: – £390 a year books and equipment; – £303 a year travel
Research supplementary grants	As for undergraduate income
Social work bursaries	Taken into account in full
Teaching training salaries	Taken into account in full

Other

Professional and career development loan	Disregarded: tuition and course cost payments Taken into account: payments for living costs
Professional study loan	Disregarded: tuition and course cost payments Taken into account: payments for living costs
Institutional bursaries	Disregarded: tuition and course cost payments Taken into account: payments for living costs

3. Dividing income throughout the year

The annual amount of your loan and grant is divided over the number of weeks in, usually, a standard academic year to arrive at the weekly amount that is used in the calculation of income-related employment and support allowance (ESA), income support (IS), income-based jobseeker's allowance (JSA), housing benefit (HB) and council tax benefit (CTB). Rules specify exactly the weeks over which the loan and grant are taken into account.

If your loan covers extra weeks of study beyond the usual academic year, that part of the loan is just included in with the rest of the loan. It does not extend the number of weeks over which your loan is taken into account for benefit purposes.

Student loans for living costs

For autumn term starters, student loans are normally divided over 42 or 43 weeks from the beginning of September to the end of June. During this period your student loan is taken into account as your income in the assessment of income-related ESA, IS, income-based JSA, HB and CTB. If your income is too high, you will not be eligible for these benefits. However, your student loan is not taken into account from around the end of June to the beginning of September. Because your income goes down in these months (unless you have other income – eg, earnings), you may be able to get benefit during the summer. It is important, therefore, to make a claim from the end of June even if you were refused benefit at the start of the academic year. Make your claim in mid-June or earlier so that your benefit can start as soon as you are entitled.

Courses starting in the autumn term lasting more than a year

The student loan is divided over the number of weeks starting from the first day of the first benefit week in September until the last day of the last benefit week in June.[25] In 2010/11 this is 42 weeks. The day that starts the 'benefit week' is the same as the payday for that benefit. For HB and CTB this is a Monday.[26] For IS and JSA it is usually the day on which you first claimed.

This is the period over which your loan is taken into account as income in the benefit assessment, unless you do not count as a student at all. For example, at the start of your first year, you do not count as being a student until you actually start attending or undertaking the course. In other words, in the first year, the loan is still divided over 42/43 weeks, but the weekly amount arrived at is ignored as income until you start your course.

In the final year of study, the loan is divided over the number of benefit weeks starting from the first day of the first benefit week in September until the end of the benefit week on or before the last day of the final academic term.[27]

Example: first year, 'current system', higher education student in England
Jean is in her first year at an institution in England. She has one child aged two and is claiming HB as a lone parent. She gets a loan of £3,290 for her fees, a student loan for living costs of £6,928 for studying in London. She also gets a special support grant of £2,906, a parents' learning allowance of £1,508 and a childcare grant of £100 a week, all of which are disregarded for IS and HB.
Her first term begins on Monday 4 October 2010. Her IS benefit week starts on a Monday. Her student loan is divided over the weeks from Monday 6 September 2010 until Sunday 26 June 2011 (42 weeks). However, as she is a first-year student, her loan is not taken into account until she starts her course on Monday 5 October. So, from Monday 6 September until Sunday 3 October 2010, her student loan income will not be taken into account for benefit purposes. From Monday 4 October 2010 to Sunday 26 June 2011 her student loan income is £138.45 for benefit purposes. From Monday 27 June until Sunday 4 September 2011 her student loan income is nil again for benefit purposes.

	£
The weekly loan income taken into account is:	
Loan	6,928.00
Less disregards for books and equipment (£390)	
and travel (£303)	6,235.00
Divided by 42 weeks	148.45
Less £10 weekly loan disregard	138.45

£138.45 is taken into account as weekly income from her loan between 5 October 2009 and 27 June 2010. She also receives £54.67 a week child tax credit and £20.30 child benefit, which brings her weekly income for HB purposes to £213.42.

Her IS applicable amount is £65.45 and her HB applicable amount is £140.42 a week. From Monday 4 October 2010 to Sunday 26 June 2011 she is not entitled to IS because her income is higher than the IS applicable amount. From Monday 27 June until Sunday 4 September 2011 her weekly income from her loan and grants is nil. Jean should claim again on 27 June 2011.

Example: final year, 'current system' higher education student in Northern Ireland

Graham is in his final year. He is claiming IS as a disabled student studying at an institution in Northern Ireland. He gets a student loan of £4,480. His parents are assessed to make a contribution of £890 towards his living costs, but this year they are refusing to pay. His parental contribution is not taken into account because he is a disabled student.

His first term started on Tuesday 14 September 2010 and his final term ends on Friday 10 June 2011. His student loan is divided over the weeks from Monday 6 September 2010 until Sunday 5 June 2011 (40 weeks).

	£
The weekly loan income taken into account is:	
Loan	4,480.00
Less disregards for books and equipment (£390)	
and travel (£303)	3,787.00
Divided by 40 weeks	94.68
Less £10 weekly loan disregard	84.68

£84.68 is taken into account as weekly income from his loan between 6 September 2010 and 5 June 2011.

For examples of calculations for 'old system' students, see the 2006/07 edition of this *Handbook*.

Courses not starting in the autumn term

Your student loan is divided over the number of weeks starting from the first day of the first benefit week on or after the beginning of a standard academic year and ending on the last day of the last benefit week on or before the last day of the academic year, but excluding benefit weeks that fall entirely within the quarter that is taken by the Department for Work and Pensions (DWP) to be the longest vacation.[28] '**Academic years**' in this case are 12 months beginning on 1 January, 1 April or 1 July for courses that begin in winter, spring or summer respectively.[29] '**Quarters**' are 1 January to 31 March, 1 April to 30 June, 1 July to 31 August, 1 September to 31 December.[30]

> *Example*
>
> Anya's course begins on Monday 3 January 2011. The main vacation is 11 June to 18 September 2011. She is claiming HB. Her loan is divided over the weeks from Monday 3 January 2011 to Sunday 26 June 2011 and from Monday 5 September 2011 until Sunday 25 December 2011. From 27 June 2011 to 4 September 2011 her student loan income will be nil for benefit purposes.

Courses lasting one year or less

Your loan is divided over the number of weeks from the first day of the first benefit week on or after the start of a standard academic year until the last day of the last benefit week on or before the last day of the final term. The academic year is taken to begin on 1 September, 1 January, 1 April or 1 July, depending on whether your course begins in the autumn, winter, spring or summer. The resulting weekly amount is then taken into account from the point you actually start attending or undertaking the course.

If you leave your course early

If you abandon your course early or are dismissed from it before you have had the final instalment of your student loan in that academic year, the loan continues to be taken into account up until the end of the term in which you leave. The end of term is taken to be the end of December if you leave in the autumn term, the end of March if you leave in the winter term, the end of June if you leave in the spring term and the end of August if you leave in the summer.

The amount of loan taken into account is that which remains from the loan that was paid from the start of the standard academic year (eg, 1 September for students whose courses begin in the autumn – see p242) to the end of the term in which you left, having subtracted that part of the loan (including disregards for books, equipment and travel) that would have been treated as your weekly income in a normal benefits calculation up until the day you left.[31] The examples below illustrate how this amount is calculated.[32]

> *Example*
>
> Nick studies in Birmingham. He abandons his course on 1 November 2010. He is in the second year of a three-year course and is claiming IS. His benefit week starts on a Monday.

Work out weekly amount of annual loan

	£
Loan	4,950.00
Less disregards (£693)	4,257.00
Divided by 42 weeks	101.36

Work out amount of loan prior to leaving the course

Multiply the weekly amount of annual loan by the number of benefit weeks from the week after the one that includes the start of the academic year until the end of the benefit week that includes the day Nick left the course.

Multiply weekly loan (£101.36) by
9 weeks (6 September to 7 November 2009)   £912.24

Work out amount of loan since leaving the course

To do this, add the loan instalments paid for the terms up to the one in which Nick left, deduct disregards and deduct the loan worked out for the period prior to leaving.

	£
Loan up to end of term (33% of £4,950)	1,633.50
Less disregards (£693)	940.50
Deduct amount of loan prior to leaving (£912.24)	= 28.26

Work out weekly amount of loan from leaving course to end of term

Divide the total amount of loan for the period since leaving the course by the number of weeks left in the term. Count from the benefit week that includes the day Nick left the course until the benefit week that includes the end of term – ie, end of December, March, June or August.

Divide £28.26 by eight weeks
(8 November 2010 to 26 December 2010)   £3.53

£3.53 a week is taken into account from 8 November 2010 until 26 December 2010.

If you leave your course nearer to the end of term, this formula could result in there being no loan income taken into account for the remainder of the term. Note that if you repay the loan, it is nevertheless taken into account as income until the end of term.[33] So you could be refused ESA, IS or JSA despite having no other money to live on. However, if the Student Loans Company asks you to repay the loan rather than you repaying voluntarily, guidance tells DWP decision makers to disregard the loan as income from the date of the request.[34]

Grants

Higher education grants

The higher education (HE) maintenance grant for full-time undergraduate students in the 'current system' who do not have a benefits claim in their own right, and the adult dependants' grant paid by the Department for Business, Innovation and Skills (BIS), the Welsh Assembly or the Department for Employment and Learning in Northern Ireland (DELNI), are taken into account over the duration of the course, whether it comprises 52 weeks or fewer. They are treated as income over the same period as the student loan, if you have one or are eligible for one.[35] This is the case even though BIS guidance says that such grants cover 52 weeks.

Example

Fiona has a student loan (£4,950) and an adult dependants' grant (£2,642) totalling £7,592. She is claiming IS. She is in the second year of a three-year course and her first term starts in September. Her loan and grant are divided over 42 weeks from Monday 5 September 2010 until Monday 27 June 2011.

The weekly loan and grant income taken into account is:

	£
Total grants and loan	7,592.00
Less disregards for books and equipment (£390) and travel (£303)	6,899.00
Divided by 42 weeks	164.26
Less £10 weekly loan disregard	154.26

£154.26 is taken into account as weekly income from her loan and grants between 6 September 2010 and 27 June 2011. Her weekly income from her loan and grants between 28 June and 4 September 2011 is nil. If she is refused IS during the year because her income is too high, she should claim again on 28 June 2011.

Example

Dave receives a student loan of £5,475 and an HE maintenance grant of £2,906 to do his full-time undergraduate degree in London. This is his first year and his first term begins on Monday 4 October 2010. Dave lives with his partner, Kareen, and their two children. Kareen claims JSA and her benefit week starts on a Monday. Dave's student loan and maintenance grant will be taken into account when working out Kareen's JSA. His student loan and maintenance grant are divided over the 42 weeks from Monday 6 September 2010 to Sunday 26 June 2011. However, as he is a first year student, his loan and grant are not taken into account until he starts his course on Monday 4 October. So, from Monday 6 September until Sunday 3 October 2010, his student loan and grant income are not taken into account for Kareen's benefit purposes. From Monday 4 October 2010 to Sunday 26 June 2011 his student loan and grant income will be included in the calculation to determine the amount of JSA Kareen receives. From Monday 27 June until Sunday 4 September 2011 his student loan and grant income is nil again for benefit purposes.

Healthcare student bursaries

There are two types of bursary available to allied health professionals. A non-means-tested bursary is available in England for nursing, midwifery and operation department practitioner students studying a diploma course, and in Northern Ireland for nursing and midwifery students on both degree and diploma courses. If you are studying for a degree in England, Wales or Northern Ireland, a means-tested bursary is available. In addition to the means-tested bursary, you can receive a non-means-tested reduced rate loan from BIS or DELNI.

Dependants' grants and other allowances may be means tested (see Chapter 6 for more details).

The income from both types of bursary, dependants' allowance and single parent addition are taken into account. As these are paid in monthly instalments, they are taken into account over 52 weeks. The reduced rate loan should be treated over the same period as other student loans. The NHS childcare grant is disregarded in full.

Social work bursaries

Social work bursaries in England and Wales should be taken into account for the period they are paid. In England, this is 52 weeks.

In England, the element paid for travelling expenses should be disregarded.[36] However, this is not usually specifically identified, so benefits offices may take the full bursary into account. Speak to an adviser for assistance.

Any amount paid for tuition fees (eg to an 'old system' student) should also be disregarded.

In Northern Ireland, the social work incentive bursary is disregarded.

Postgraduate grants

A postgraduate award that is assessed for study throughout the calendar year is taken into account for the number of benefit weeks within the full calendar year.[37]

Students on a Postgraduate Certificate of Education course may get the same student loan and grants as undergraduates, and these are treated in the same way as undergraduate loans and grants.

If you leave your course early

For income-related ESA, IS and income-based JSA, if you abandon your course or are dismissed from it, your grant continues to be taken into account until the end of the term or vacation in which you stop being a full-time student or, if earlier, until you repay the grant or the period for which the grant is payable ends.[38]

For HB and CTB, your grant is taken into account until the grant provider asks you to repay it.[39]

4. Hardship funds and other payments

Hardship funds, and Access to Learning, Financial Contingency and discretionary support funds

Hardship funds are treated differently from student grants and loans. Hardship funds include payments from the:[40]

- Access to Learning Fund;
- Welsh Financial Contingency Fund;
- Northern Irish Hardship Fund;
- further education (FE) discretionary support funds.

In general, if the payment is for living costs, it is taken into account in full if it counts as capital, or with up to a £20 a week disregarded if it counts as income. If the payment is for other costs, it is disregarded. Ask your college for a letter saying what the payment is for and how it is paid.

Lump-sum payments count as capital. Regular payments count as income.

Grants from FE funds specifically for childcare are disregarded altogether.[41]

Lump-sum payments

Lump-sum payments are taken into account as capital if they are intended and used for food, ordinary clothing or footwear, household fuel, rent met by housing benefit (HB), housing costs met by income support (IS), council tax or water charges.[42] Although taken into account as capital, they only affect your benefit if they bring your capital above the £6,000 lower limit (see p252 for details). Payments for school uniforms or sports clothes or sports shoes are ignored, as these do not count as 'ordinary clothing or footwear'.

Regular payments

Regular payments are taken into account as income if they are intended and used for food, ordinary clothing or footwear, household fuel, rent met by HB, housing costs met by IS, council tax or water charges.[43] But up to £20 a week is disregarded. You cannot get the £20 disregard in full as well as the full disregards available on a student loan, widowed parent's allowance or war pensions. If you get one of these other payments in addition to a hardship payment, your maximum weekly disregard is £20. For example, if you have a student loan and receive a war pension, £10 a week is disregarded from each. If you also receive regular payments from a hardship fund, these would count in full as you have already used up your £20 disregard.

Regular payments intended and used for anything else, such as childcare expenses, are completely disregarded.

Payments before a course starts or before a loan is paid

A payment from a hardship fund made before the course starts is always ignored as income, even if it is for living costs. A payment made before you get the first instalment of your student loan is ignored as income, provided it is intended to tide you over until your loan is paid.

Institutional bursaries

Bursaries paid by institutions for living costs are treated as income over the period for which they are paid.

Voluntary or charitable payments

Regular voluntary or charitable payments are ignored for income-related employment and support allowance (ESA), IS, jobseeker's allowance (JSA), HB and council tax benefit. For IS and JSA, if paid as a lump sum, the payment is taken into account as capital whatever it is intended for.

Professional and career development loans

Professional and career development loans are always treated as income rather than capital, no matter how they are paid.[44] The loan is taken into account if it is intended and used for food, ordinary clothing or footwear, household fuel, rent met by HB, housing costs met by IS, council tax or water charges. Once the period of education supported by the loan is completed, the loan is disregarded altogether, whatever it was originally intended for.

5. Earnings

Your earnings and the earnings of your partner, if you have one, are taken into account in the benefit assessment. It is your net weekly earnings that are taken into account – ie, after deducting:

- income tax;
- Class 1 national insurance contributions;
- half of any contribution you make towards a personal or occupational pension.

Some of your earnings are disregarded. The highest disregard that applies in your circumstances is deducted:

- £25 for lone parents claiming housing benefit (HB) or council tax benefit (CTB) who are not claiming income support (IS), income-related employment and support allowance (ESA) or income-based jobseeker's allowance (JSA);
- £20 for lone parents claiming IS, ESA or JSA;
- £20 for someone who gets a disability premium;
- £20 for someone who gets a carer premium;

- £20 for part-time firefighters and some other emergency auxiliaries;
- £10 for couples, whether one or both of you are working;
- £5 for single people.

For HB and CTB only, there is an additional disregard (£17.10) for some people working 16/30 hours a week.

For HB and CTB, childcare costs for registered childminders, nurseries and playschemes can be disregarded from earnings in some circumstances. Childcare costs of up to £175 a week for one child or £300 for two or more children are deducted from weekly earnings for:

- lone parents who are working;
- couples who are both working;
- couples, where one is working and one is incapacitated or in hospital or prison.

In each case, the work must be for 16 hours or more a week.

For full details of the way earnings are treated, see CPAG's *Welfare Benefits and Tax Credits Handbook*.

6. **Benefits and tax credits**

Some benefits are taken into account in the assessment of income support (IS), income-based jobseeker's allowance (JSA), income-related employment and support allowance (ESA), housing benefit (HB) and council tax benefit (CTB), and others are ignored or partially ignored.

Benefits and tax credits **taken into account in full** include:

- child tax credit (CTC) for HB and CTB;
- carer's allowance;
- contributory ESA;
- contribution-based JSA;
- incapacity benefit;
- most industrial injuries benefits;
- retirement pension;
- working tax credit.

Benefits and tax credits **completely disregarded** include:

- attendance allowance;
- child benefit;
- CTC for IS, JSA and income-related ESA;
- disability living allowance;
- social fund payments.

Benefits and tax credits **partly disregarded** include:
- widowed mother's allowance and widowed parent's allowance, which have £10 a week disregarded for ESA, IS and JSA, £15 a week for HB and CTB (but you do not get this disregard if you already have £10 disregarded from a student loan or £20 disregarded from hardship fund payments).

7. Maintenance

For housing benefit, council tax benefit, income support, jobseeker's allowance and income-related employment and support allowance, maintenance paid to you by a former partner or your child's other parent is disregarded completely.

8. Savings and capital

There are limits on the amount of savings or capital you can have and still claim benefit. These limits are described below. Some kinds of capital are not counted in the assessment. For details see CPAG's *Welfare Benefits and Tax Credits Handbook*.

You cannot get income support, income-based jobseeker's allowance, housing benefit (HB) or council tax benefit (CTB) if your savings or other capital are above £16,000.

If your capital is £6,000 or less it does not affect your benefit at all.

If your capital is between £6,000.01 and £16,000, you are treated as though you have income from this capital of £1 a week for every £250 or part of £250 between these limits. This is referred to as 'tariff income'. For example, if you have savings of £6,525, your tariff income is £3 a week.

These limits are different if you or your partner have reached the qualifying age for pension credit (see p165). All your capital is ignored if you or your partner get pension credit guarantee credit. Otherwise, tariff income of £1 for each £500 or part of £500 between £10,000.01 and £16,000 is taken into account in the assessment of HB and CTB.

Notes

2. Grants and loans
1 Memo DMG JSA/IS 130 para 4
2 **IS** Reg 66A(3) and (4) IS Regs
  HB Reg 64(3) and (4) HB Regs
3 **IS** Reg 66A(4)(a) IS Regs
  HB Reg 64(4) HB Regs

4 **IS** Reg 67A(5)b IS Regs
JSA Reg 136(5) JSA Regs
HB Reg 64(5) HB Regs
CTB Reg 51(5) CTB Regs

5 **IS** Reg 41(6) IS Regs
JSA Reg 104(5) JSA Regs
HB Reg 41(4) HB Regs
CTB Reg 31(4) CTB Regs

6 **IS** Reg 62(2) IS Regs
JSA Reg 131(2) JSA Regs
See also Memo DMG JSA/IS 130 para 7,
July 2006

7 **IS** Reg 62(2)(a) IS Regs
HB Reg 59(2)(a) HB Regs

8 **IS** Reg 62(2) IS Regs
JSA Reg 131(2) JSA Regs
See also Memo DMG JSA/IS 130 para 6,
July 2006

9 **IS** Reg 62(2) IS Regs
JSA Reg 131(2) JSA Regs
See also Memo DMG JSA/IS 130 para 7,
July 2006

10 **IS** Reg 62(2)(c) IS Regs
HB Reg 59(2)(b) HB Regs

11 paras 5.246-5.249 GM

12 **IS** Reg 62(2)(h) IS Regs
HB Reg 59(2)(g) HB Regs

13 **IS** Reg 62(2)(g) and (h) IS Regs
JSA Reg 131(2) JSA Regs
HB Reg 59(2) HB Regs

14 **IS** Reg 62(2)(a) IS Regs
JSA Reg 131(2)(a) JSA Regs
See also Memo DMG JSA/IS 130 para 8,
July 2006

15 **HB** Reg 59(6) HB Regs

16 **IS** Reg 62(2)(c) IS Regs
HB Reg 59(2)(b) HB Regs

17 **IS** Reg 62(2)(h) IS Regs
HB Reg 59(2)(g) HB Regs

18 paras 30121-30125 Vol 6 DMG

19 paras 5.361-5.364 GM

20 **IS** Sch 9 para 11(a) IS Regs
HB Sch 5 para 11 HB Regs

21 p15, ALG Guidance 2010/11

22 p15, ALG guidance 2010/11

23 **IS** Reg 68 IS Regs
JSA Reg 138 JSA Regs
HB Reg 68 HB Regs
CTB Reg 55 CTB Regs

24 **IS** Reg 66B IS Regs
JSA Reg 136A JSA Regs
HB Reg 65 HB Regs
CTB Reg 52 CTB Regs

3. **Dividing income throughout the year**

25 **IS** Reg 66A(2)(c) IS Regs
HB Reg 64(2)(d) HB Regs

26 **HB** Reg 2 HB Regs
CTB Reg 2 CTB Regs

27 **IS** Reg 66A(2)(b) IS Regs
HB Reg 64(2)(d) HB Regs

28 **IS** Reg 66A(2)(aa) IS Regs
HB Reg 64(2)(b) HB Regs

29 **IS** Reg 61(1) IS Regs
HB Reg 53(1) HB Regs

30 **IS** Reg 66A(2)(aa) IS Regs
HB Reg 64(2)(b) HB Regs

31 **IS** Reg 40(3A) IS Regs
HB Reg 40(7) HB Regs

32 See also HB/CTB Circular A31/2001 Part
6 and Annex D for guidance and a
sample calculation, together with
HB/CTB Circular A39/2001 para 19

33 CJSA/549/2003

34 para 30305 Vol 6 DMG

35 **IS** Reg 62(3B) IS Regs
HB Reg 59(7) HB Regs

36 **IS** Reg 62(2)(h) IS Regs
HB Reg 59(2)(g) HB Regs
CTB Reg 46(2)(g) CTB Regs

37 **IS** Regs 61 and 62(3)(a) IS Regs
HB Regs 53 and 59(5)(a) HB Regs

38 **IS** Reg 29(2B) IS Regs
JSA Reg 94(2B) JSA Regs

39 *Leeves v Chief Adjudication Officer*,
reported as R(IS) 5/99

4. **Hardship funds and other payments**

40 **IS** Reg 61 IS Regs
HB Reg 53 HB Regs

41 **IS** Reg 61(1) IS Regs
JSA Reg 130 JSA Regs
HB Reg 53(1) HB Regs
CTB Reg 43(1) CTB Regs

42 **IS** Reg 68 IS Regs
HB Reg 68 HB Regs

43 **IS** Reg 66B IS Regs
HB Reg 65 HB Regs

44 **IS** Reg 41(6) IS Regs
HB Reg 41(4) HB Regs

Chapter 21

How income affects tax credits

This chapter covers:
1. Working out your income (below)
2. Grants and loans (p255)
3. Earnings (p256)
4. Benefits (p257)
5. Other income (p258)

This chapter explains how HM Revenue and Customs treats your income when working out your entitlement to tax credits. It outlines the type of student income that is taken into account, as well as how other income, such as earnings, is treated. Most forms of student support are, however, disregarded for tax credit purposes. The rules apply to both part-time and full-time students.

For details of the rules of entitlement to tax credits, see Chapters 18 and 19.

1. Working out your income

Step 1 **Add together all taxable income from the previous full tax year.**
Add all of your taxable benefits and income from employment or self-employment from the previous full tax year. Use the current full tax year if your income is lower, or more than £25,000 higher, than the previous year's income. After April 2011, this figure will be £10,000.

Step 2 **Add any relevant student income.**
Add any relevant student income – adult dependants' grant, or living costs elements of a professional and career development loan (see p256) – from the same period.

Step 3 **Add any other relevant income.**
Add any other relevant forms of income from the same period.
This is the total income on which your claim will be assessed.

Step 4   **Calculate any excess.**

If your total income is less than £16,190 for child tax credit or £6,420 for working tax credit, you will receive the maximum to which you are entitled. If it is more than £16,190 (or £6,420), subtract £16,190 (or £6,420) from the total amount. Divide the remainder by 100 and multiply by 39 (41 after April 2011). This is the amount that should be subtracted from your total maximum entitlement (see Chapters 18 and 19 for details of how this is calculated) to give the amount you will receive.

2. **Grants and loans**

Most grants and loans are disregarded when calculating a student's income for tax credit purposes (see below).[1] The following are the exceptions.

- Adult dependants' grant. Any grant received for an adult dependant is included in the calculation.
- Professional and career development loan. Any part of this paid for living costs for the period supported by the loan is taken into account in full.[2]

Grants and loans checklist

Student support	Treatment
Further education income	
Adult learning grant	Disregarded
Care to Learn grant	Disregarded
Childcare fund	Disregarded
Education maintenance allowance	Disregarded
Further education award (Northern Ireland)	Disregarded
Discretionary support funds grant	Disregarded
Special educational needs allowance	Disregarded
Travel grant or expenses	Disregarded
Welsh Assembly learning grant	Disregarded
Undergraduate income	
Access to Learning Fund grant	Disregarded
Adult dependants' grant	Taken into account in full
Childcare grant	Disregarded
Disabled students' allowance	Disregarded
Financial Contingency Fund grant	Disregarded
Hardship funds	Disregarded
Higher education grant	Disregarded

Institutional bursaries or scholarships	Disregarded
Maintenance grant	Disregarded
NHS dependants' grant for children	Disregarded
NHS healthcare bursary	Disregarded
Northern Ireland higher education bursary	Disregarded
Nursing and midwifery bursary	Disregarded
Parents' learning allowance	Disregarded
Part-time students' grant for course costs	Disregarded
Part-time students' grant for fees	Disregarded
Social work bursary	Disregarded
Special support grant	Disregarded
Student loan for living costs (including any means-tested element where appropriate)	Disregarded
Travelling expenses	Disregarded
Tuition fee grant	Disregarded
Tuition fee loan	Disregarded
Welsh Assembly learning grant	Disregarded

Postgraduate income

Books and equipment expenses	Disregarded
British Academy grant	Disregarded
Research Council studentship or scholarship	Disregarded
Residential study	Disregarded
Social work bursary	Disregarded
Supplementary grants	As for undergraduate income
Teacher training grant	Disregarded
Tuition fees grant or loan	Disregarded

Other income

Professional and career development loan	Disregarded, except for any amount applied or paid for living expenses during the period supported by the loan, which is taken into account in full

3. **Earnings**

Your gross earnings from the last full tax year plus those of your partner (if any) are taken into account in the tax credit assessment. 'Gross earnings' means all income before any income tax or national insurance contributions are deducted. It also includes tips, overtime pay, taxable expenses and, ignoring the first

£30,000, taxable payments related to the termination of employment such as redundancy pay and strike pay.[3] If you make any contributions to a personal or occupational pension approved by HM Revenue and Customs, these contributions should be disregarded.[4] The first £100 a week of statutory maternity, paternity and adoption pay is disregarded, but payments above this are included.[5] Statutory sick pay is included in full.[6] Any payments which are exempt from income tax should be ignored for the purposes of tax credits.

For full details of the way earnings are treated, see CPAG's *Welfare Benefits and Tax Credits Handbook*.

4. Benefits

Generally speaking, benefits that are not taxable are disregarded when calculating tax credits, and benefits that are taxable are included. For full details of the way social security benefits are treated, see CPAG's *Welfare Benefits and Tax Credits Handbook*.

Benefits **disregarded** include:[7]
- child benefit;
- disability living allowance;
- income-related employment and support allowance (ESA) (child tax credit only – cannot be claimed with working tax credit);
- guardian's allowance;
- housing benefit;
- lower rate of short-term incapacity benefit (IB);
- income support (except to strikers);
- income-based jobseeker's allowance (JSA);
- industrial injuries benefit;
- maternity allowance;
- social fund payments;
- most war pensions;[8]
- increases for a child or adult dependant paid with any of the above benefits.

Benefits **taken into account** in full include:
- bereavement allowance;
- carer's allowance;
- contributory ESA;
- long-term IB;
- higher rate of short-term IB;
- contribution-based JSA (although amounts above the 'taxable maximum' are ignored. In practice, people are not paid above this amount so in the majority of cases all contribution-based JSA will be included);
- increases for a child or adult dependant paid with any of the above benefits.

Benefits **partly taken into account** include state retirement pension (and private and occupational pensions) and widows' pensions. These are included in tax credit calculations, although the first £300 of the total income from pensions, income from capital, and foreign or notional income is disregarded.

5. **Other income**

This is a brief outline of how other income is treated. For further details, see CPAG's *Welfare Benefits and Tax Credits Handbook*.

Income from self-employment

Your taxable profits are taken into account less any personal pension contributions.

Savings and investments

Savings and investments are ignored as the tax credit assessment is based on income only. Any taxable income from your savings and investments is included, although the first £300 of the total income from pensions, income from capital, and foreign or notional income is disregarded.

Property

As with savings and investments, the capital value of any property is ignored, but any taxable rental income is included, although the first £300 of the total income from pensions, income from capital, and foreign or notional income is disregarded.[9]

Note that it is possible to rent a room in your own home tax free, as long as the rental income does not exceed £4,250 per year, and such income would not be taken into account when assessing tax credits.

Maintenance

Regular maintenance from an ex-partner is ignored, regardless of how the arrangement was made. Similarly, any support received from an ex-partner for your child(ren) is also ignored.[10]

Notes

∙∙

1. **Grants and loans**
   1 Reg 8 TC(DCI) Regs
   2 Reg 19(c) table 8 para 2 TC(DCI) Regs

3. **Earnings**
   3 Reg 4 TC(DCI) Regs
   4 Reg 3(7)(c) TC(DCI) Regs
   5 Reg 4(1)(h) TC(DCI) Regs
   6 Reg 4(1)(g) TC(DCI) Regs

4. **Benefits**
   7 Reg 7(3) TC(DCI) Regs
   8 Reg 5 TC(DCI) Regs

5. **Other income**
   9 Reg 11 TC(DCI) Regs
   10 Reg 19 table 6 para 10 TC(DCI) Regs

22

Chapter 22

How income affects health benefits

This chapter covers:
1. Working out your income (below)
2. Grants and loans (p261)
3. Hardship funds and other payments (p265)
4. Earnings (p266)
5. Benefits and tax credits (p266)
6. Maintenance (p267)
7. Savings and capital (p267)

This chapter explains how your income is treated when your entitlement to health benefits under the NHS low income scheme is worked out. It outlines the type of student income that is taken into account and how much can be disregarded, as well as how other income, such as earnings, is treated. It applies to both part-time and full-time students.

If you are not otherwise exempt from healthcare costs (see Chapter 11) and have less than £16,000 (£23,250 if you are in a care home in England, or £22,000 in Wales) a year in property, savings, or other assessed income or capital, you are eligible to apply for at least some assistance.

The exact amount of help you receive depends on the amount of excess weekly income (if any) you are assessed as having, once it is offset against a personal allowance and your housing costs. The NHS Business Services Authority calculates this from the information provided on Form HC1.

1. Working out your income

The way that student income is taken into account for health benefits is broadly the same as for means-tested benefits.

Step 1	**Apply annual disregard.**

Step 1   **Apply annual disregard.**
From the student loan, deduct the disregarded amount of £693 for books, equipment and travel.

Step 2   **Divide income throughout the year.**
Divide the annual amount of loan by 52 weeks, unless you are in the final or only year of your course, in which case you should divide by the number of weeks between the start and finish of your course.

Step 3   **Weekly disregard.**
Unlike the means-tested benefits assessment, there is no weekly disregard of £10 on the student loan, unless you receive a premium in your applicable amount, an allowance because of deafness (separate to any disabled students' allowance), or you are not a student but your partner is. If you fall into any of these categories, disregard £10.

Step 4   **Add other income to weekly loan amount.**
Add together any other weekly income (except for 'mandatory' awards such as research council awards or non-means-tested NHS bursaries) – eg, from hardship funds or a professional and career development loan (see pp265–266), earnings (see p266), tariff income from capital (see p267), benefits and tax credits (see p266) – ignoring any amount that is disregarded.

Step 5   **Divide mandatory grant income over 52 weeks.**
Divide any mandatory grant or bursary over 52 weeks and add this to the weekly amounts where appropriate. Sums in excess of a maintenance grant are disregarded. This total, added to the weekly loan total calculated at Step 4, is the amount of income used in the health benefit assessment.

---

2. Grants and loans

Student loan

A student loan includes:
- the maximum loan for living costs for which you are eligible, including any means-tested element (where applicable). This is taken into account as your income whether or not you apply for it. The Government believes that it is the primary source of public support to students and, therefore, should be fully exhausted before further support is given;
- any payments for extra weeks' attendance.

The NHS Business Services Authority disregards £693 for books, travel and equipment from the annual student loan.

Grants

In general, grants intended for living costs (such as the old maintenance grant, the NHS bursary and the social work bursary) are taken into account and grants for other costs are disregarded. For details of how Access to Learning Fund and other hardship grants are treated, see p265.

An amount of any maintenance grant or Welsh Assembly learning grant paid to 'current system' system students subject to variable or flexible tuition fees is taken into account, but amounts above this are ignored.[1] The amounts taken into account are as follows:

Student cohort	Amount taken into account
England 2009 cohort	£1,453
England All other current system students	£1,292
Wales 2010 cohort	£2,844
Wales All other current systems students	£1,288
Northern Ireland	£1,318

Institutional bursaries and scholarships are taken into account if they are paid for living costs.

If you are *not* eligible for a student loan for living costs, £693 for books, travel and equipment is deducted from your grant.

Social work bursaries are usually divided over the number of weeks of study, except where classroom weeks exceed 45, in which case they are divided by 52.

Teacher training bursaries are divided over the number of days they are paid, then multiplied by seven to give a weekly amount. The £693 disregard is not applied.

Grants in further education

The following further education grants are **disregarded**:
- education maintenance allowance;
- adult learning grant;
- Care to Learn grant;
- travel expenses allowance.

Grants in higher education

The following higher education (HE) grants are completely **disregarded**:
- HE grant for 'old system' students;

- Welsh Assembly learning grant for 'old system' students;
- part-time course costs grant;
- childcare grant;
- parents' learning allowance;
- disabled students' allowance;
- travel expenses;
- tuition fees grants and loans.

The following grants are **taken into account**:
- adult dependants' grant;
- teacher training bursary;
- nursing and midwifery bursary;
- social work bursary.

Postgraduate grants

Any research council or other maintenance grant and dependants' allowances are taken into account. Supplementary grants are treated in the same way as those for undergraduates (see p262). Ignore:
- grants for tuition fees;
- grants for residential study away from your normal home;
- grants intended to meet the costs of books and equipment.

Grants and loans checklist

Student support	Treatment
Further education income	
Adult learning grant	Disregarded
Care to Learn grant	Disregarded
Education maintenance allowance	Disregarded
Discretionary support funds grant	Taken into account if paid for basic living
Financial Contingency Fund grant	costs, disregarded if paid for other items such as childcare
Travel expenses allowance	Disregarded
Welsh Assembly learning grant for further education	Disregarded
Undergraduate income	
Access to Learning Fund grant	Taken into account if paid for basic living
Financial Contingency Fund grant	costs (as capital if not regular payments),
Northern Irish hardship funds	disregarded if paid for other items
Adult dependants' grant	Taken into account in full
Childcare grant	Disregarded
Disabled students' allowance	Disregarded

Higher education grant	Disregarded
Institutional bursaries or scholarships	Taken into account if paid for living costs
Loan (including any means-tested element where appropriate)	Taken into account Disregarded: – £693 a year for books, travel and equipment; *and* – £10 a week in certain circumstances (see p266)
Maintenance grants (including Welsh Assembly learning grant for 'new system' students)	Any sum in excess of £1,288 (£1,453 for '2009 cohorts' or £1,788 in Northern Ireland, see p262)
NHS healthcare bursary, Nursing and midwifery bursary	Means tested: taken into account in full Non-means tested: taken into account, except for £693 a year disregard for books, travel and equipment
Parents' learning allowance	Disregarded
Part-time grant for course costs	Disregarded
Part-time grant for tuition fees	Disregarded
Social work bursary	Taken into account, with £693 a year disregard if you are not entitled to a student loan
Special support grant	Disregarded
Teacher training bursary	Taken into account
Travelling expenses	Disregarded
Tuition fee grant	Disregarded
Tuition fee loan	Disregarded
Welsh Assembly learning grant for 'old system' students	Disregarded

Postgraduate income

Books and equipment	Disregarded
Research council studentship or scholarship	Taken into account, except for an annual £693 books, travel and equipment disregard
Residential study	Disregarded
Social work bursary	Taken into account
Supplementary grants	As for undergraduate income
Teacher training salary	Taken into account
Tuition fees grant or loan	Disregarded

Example

Oliver is a first-year full-time undergraduate in Wales. He receives the maximum away-from-home student loan (£1,901), the maximum Assembly learning grant for 'new system' students (£5,000) and £20 a week from his parents for food and bills.

When calculating his income for health benefits purposes, subtract £693 from his student loan, to give £1,208 and include the first £2,844 of his Welsh Assembly learning grant. This gives £4,052. Divide this by 52 weeks (to give £77.92). The £20 a week he gets from his parents is added to this figure and his income is, therefore, assessed to be £97.92 a week.

This income would then be set against the appropriate income support personal allowances, housing and other costs to determine whether or not it exceeds or falls short of Oliver's requirements. If it does fall short, he would receive full support. If his income exceeds this amount, he may receive partial support, depending on the level of excess.

3. Hardship funds and other payments

Access to Learning Fund and other hardship funds

Discretionary support provided when you are in financial difficulty is treated differently from other student grants and loans. This support can include:

- higher education (HE) Financial Contingency Fund, Northern Irish hardship funds or Access to Learning Fund;
- further education (FE) discretionary support funds or Financial Contingency Fund.

In general, if the payment is for living costs, it is taken into account in full if it counts as capital, or with up to a £20 a week disregard if it counts as income. If the payment is for other costs, it is disregarded. For example, an FE discretionary support funds grant solely for childcare costs is disregarded. Ask your college for a letter saying what the payment is for and how it is paid.

Lump-sum payments count as capital. Regular payments count as income.

Lump-sum payments

Lump-sum payments are taken into account as capital if they are intended and used for living costs such as food, ordinary clothing or footwear, household fuel, rent, council tax or water charges. Payments for anything else are disregarded. Although taken into account as capital, this only affects your entitlement if it brings your capital above the £16,000 lower limit. See p267 for details.

Regular payments

Regular payments are taken into account as income if they are intended and used for food, ordinary clothing or footwear, household fuel, rent, council tax or water charges. Up to £20 a week is disregarded. You cannot get the £20 disregard in full as well as the full disregards available on a student loan or voluntary and charitable payments (or on widowed parent's allowance or war pensions). If you get one of these other payments as well as a payment from the Access to Learning Fund (or equivalent), your maximum weekly disregard is £20.

For example, if you have a student loan for living costs and regular payments from the Access to Learning Fund, £10 a week is disregarded from each. If you also receive regular payments from a charity, these would count in full as you have already used up your £20 disregard on the loan and the hardship fund payment.

Regular payments intended and used for anything else, such as childcare expenses, are completely disregarded.

Voluntary or charitable payments

These are treated in the same way as hardship fund payments.

Professional and career development loans

Professional and career development loans are always treated as income, not capital, no matter how they are paid. The loan is taken into account if it is intended and used for living costs – eg, food, ordinary clothing or footwear, household fuel, rent, council tax or water charges. Once the period of education supported by the loan is completed, the loan is disregarded altogether, whatever it was originally intended for.

4. Earnings

Your earnings and the earnings of your partner, if you have one, are taken into account in the health benefits assessment. It is your net weekly earnings that are taken into account – ie, deducting:

- income tax;
- Class 1 national insurance contributions;
- half of any contribution you make towards a personal or occupational pension.

5. Benefits and tax credits

If you receive income support (IS), income-based jobseeker's allowance (JSA), income-related employment and support allowance (ESA) or child tax credit, you automatically get free health benefits (see Chapter 11).

Housing benefit and council tax benefit are effectively disregarded, as the NHS Business Services Authority only takes into account the rent and council tax paid directly by the applicant when determining need.

Benefits and tax credits **taken into account** in full include:

- carer's allowance;
- contribution-based JSA;
- contributory ESA;
- incapacity benefit;
- most industrial injuries benefits;
- retirement pension;
- working tax credit.

Benefits and tax credits **completely disregarded** include:

- attendance allowance;
- child benefit for IS and JSA, once your IS or JSA no longer includes allowances for children;
- disability living allowance;
- social fund payments.

Benefits and tax credits **partly disregarded** include:

- widowed mother's allowance and widowed parent's allowance, which have £10 a week disregarded. **Note:** you do not receive this disregard if you already have £10 disregarded from a student loan or £20 disregarded from hardship fund payments.

6. **Maintenance**

Regular maintenance payments (eg, child support and parental or spousal contributions towards maintenance) count as income. As a general rule, income will normally be taken into account in the week in which it is paid, subject to a weekly disregard of £5, £10 or £20 depending on circumstances. Irregular payments are averaged over the 13 weeks prior to your claim, and lump sums are treated as capital.

7. **Savings and capital**

There are limits on the amount of savings or capital you can have and still claim health benefits.

You cannot get health benefits if your savings or other capital is above £16,000.

If your capital is £6,000 or less, it does not affect your benefits at all. If your capital is between £6,000.01 and £16,000 (a higher limit if you are in a care home), you are treated as though you have an income from this capital of £1 a week for every £250 (or part of £250) between these amounts. This is referred to as 'tariff income'. For example, if you have savings of £6,525, your tariff income is £3 a week.

Notes

2. Grants and loans
1 The National Health Service (Travel Expenses and Remission of Charges) Amendment (No.2) Regulations 2006 No.2171

Part 4

Other issues

Chapter 23

Council tax

This chapter covers:
1. What is council tax (below)
2. Who pays council tax (p272)
3. Council tax benefit (p278)
4. Second adult rebate (p278)

Basic facts

– Council tax is a local tax on residential dwellings.

– You do not pay council tax if you are under 18.

– Council tax does not apply in Northern Ireland.

– Full-time students sharing accommodation solely with other full-time students do not pay council tax.

– Full-time students sharing accommodation with non-students do not pay.

– Full-time students who own the home in which they live, and who live with non-students may be liable, but may be exempt or get a discount.

– Full-time students liable to pay council tax can claim council tax benefit if they get income support or income-based jobseeker's allowance, or if they have children, are disabled or are aged 60 or over. Part-time students are eligible to claim benefit whatever their circumstances.

– Since April 2006, a full-time student sharing with others – who all get income support, jobseeker's allowance or pension credit, and do not pay rent to the student – qualifies for a second adult rebate of 100 per cent.

1. **What is council tax**

Council tax is a tax on residential dwellings and is paid to the local authority. There is one amount to pay and one bill for each dwelling unless it is exempt from council tax. A 'dwelling' includes a self-contained flat.

Each dwelling is allocated a valuation band from A to H based on property values in 1991 (2005 in Wales). Council tax is lowest for those in Band A.

Some dwellings are exempt from council tax. If the dwelling is exempt, there is no council tax to pay for anyone who lives there or for a non-resident owner. There are also exemptions specifically for students and these are described below.

Properties occupied solely by students are usually exempt, with the local authority receiving additional funds from central government in place of the council tax that would have been paid. Students who share with non-students are also exempt from payment of council tax, although the property itself is not exempt. If you are a student and you are liable, the amount to pay may be reduced if you are eligible for council tax benefit or second adult rebate (see p278).

2. **Who pays council tax**

As a student, you may be exempt from paying council tax if:
- the accommodation in which you live is exempt (see p275); *or*
- you are not liable to pay (see p275).

If neither of these applies, it may be possible to reduce the council tax bill if:
- the liable person can get a discount (see p277); *or*
- the liable person can get council tax benefit (CTB – see p278) or second adult rebate (see p278).

Who counts as a student

If you are aged under 20, whether you count as a student for council tax purposes depends on whether you are on an advanced or non-advanced course. For older students, one rule applies whatever level of course you do.

Under 20 in non-advanced education

You are regarded as a 'student' for council tax purposes if you are aged 19 or under and on a non-advanced course of more than 12 hours a week.[1]

A '**non-advanced course**' is one below the level of a foundation degree, honours degree, higher national certificate (HNC), higher national diploma (HND) or NVQ Level 4. It includes A levels, advanced vocational certificates of education (AVCEs), national diplomas and national certificates. The course must last more than three months.[2] It does not include:
- evening classes;[3]
- correspondence courses;[4]
- courses taken as a result of your office or occupation.[5]

The hours that count are those required by the course rather than those you actually do, if they are different.

To work out your hours, average out over term times the hours required under the course for tuition, supervised study, exams, and supervised exercise, experiment, project and practical work.[6]

You are treated as a student for each day from the day you start the course until the day you complete it, abandon it or are dismissed from it.[7] So you count as a student during term times, during short vacations at Christmas and Easter, and during the summer if your course continues after the summer. If your course ends in the summer and you begin a different one in the autumn, you do not count as a student in the summer between courses.[8] However, you might still have a 'status discount' (see p277).

> **Example**
> Drew is 18 and taking three A levels at college. Including his classes, exams and supervised study, his course hours are 18 a week. He is a student for council tax purposes.

Under 20 in higher education

The rules are the same as they are for those aged 20 or over (see below).

20 or over in non-advanced or higher education

You are regarded as a 'student' for council tax purposes if the course requires attendance for at least 21 hours a week in at least 24 weeks each academic year.[9]

Hours include periods of study as well as tuition. If you are on a sandwich course, include required periods of work experience.

To count as a student you must be enrolled on a course with an educational institution. You are a student from the day you begin the course until the day you complete it, abandon it or are no longer permitted by the educational institution to attend it.[10] So if you take time out and are not enrolled on the course during that period, you do not count as a student for council tax purposes and you may become liable for council tax. However, if this is the case, you may wish to check to see if you are eligible for council tax benefit (see p278).

On the other hand, if you take time out but are still enrolled on the course, you continue to count as a student so long as you have not abandoned it completely and the institution has not said you can no longer attend the course. Because the law says you are not a student if you are 'no longer permitted by the institution to attend', it suggests that your dismissal from the course must be final. So you could argue that if you are temporarily suspended from the course but still registered, you do still count as a student. In an informal letter, written in 1996, the former Department of the Environment (then responsible for the council tax) stated:

> In our view a period of intercalation will remain within the period of a course. . . and therefore, provided that the person remains enrolled at the education establishment, they will continue to fall within the definition of a full-time student.[11]

Your college or university determines the number of hours. You may need evidence from it to prove to the local authority that you count as a student. Colleges and universities are required by law to provide you with a certificate if you ask for one while you are a student or up to a year after you leave the course.[12] After that, they may still give you a certificate, but are not legally required to do so. The certificate must contain:[13]

- the name and address of the institution;
- your full name;
- your term-time address and home address (if known by the institution);
- a statement that you are (or were) a student – ie, that you are enrolled on a course requiring attendance of at least 21 hours a week over at least 24 weeks a year; *and*
- the date you became a student and the date your course ends.

Postgraduate students

Full-time postgraduate students are regarded as 'students' for council tax purposes in the same way as other full-time higher education students.

In the past, some postgraduate research students have had difficulty in securing council tax exemption because local authorities have considered that their periods of 'study, tuition or work experience' do not meet the requirements of the regulations, and that, in particular, research does not count as 'study'. This has been successfully challenged in an appeal in Kent[14] and, although it does not set a legal precedent, local authorities are obliged to take such decisions into account when making their own decisions.

Other postgraduate students have had difficulty in securing exemption during the thesis 'writing-up' period after the formal end of the course. While some local authorities are sympathetic and will extend student status after the end of the course, others have been known to regard such students as liable as they are no longer 'within the period of their course'. A High Court ruling in 2008 in the case of *Fayad vs Lewisham*[15] has served to harden some local authorities' views (although in that case, the student was trying to claim exemption for a writing-up period lasting more than two years). Indeed, the case has been used by some local authorities to suggest that PhD students are ineligible for exemption even during the formal period of the course, but this should be challenged as the ruling related only to a writing-up period.

If this affects you, seek advice from your students' union or institution's advice centre.

Note: students who have completed their undergraduate course and intend to start a postgraduate course in the following academic year are not exempt as they are not within the period of either course. Depending on your circumstances, however, you may be able to claim council tax benefit or a discount on the bill (see pp277–278).

Exempt dwellings

A dwelling is exempt if everyone who occupies it is:[16]
- a student; *or*
- a student's overseas partner, if s/he entered the UK on a visa that denies the right to work or claim benefits. If the partner has the right to work but not to claim benefits, s/he should come under this exemption; *or*
- under age 18; *or*
- under age 20 and left non-advanced education at school or college after 30 April – this only applies between 1 May and 31 October of the year they left school or college; *or*
- 'severely mentally impaired'.

An unoccupied dwelling is exempt for up to four months if it is the main residence of a student (and not of anyone else who is not a student) and it was last occupied by one or more students. This allows an exemption to continue, for example, to the student's term-time accommodation through the summer vacation. Dwellings left unoccupied by a student owner are exempt indefinitely as long as the owner has been a student since s/he last occupied the dwelling or within six weeks of leaving it. Unoccupied dwellings which are substantially unfurnished are exempt for up to six months. If you are liable for council tax and anyone who is jointly liable with you is also a student, and the dwelling is no one's main residence, the dwelling is exempt without time limit.

If the dwelling is exempt, there is no council tax to pay.

There are a number of other exemptions that are not specifically aimed at students. For details see CPAG's *Council Tax Handbook*.

Who is liable for council tax

Most full-time students are not liable to pay council tax. This is because either the dwelling is exempt because everyone who lives there is a full-time student or, if a student lives with non-students, s/he is deemed exempt from liability for the council tax due on the property.

If the dwelling is not exempt from council tax, at least one person is liable for the bill. Who that is depends on her/his position in a liability hierarchy. The person who comes first (highest up) in the hierarchy is the one who is liable to pay. If there are two or more people at the same level in the hierarchy, they are usually jointly liable.

Council tax liability hierarchy
Resident with a freehold interest in the property
Resident with a leasehold on the property, or the superior leaseholder if there is more than one
Resident tenant

Resident statutory or secure tenant
Resident who is a licensee
Other resident, including a squatter

If students share accommodation with non-students who are at the same level in the hierarchy, the non-students are liable but the students are not.[17]

There does, however, remain a situation where a student may still be liable for the council tax; if you live with one or more non-students, but you are higher on the hierarchy of liability than the non-students (eg, you are the owner of the property or the only person named on the tenancy agreement), the property ceases to be exempt from council tax. However, because you are higher up on the hierarchy of liability you, and not the non-students in the property, would be liable for the council tax. In this case you may, nevertheless, be entitled to a discount on the bill or to CTB, depending on your circumstances.

Example: joint tenants

Three students, Pooja, Joey and Zarah, share a flat as joint tenants. While they are all students the flat is exempt and there is no council tax to pay. Joey drops out of his course. The flat is no longer exempt and Joey is solely liable for the whole council tax bill (although there is a discount). Pooja and Zarah are not liable for any council tax. Joey should apply for CTB if his income is low.

Examples: students who remain liable

Antonia is studying full time and owns the flat in which she lives. She rents out a room to a friend who is not a student. Antonia is liable for the council tax. As there is only one non-student at the property, there is a 25 per cent discount on the bill. Her friend is not liable for any council tax.

Raj is studying full time and rents the flat in which he lives. He sublets a room to a friend who is also a student. Raj is higher up on the hierarchy of liability, but, as both of them are students, the flat is exempt and the bill is nil.

Joint and several liability

Joint and several liability means that, in legal terms, you can be held liable for all or part of a bill, even though there may be more than one person named. This gives the local authority the right to pursue as many or as few people for payment of the bill as it likes, regardless of how many liable residents are, or were, in the property.[18]

In practice, local authorities will try to bill as many liable people as possible. If they cannot contact all of the liable people, those who they can contact can be required to take on the total debt between them.

Couples

Normally, couples (of the same or opposite sex, and whether married, in a civil partnership or cohabiting) who live together are jointly liable for the council tax. Students, however, are exempt from this rule. If you have a non-student partner who is liable for council tax, you are not jointly liable while you are a student.[19]

Discounts

The full council tax bill assumes that there are two adults living in the dwelling. You get a discount of 25 per cent if there is only one person living there. You get a discount of 50 per cent if there is no one living there. Full-time students who are liable can get a 100 per cent discount if the people they share with do not pay them rent and all receive income support, jobseeker's allowance or pension credit (see below). You also get a discount if there is no one or just one adult living there, other than people in certain specified circumstances. These people are sometimes described as 'invisible' (because they are disregarded when counting how many live in the dwelling) or as having a 'status discount'.

The following people are disregarded in this way:
- anyone under 18 years old;
- anyone aged 18 or over for whom child benefit is payable;
- full-time students;
- partners of students who are not British citizens and whose immigration status prevents them from taking up paid employment or accessing social security benefits (though not necessarily both);
- someone under age 20 who was on a non-advanced course of education and who left school or college after 1 May – the status discount lasts from 1 May until 31 October;
- student nurses – ie, those studying for registration;
- apprentices training for an NVQ and on low pay;
- others – eg, carers, hospital patients and trainees (see CPAG's *Council Tax Handbook*).

Disability reduction

The council tax bill is reduced to the valuation band below your own band if you or anyone else (adult or child) who is resident in the dwelling is substantially and permanently disabled and uses a wheelchair indoors or needs an extra room.

3. **Council tax benefit**

Council tax benefit (CTB) is administered by local authorities and helps pay the council tax. To get CTB you must meet all of the following conditions.

- You are liable for council tax. Most full-time students are not liable for council tax and have no need to claim benefit.
- You do not count as a student, or you do count as a student but are still eligible for CTB (see below).
- You are 'habitually resident' in the UK, Ireland, Channel Islands or the Isle of Man and not a 'person subject to immigration control'. These terms are explained in CPAG's *Welfare Benefits and Tax Credits Handbook*.
- You have no more than £16,000 capital.[20] There is no capital limit if you are aged 60 or over and getting the pension credit guarantee credit.
- Your income is sufficiently low. CTB is means tested so the amount you get depends on how much income you have.

Students eligible for council tax benefit

Part-time students can claim CTB. If you are a full-time student you cannot claim CTB unless:[21]

- you are under 19, or aged 19 and you started your course when you were under 19 and not in higher education;
- you are a full-time student aged 20 or over or aged 19 when you started your course, or aged under 19 if you are in higher education, and:
  – you get income support (IS), income-related employment and support allowance or income-based jobseeker's allowance (JSA); *or*
  – you are a lone parent or part of a full-time student couple with a child; *or*
  – you are a disabled student.

The way 'full-time student' is defined is the same as for housing benefit (HB – see p143). **Note:** it is *not* the same as the council tax definition described in this chapter. The groups of students eligible for CTB are the same as those eligible for HB (see p139).

You can get a claim form for CTB from the local authority. There is usually one form for claiming both CTB and HB. If you are claiming IS or income-based JSA, you claim CTB at the same time. You can claim backdated CTB if you receive a council tax bill for a past period on the grounds that the local authority has only just notified you of liability.

4. **Second adult rebate**

All students who are liable for council tax can claim second adult rebate. The law refers to this rebate as 'alternative maximum council tax benefit'. It is intended for people whose bill is higher because they live with others who cannot get a status discount and who cannot make a full contribution towards a share of the bill. You can only get a second adult rebate if you live with someone else who is not a full-time student.

Whether you get a rebate or not depends on the income of the people who share with you. Your own income or capital is ignored.

You can get a second adult rebate if:
- you are liable for council tax; *and*
- you have a 'second adult' (see below) living with you; *and*
- the second adult is on income support (IS) or income-based jobseeker's allowance (JSA), or has a low income; *and*
- you do not get rent from a tenant or sub-tenant (arguably rent from students or others who have a status discount should not disbar you from getting second adult rebate);[22] *and*
- you are in a couple and one or both of you are students or have a status discount for some other reason; *and*
- you are jointly liable for the council tax and all of those jointly liable are, or all but one are, students or have a status discount for some other reason.

A '**second adult**' is someone aged 18 or over who is a non-dependant (ie, someone who lives with you on a non-commercial basis), and is not a student and does not have a status discount for any other reason.

If you are eligible for second adult rebate and for council tax benefit, the local authority will decide which is worth the most to you. You cannot get both at the same time. If you get a second adult rebate, you get a reduction of 25 per cent, 15 per cent or 7.5 per cent depending on the income of the second adult.

Where a full-time student shares with others who all get either IS, JSA or pension credit and do not pay rent to the student, the discount can be 100 per cent. As the rules around second adult rebate are complex, you should get advice from your students' union, institution or local Citizens Advice Bureau.

Examples

Terry and his wife, June, live with their daughter, Minnie, aged 22. June is a student. Minnie is claiming JSA. Terry rents their house from a housing association. Terry can claim second adult rebate. Minnie is the second adult.

Dean is a student and he owns the flat he shares with his brother, Steve. Steve is aged 19 and works for the minimum wage. Dean can claim second adult rebate. Steve is the second adult.

Notes

2. **Who pays council tax**
1 Sch 1 para 5(1) CT(DD)O
2 Sch 1 para 6(1)(a) CT(DD)O
3 Sch 1 para 6(1)(e) CT(DD)O
4 Sch 1 para 6(1)(c) CT(DD)O
5 Sch 1 para 6(1)(d) CT(DD)O
6 Sch 1 paras 5(3) and 6(2) CT(DD)O
7 Sch 1 para 3 CT(DD)O
8 Sch 1 para 5(2) CT(DD)O
9 Sch 1 para 4(1) CT(DD)O
10 Sch 1 para 3 CT(DD)O
11 Council tax information letter 5, 29 April
  1996
12 Sch 1 para 5 LGFA 1992
13 Art 5 CT(DD)O
14 Kent Valuation Tribunal – appeal
  2220M23702/148C/1
15 [2008] EWHC 2531 (Admin)
16 Reg 3 CT(ED)O
17 s74 LGA 2003
18 s6 LGFA 1992
19 ss9 and 77 LGFA 1992

3. **Council tax benefit**
20 Reg 33 CTB Regs
21 Reg 45(2) CTB Regs

4. **Second adult rebate**
22 s131(6)(a) and (7) SSCBA 1992

Chapter 24

· ·

Tax and national insurance

This chapter covers:
1. Income tax (below)
2. National insurance (p285)
3. Further information (p288)

This chapter provides a brief introduction to income tax and national insurance (NI) as they affect full-time students. More information is available on the HM Revenue and Customs (the Revenue) website www.hmrc.gov.uk and you can find its contact details at www.hmrc.gov.uk/menus/contactus.shtml. The Revenue's taxes helpline number is 0845 300 0627; the helpline for NI queries is 0845 302 1479.

In principle, students are not in any special position with regard to income tax. However, most educational grants and scholarships, most research awards, student loans, and grants from discretionary funds do not normally count as taxable income. This means that most full-time students do not have to pay income tax or NI contributions on their student support.

1. Income tax

Rates and allowances

Income tax is charged on assessable income (income from all sources not subject to tax exemption) arising during a tax year (6 April to the following 5 April). The rates for the tax year 2010/11 are listed below.[1]

· ·

Income tax rates 2010/11

20 per cent basic rate on taxable income up to £37,400

40 per cent higher rate on taxable income above £37,400 up to £150,000

50 per cent additional rate on taxable income above £150,000

· ·

Every person resident in the UK has a personal allowance. This is an amount of yearly income on which you do not have to pay tax. It is deducted from total taxable income before the rate bands are applied. There may also be other tax allowances that you could claim, depending on your personal circumstances.

Income tax allowances 2010/11

Personal allowance[2]	£6,475
Blind person's allowance (additional)[3]	£1,890

Note that if your income exceeds £100,000, your personal allowance is reduced by £1 for every £2 of additional income.

For the 2011/12 tax year, the personal allowance will rise to £7,475. However, the higher rate threshold will reduce at the same time so that those with higher incomes will not benefit from the increase.

The blind person's allowance (BPA) is available for people with sight impairment. Despite its name, it is important to note that you do not have to be entirely without sight to claim it. You can claim BPA if either:

- you are registered blind with a local authority in England and Wales; *or*
- for those people living in Scotland/Northern Ireland, your sight is so bad as to stop you doing any work for which eyesight is essential.

Example

Alice earns £13,200 in her placement year from September 2010 to August 2011, so £7,700 is earned in the months to 5 April 2011 (the 2010/11 tax year) and £5,500 from 6 April 2011 (the 2011/12 tax year). In each tax year, she has a personal allowance; so in 2010/11, she pays no tax on the first £6,475 and 20 per cent on the remaining £1,225 – ie, £245. She should pay no tax in 2011/12 assuming she does not work after August 2011 for the rest of the tax year. Note, however, that she will have tax deducted from her pay in 2011/12 but will be able to claim it back after she stops work or at the end of the tax year.

Non-domiciles

Most students coming from overseas will be regarded as non-domiciled (generally if you and/or your father were born outside the UK). This means different rules apply in some cases, but much will depend on your own circumstances. More information is available in the Revenue's *Coming to the UK to study?* guide (see www.hmrc.gov.uk/cnr/guide-int-students.pdf).

Marriage and civil partnerships

The incomes of a husband and wife, and those of civil partners, are taxed separately; each of them is responsible for his or her own tax affairs.

Sponsorships and scholarships

Sponsorships and scholarships are not usually taxable, provided they do 'no more than support a student during a period of study'.[4] If you are required to work in a company or organisation and its sponsorship is part-payment for this, see the section on 'placement students' below.

Bank and building society interest

Banks and building societies have to deduct income tax from interest payments before they are credited to your savings account. However, if you believe your total income will not exceed your personal allowances over the tax year, you can fill out Form R85 and give it to your bank or building society who will then pay the interest without deducting tax. If tax is deducted from your interest and you are not due to pay any, or if the tax deducted is more than you are due to pay, you can claim the tax back by completing Form R40.

Tax rates for savings income 2010/11

10 per cent starting rate	£0 – £2,440
20 per cent basic rate	£2,441 – £37,400
40 per cent higher rate	£37,401 – £150,000
50 per cent additional rate	above £150,000

Note that if you have other taxable income (for example, from earnings) above the 10 per cent starting rate for savings, this limit would not apply, and it may be reduced if your other income is above your personal allowance but not above the 10 per cent band.

For more information on receiving your interest without tax being deducted and about claiming tax back, see www.hmrc.gov.uk/incometax/tax-free-interest.htm, which also has links to Forms R40 and R85.

Dividends on shares are also taxed – at 10 per cent up to the basic rate limit of £37,400, then at 32.5 per cent up to the higher rate limit and finally 42.5% at the additional rate for any amount above that. If you have shares in a UK company, when you get your dividend it should be accompanied by a tax credit voucher which shows the amount of the dividend payable and the amount of the tax credit that goes with that dividend. **'Dividend income'** for tax purposes is the dividend plus the tax credit.[5]

The tax credit is not tax deducted on your behalf; rather, it represents the fact that the company paying the dividend has paid tax on the profits used to pay the dividend. The tax credit, which is 10 per cent of the dividend income, can therefore be set against your tax liability on the dividend but it can never be refunded even if you are a non-taxpayer. Put another way, as some tax has already been paid on these earnings, the amount you have to pay is reduced accordingly.

Paying tax on your earnings

Vacation and part-time earnings

Students who are employed during vacations would normally expect to have tax deducted at source under the pay-as-you-earn (PAYE) system. However, if your overall income will not exceed your personal allowance over the whole tax year (see p282), you should ask your employer if you can complete the Form P38(S), which enables the employer to pay your wages without deducting any tax. This does not apply to evening or part-time work outside normal holiday times, or to vacation work where you expect your income to be more than the personal allowance. In these instances, you are required to complete Form P46, unless you have a P45 from a previous employer.

> **Example**
> Jamie takes a job during the summer vacation. He will work 24 hours a week and earn £7.50 an hour. The job is for eight weeks. Jamie will not work during term time so his annual income for income tax purposes is £1,440. This is below his personal allowance of £6,475 so he can ask his employer to complete Form P38(S).

Note that the Revenue intends to scrap the P38(S) form from 6 April 2011.

Placement students

Wages or salaries paid to placement students during periods of practical experience (including sandwich courses) are taxable as earned income under PAYE, subject to the usual tax-free allowances. However, if an employer sponsors your study, any wages/salary paid for periods spent at college, while normally taxable, can be paid tax free if:

- you are enrolled in college for at least one academic year; *and*
- attendance at college amounts to at least 20 weeks' full-time instruction within that academic year; *and*
- your earnings, including lodging or subsistence allowances, do not exceed £15,480 (excluding any fees paid by the employer).

These rules also apply if you are being released by your employer to study a course but continue to be paid as a full-time employee. For further guidance see www.hmrc.gov.uk/students/wf27_1.htm.

How income tax is paid

Employed earners

Under the PAYE system, tax is deducted by your employer from each wage payment, using a code number. Due to the way PAYE works, it is not uncommon for students to pay too much tax and have to contact the Revenue to claim it back.

Self-employed earners

If you are self-employed, you will usually be required to complete a self-assessment return and pay tax directly to the Revenue. Key tax payment dates are 31 January and 31 July. If you need help with your return, there is a specific self-assessment helpline: 0845 900 0444.

Tax and benefits

Some state benefits are taxable and some are not. For example, income support is not normally taxable and housing benefit is not taxable, but jobseeker's allowance (JSA) (both contribution-based and income-based) is taxable. However, tax is not deducted while benefit is paid but instead reduces the refund you might otherwise receive through the PAYE system when you either return to work or reach the end of the tax year, whichever is sooner.[6]

2. National insurance

National insurance (NI) is the government scheme to ensure that all those who earn above a certain amount contribute to the social security system. Paying into the scheme can entitle you to a range of benefits, including the state pension, depending on the type of contributions you pay. HM Revenue and Customs' (the Revenue) National Insurance Contributions Office keeps records of everyone's contributions and should issue you an NI number shortly before your 16th birthday.

Employers need an NI number for each employee in order to comply with taxation law. If you lose your number, or do not have one (eg, if you are an international student who is permitted to work in the UK), you must contact your local Jobcentre Plus office or, in Northern Ireland, your local Social Security/Jobs and Benefits office.

If a new number must be issued, the process can take several weeks to be completed. However, if you have lost your number, your employer can send the appropriate tax forms to the Revenue without one, and attempts will automatically be made to trace your number and inform your employer when it is found.

Who must pay national insurance contributions

Vacation or part-time work

Students are not required to pay NI contributions on any forms of student support. However, if you take up employment and your pay exceeds the earnings threshold of £110 a week (or £476 a month), you must pay Class 1 (earnings-related) contributions. Your employer deducts these from your wages. The rate of contribution for 2010/11 is 11 per cent of all earnings above the £110 a week threshold but below £844. All earnings above £844 a week incur a 1 per cent rate of contribution.[7] Note that even if you have signed a P38(S) for vacation work (see p284), it will only apply for income tax purposes and you will still have to pay NI contributions as normal.

> **Example**
>
> Bob earns £900 a week. He pays no NI contributions on the first £110. He pays 11 per cent on the next £734 (£80.74) and 1 per cent on the remaining £56 (£0.56). His weekly NI contribution is, therefore, £81.30.

If you are self-employed, you have to pay flat-rate Class 2 contributions of £2.40 for each week of self-employment if your income exceeds £5,075 in the 2010/11 tax year. If you have a lower income, you can apply for an exception from Class 2.[8] You also have to pay Class 4 contributions of 8 per cent on profits or gains between £5,715 and £43,875 and 1 per cent on any amount above this.[9]

Postgraduate students
If you are a research student, you should check if you are liable for Class 1 or Classes 2 and 4 contributions if you are paid for teaching or demonstrating.

Placement students
Placement students are liable to pay Class 1 contributions while receiving wages/salaries for periods of work experience, although this income can be classed as exempt scholarship income for periods spent attending college.

Note: if you have been released from work to take a course but continue to be paid by your employer, some of this income can qualify as scholarship income and is exempt from contributions.

Age limits
No NI contributions are payable if you are under the age of 16 or over state pension age, although you may have to apply for an exemption if your earnings would otherwise attract contributions.

Voluntary contributions

Your entitlement to the state retirement pension depends on your having paid NI contributions at a certain level for a set number of years during your 'working life'. For anyone retiring after 6 April 2010, enough contributions for 30 years must have been paid to receive a full basic pension.

Reduced rates of the basic state pension are possible but NI contributions must still have been made at the correct rate for at least 25 per cent of the required time.

However, if you have not paid this amount of contributions you can pay voluntary contributions to make up the 'missing' years. These contributions are paid at a flat rate under Class 3; the rate for 2010/11 is £12.05 a week.[10]

You can preserve your entitlement to only the state pension and to widows' and bereavement benefits in this way. If you do not have a recent record of employment, you cannot gain access to short-term benefits (eg, contribution-based jobseeker's allowance (JSA), contributory employment and support allowance (ESA) and maternity benefit) by paying Class 3 contributions.

Deciding whether to pay voluntary contributions

Before committing yourself to paying voluntary Class 3 contributions, contact the State Pension Forecasting Team on 0845 300 0168 or online at www.direct.gov.uk/statepension to establish your likely pension at retirement age and, therefore, whether it is necessary to make voluntary contributions in light of your personal circumstances and overall contribution record. This is especially relevant if you are a mature or postgraduate student, have taken time out of work for children or caring duties (in which case you might be awarded NI 'credits'), or have lived abroad for long periods of time during your working life. Under the current rules, most younger students will not have a reduction to any pension entitlement by not paying contributions during their studies, as they will have sufficient time after completing full-time education in which to qualify for full pension rights.

Voluntary contributions may generally only be paid up to the end of the sixth tax year after they were 'due' other than in exceptional circumstances.

If you are thinking of replacing the additional state pension with a personal or occupational pension (known as 'contracting out'), always check which would be the most advantageous for your personal circumstances. Pension Service leaflets are available from Jobcentre Plus offices and Citizens Advice Bureaux or from www.direct.gov.uk/en/Diol1/DoItOnline/DG_179755.

Contribution rates

Contribution rates 6 April 2010 to 5 April 2011

Contribution type	Weekly earnings	Employee's contribution
Class 1	Below £110 (earnings threshold)	Nil
	£110.01–£844	11% (in additional state pension)
		9.4% (contracted out of additional state pension)
	£844.01 and over	1%
Class 2 (self-employed)		£2.40 flat rate a week of self-employment

Class 3 (voluntary)		£12.05 a week flat rate
Class 4 (self-employed)	On profits between £5,715–£43,875	8%
	On profits above £43,875	1%

National insurance contributions and benefits

- **Class 1 contributions** may later entitle you to contributory ESA, contribution-based JSA, basic state pension, bereavement allowance and widowed parent's allowance. If you are a low earner, you can build up an entitlement to contributory benefits if you are earning between the 'lower earnings limit' (£97 a week for 2010/11) and the earnings threshold of £110 a week, even though you are not actually paying NI contributions.
- **Class 2 contributions** may later entitle you to contributory ESA, basic state pension, bereavement allowance and maternity allowance.
- **Class 3 contributions** allow you to top up your benefit entitlement to possibly provide you with a higher state pension, and widows' and bereavement benefits.
- **Class 4 contributions** do not lead to any social security benefit entitlements.

The exact level of necessary NI contributions varies depending on the benefit. Paying NI contributions does not entitle you to benefits you would not otherwise be able to claim as a student.

3. **Further information**

- HM Revenue and Customs website: www.hmrc.gov.uk.
- Information for students: www.hmrc.gov.uk/students.
- Address of your nearest HM Revenue and Customs office: www.hmrc.gov.uk/menus/contactus.shtml.
- Information on tax issues for students from the Low Incomes Tax Reform Group: www.litrg.org.uk.

Notes

1. **Income tax**
   1 s1 FA 2010
   2 s1 FA 2010
   3 s1 FA 2010
   4 s776 IT(TOI)A 2005 and the Revenue's
     EIM06220
   5 s8 ITA 2007
   6 ss671-75 IT(EP)A 2003 and part 8
     IT(PAYE) Regs

2. **National insurance**
   7 s5 SSCBA 1992 and reg10 SS(C) Regs
   8 s11 SSCBA 1992
   9 s15 SSCBA 1992
   10 s13 SSCBA 1992

Chapter 25

· ·

Time out from studies

This chapter covers:
1. Time out because of ill health (below)
2. Time out because of pregnancy or children (p293)
3. Time out to be a carer (p295)
4. Re-sits (p296)

This chapter provides a checklist of student support and benefits that you may be eligible for if you have to take time out from your studies. You must meet the usual rules of entitlement. For more details about a specific benefit, including how to claim, see the relevant chapter.

1. **Time out because of ill health**

Full-time students

If you are a full-time student, your entitlement to benefits depends on your age, how long you have been ill, whether you have paid any national insurance (NI) contributions and whether you need personal care or have mobility difficulties. Once you have recovered from your illness, you may be able to 'sign on' for certain benefits such as jobseeker's allowance until you can return to your course.

Note: this chapter assumes you are claiming on the grounds of ill health for the first time and are, therefore, claiming employment and support allowance (ESA). However, if your period of ill health can link to a previous period, you may be able to claim income support and incapacity benefit instead (see Chapters 13 and 14).

From the start of your ill health

You are eligible for contributory ESA after three 'waiting' days if you have paid sufficient NI contributions in recent years (see Chapter 10).

After three months

You can claim disability living allowance (DLA) if you need personal care or have mobility difficulties. You are eligible for this after three months if your disability is likely to last at least another six months.

If you get DLA you can also claim income-related ESA, and housing benefit (HB) to help with rent (and rates if you live in Northern Ireland), as well as council tax benefit (CTB) if you are liable.

After 28 weeks

You can claim:

- contributory ESA in youth from your 19th birthday (or age 16, 17 or 18 if your course is less than 21 hours a week, not including any hours of tuition that would not be suitable for someone of the same age who is not disabled). Ask your doctor for a backdated medical certificate for 28 weeks of limited capability for work. If you are already 20 by the time you have had 28 weeks of limited capability for work, you can still claim as long as you do so straight away, and as long as your limited capability for work started before your 20th birthday. Otherwise, if you are over 20 but under 25, you can claim contributory ESA in youth only if you leave the course;
- HB to help with your rent (and rates in Northern Ireland if you are liable);
- CTB to help with your council tax if you are liable.

The 28-week period runs from the day your limited capability for work begins, not from the day you leave your course. See p120 for how your limited capability for work is assessed. You do not need to have been working to count as having limited capability for work. **Note:** you can have limited capability for work but still be able to study, so contributory ESA can continue when you return to college or university.

Once you have recovered

Once you have recovered, you may need to wait some time before you are readmitted to your course. During this time you can claim:[1]

- jobseeker's allowance (JSA). You need to 'sign on' at your Jobcentre Plus office;
- HB;
- CTB.

You can claim from the day you recover until the day before the college or university agrees you can return to your course – up to a maximum of one year. You cannot claim the above benefits if you get a grant or loan during this period. Once the student support stops, you can claim.

Student support

Full-time undergraduate students under the 'old' or 'current' system of support (see Chapters 2, 3 and 4) receiving a student loan paid for living costs, higher education grants and supplementary grants may have their student support suspended after 60 days' absence because of ill health.[2] However, local authorities, Student Finance England (SFE) and education and library boards (ELBs) have the discretion to continue making student loan payments for living costs for the rest of the academic year.[3]

Your college or university should write to your local authority/SFE/ELB explaining why it has suspended you from your course. You should also contact your local authority/SFE/ELB in writing and request that it continues to pay you while you are ill.

Any student who is personally eligible can also apply to the college or university for discretionary help from the hardship fund, Access to Learning Fund or Financial Contingency Fund.

If you receive a bursary from your college or university and want to take time out from your studies, you should check with the institution to see if it will continue to be paid while you take the time out and what will happen when you return to your studies.

Example

Kerry is 23. She is studying for a degree in engineering at Manchester University.

She completed her first year on a full-time basis from September 2009 to July 2010, for which she received a full student loan for tuition fees, a full student loan for living costs, a full maintenance grant and a £500 institutional bursary. She begins her second year in September 2010 and receives the same support. In February 2011 she has to suspend her studies because of illness. She will not be paid any further fee loan until she returns to her studies. She continues to receive her student loan for living costs and maintenance grant for 60 days. She applies to SFE to have her student loan and grant payments extended while she is ill. SFE agrees to continue her loan payments, but not her grant payments until she recovers from her illness, which is in June 2011. She applies to her institution for her bursary to continue to be paid. The institution agrees to this. Kerry agrees with her institution to return to her studies in January 2012. She can claim JSA from June 2011 until she returns to her studies in January 2012.

If you are receiving an adult learning grant (ALG) and need to interrupt your studies for any reason, the guidance previously stated:[4]

> Some ALG learners may require long-term absence, for example, maternity leave, severe medical conditions or jury service. In these circumstances, a learning programme should be agreed that, where possible, enables the learner to continue their studies, should they wish to do so. The aim should be to ensure that the minimum requirement of 450 guided learning hours over the academic year is achieved.

No mention is made of long-term absence in the 2010/11 guidance. You may be able to argue that your circumstances should be assessed and consideration given to how the course and payment of ALG can continue – speak to the student services department at the college or learning provider.

Part-time students

If you are a part-time student, you can claim income-related ESA as soon as you are ill and incapable of work, whether or not you get DLA.

From the start of your ill health

If you are already getting JSA, you continue to receive it for two weeks. After two weeks, you need to claim ESA instead.

You can claim:

- ESA if your income is low or you have paid enough NI contributions;
- HB;
- CTB.

After three months

You can claim DLA if you need personal care or have mobility difficulties. You are eligible for this after three months if your disability is likely to last for at least another six months.

After 28 weeks

If you have not paid enough NI contributions to claim contributory ESA at the start of your illness, and your income is too high to allow you to claim income-related ESA, you can claim contributory ESA after 28 weeks if your ill health began before your 20th birthday. This is called contributory ESA in youth (see p117). The earliest you can claim is your 16th birthday. You should send in a backdated medical certificate from your doctor for 28 weeks with your claim. As your 'limited capability for work' must have begun before your 20th birthday, the latest you can claim is 28 weeks (the qualifying period) plus three months (the automatic backdating period allowed in ESA claims) after the day before your 20th birthday.

In this case, you must ask for your claim to be backdated for three months and supply a medical certificate covering both the qualifying period and the backdating period.

The 28-week period runs from the day your 'limited capability for work' begins, not from the day you leave your course. See p120 for how limited capability for work is assessed.

Once you have recovered

You can claim JSA if you are available for work.

2. **Time out because of pregnancy or children**

Student support

If you are a full-time undergraduate student receiving a student loan paid for living costs and any grants for living costs, your local authority, Student Finance

England (SFE) or education and library board (ELB) has the discretion to continue making these payments for the rest of that academic year.[5]

Your college or university should write to your local authority/SFE/ELB explaining why it has suspended you from your course. You should also contact your local authority/SFE/ELB in writing and request that it continues to pay you while you are taking time out.

If you are an NHS-funded healthcare student in England or Wales, you can continue to receive your bursary while on maternity leave. Contact NHS Student Bursaries in England or the NHS Student Awards Unit in Wales for details.

You could also apply to your college or university for support from the Access to Learning Fund, Financial Contingency Fund or hardship funds.

If you receive a bursary from your college or university and want to take time out from your studies, you should check with the institution to see if this will continue to be paid while you take the time out and what will happen when you return to your studies.

If you receive an adult learning grant, see p292.

Benefits

There is no provision for pregnant full-time students to claim income support (IS) or housing benefit (HB).

As a part-time student, you can claim IS once you reach the 11th week before your 'expected week of childbirth', or earlier if your pregnancy has made you ill and incapable of work.

If you have an employer, you may be able to get statutory maternity pay. If you are not working now but have worked recently, you may be able to get maternity allowance.

You can claim a health in pregnancy grant from the 25th week of pregnancy, although note that these grants will be scrapped from January 2011. See p132.

Once the baby is born there are various benefits you can claim. See Chapter 16 for more details.

Lone parents

Once the baby is born, a lone parent can claim the following while studying full time:

- child benefit;
- child tax credit (CTC);
- IS until your youngest child is 10 (seven from 25 October 2010 – see p174);
- jobseeker's allowance (JSA) in the summer vacation (for those who are not eligible for IS, or those who are eligible but would prefer to claim JSA instead – see p190);
- HB;
- council tax benefit (CTB) (if liable for council tax);

- a Sure Start maternity grant of £500 (claims must be made within three months of the birth, or, in some cases, before the birth – see p209);
- Healthy Start food vouchers and vitamins (see p131).

Fathers and partners

If your partner has had a baby and you have an employer, you may be able to claim statutory paternity pay. You can claim if you are the child's father or the mother's partner (married, unmarried or of the same sex) and you will be caring for the baby or the mother.

Couples

A full-time student couple (ie, both of you are students) with a child can claim the following throughout the course:
- child benefit;
- CTC;
- HB;
- CTB (if liable for council tax).

A full-time student couple with a child can claim the following in the long vacation:
- IS (if eligible under the usual non-student rules); *or*
- JSA.

Couples can also claim a Sure Start maternity grant if one of them gets a qualifying benefit (see p209).

If you are a full-time student and a parent and you have a partner who is not a student, s/he can claim benefits for you under the usual benefit rules.

3. **Time out to be a carer**

If you are a full-time student, you may have stopped doing your course to care for someone. If you suspend your studies, your local authority, Student Finance England or education and library board has the discretion to keep paying your student loan and grant for living costs, if you have been receiving one.[6] You could also apply to your college or university for support from the Access to Learning Fund, Financial Contingency Fund or hardship funds.

If, once your caring responsibilities come to an end, you have to wait before you can return to the course, you can 'sign on' for jobseeker's allowance, and claim housing benefit and council tax benefit. You can claim for up to a year until the day from which the university or college agrees you can return to your course.[7] You are not eligible, however, if you get a grant or loan during this time.

If you receive a bursary from your college or university and want to take time out from your studies, you should check with the institution to see if this will continue to be paid while you take the time out and what will happen when you return to your studies.

If you receive an adult learning grant, see p292.

See Chapter 7 for information on claiming carer's allowance.

4. Re-sits

If you are a full-time student taking time out to re-sit exams, you are still treated as a student during your absence from the course. You cannot claim income support (IS) or jobseeker's allowance (JSA) during this time, unless you would be eligible anyway as a student – eg, as a lone parent or disabled student.

One exception applies to students taking professional qualifications set by a professional institute or some other body unconnected with their own college or university – eg, chartered accountants. They may be able to claim IS or JSA while taking time out for re-sits. If you are in this situation, you may need to be prepared to appeal and argue that caselaw supports your getting benefit.[8]

If you receive a bursary from your college or university and want to take time out from your studies, you should check with the institution to see if this will continue to be paid while you take the time out and what will happen when you return to your studies.

Notes

1. **Time out because of ill health**
   1 **JSA** Reg 1(3D) JSA Regs; para 30121 DMG
   HB Reg 56(6) HB Regs
   CTB Reg 45(7) CTB Regs
   HB/CTB Circular A32/2000 para 6
   2 Reg 112(14) E(SS) Regs
   3 Reg 112 (12)-(13) E(SS) Regs
   4 ALG Guidance, 2009/10, p17

2. **Time because of pregnancy or children**
   5 Reg 112(12)-(13) E(SS) Regs

3. **Time out to be a carer**
   6 Reg 112(12)-(13) E(SS) Regs
   7 **JSA** Reg 1 JSA Regs
   HB Reg 56(6) HB Regs
   CTB Reg 45(7) CTB Regs
   HB/CTB Circular A32/2000 para 6

4. **Re-sits**
   8 CJSA/1457/1999

Appendices

Appendices

Appendix 1

. . . .

Information and advice

Student support

Official guidance

The Department for Business, Innovation and Skills (BIS) issues guidance on existing higher education (HE) student support legislation for England and forthcoming provisions. The guidance has no legal standing, but may be quoted in an appeal. It is available at the Student Finance England website at http://practitioners.studentfinanceengland.co.uk. Guidance includes:

- notes for funding bodies on the student support regulations;
- *Student Support Update* – a monthly newsletter on HE student support and forthcoming changes;
- student support information notes containing announcements of forthcoming student support provision;
- Access to Learning Fund guidance on the framework for colleges to implement discretionary funds.

The Department for Education (DfE) and BIS also issue guidance to providers and partners on the learner support schemes in further education in England. These can be found at www.ypla.gov.uk/learnersupport and http://skillsfundingagency.bis.gov.uk/providers/programmes/ls.

Information and guidance on funding in Wales is available from the Welsh Assembly at www.wales.gov.uk/sfwpartnersub/home.

Information and support fund guidance for HE institutes in Northern Ireland is available on the Department for Employment and Learning website at www.delni.gov.uk.

Advice

Contact student advisers within institutions and students' unions for advice on student support. A list of such advisory services is available at the website of the National Association of Student Money Advisers at www.nasma.org.uk.

Social security benefits and tax credits

Publications

The following guide books are available from CPAG at 94 White Lion Street, London N1 9PF. An order form is available on CPAG's website at www.cpag.org.uk/publications, or telephone CPAG on 020 7837 7979.

- *Benefits for Students in Scotland Handbook* 2010/11, £13.50
- *Welfare Benefits and Tax Credits Handbook* 2010/11, £39. The 2011/12 edition is due April 2011. Also available online – visit http://onlineservices.cpag.org.uk for more information.
- *Council Tax Handbook*, 8th edition, £17
- *Guide to Housing Benefit and Council Tax Benefit* 2010/11, £26.00
- *The Young Person's Handbook*, 4th edition, £15.95

Official guidance

The following guidance, used by decision makers in the Department for Work and Pensions (DWP) and local authorities, is available on the DWP website at www.dwp.gov.uk/publications/specialist-guides. This guidance has no legal standing so you cannot quote it in an appeal, but it can be useful to refer decision makers to the guidance if you are seeking to have a decision overturned by an internal revision or supersession.

- *Decision Makers' Guide*
- *A Detailed Guide to Income Support*
- *A Guide to the Social Fund*

In Northern Ireland, the equivalent guidance is provided by the Department for Social Development (DSD). Advice and guidance is available on the DSD website at www.dsdni.gov.uk/index/ssa/information_for_advisors.

Legislation

- *The Law Relating to Social Security*
  - Volume 6 deals with income-related benefits (including income support, family credit and disability working allowance) and the social fund
  - Volume 8 deals with housing benefit and council tax benefit
  - Volume 11 deals with jobseeker's allowance

  This is available at www.dwp.gov.uk/publications/specialist-guides/law-volumes. These volumes are officially produced and contain updated Acts and Regulations relating to social security.
- *Social Security Legislation*, Volumes 1 to 4. Published by Sweet and Maxwell, these volumes contain updated Acts and Regulations covering social security and tax credits with explanatory commentary. Available from CPAG.
- CPAG's *Housing Benefit and Council Tax Benefit Legislation*. Published by CPAG, this contains updated Acts and Regulations and a detailed commentary. Also available online – visit http://onlineservices.cpag.org.uk for more information.

- *Decisions of the Social Security and Child Support Commissioners.* Reported decisions are available from the DWP website at www.dwp.gov.uk/commdecs. Unreported decisions are available from the website of the Tribunals Service at www.osscsc.gov.uk.

Advice

Contact your student services department or students' union for advice on studying and claiming benefits.

Appendix 2

Useful addresses

General sources of information

Child Poverty Action Group
94 White Lion Street
London N1 9PF
Tel: 020 7837 7979
Advice line for advisers only:
020 7833 4627
(2–4pm Monday to Friday)
advice@cpag.org.uk
www.cpag.org.uk

CPAG provides an advice,
information and training service to
advisers.

Educational Grants Advisory Service
Family Action
501–505 Kingsland Road
London E8 4AU
Tel: 020 7241 7459
(2–4pm on Tuesday, Wednesday
and Thursday only)
egas.enquiry@family-action.org.uk
www.family-action.org.uk/grants

EGAS gives information on
alternative sources of student
funding. Complete a student
questionnaire, available from its
website or by sending a stamped,
addressed envelope to obtain a copy.

National Union of Students
4th Floor
184–192 Drummond Street
London NW1 3HP
Tel: 020 7380 6600
www.nus.org.uk

NUS provides information on
entitlement to student support,
benefits and tax credits, along with
other student welfare issues.

**National Union of Students-Union of
Students in Ireland**
42 Dublin Road
Belfast BT2 7HN
Tel: 028 9024 4641
info@nistudents.org
www.nistudents.org

NUS-USI represents students in
Northern Ireland and can provide
advice and information on student
support and benefits.

NUS Wales
13 Lambourne Crescent
Cardiff CF4 5GF
Tel: 029 5068 0070
office@nus-wales.org.uk

NUS Wales represents students in
Wales and campaigns on student
support and other welfare issues.

Skill: National Bureau for Students with Disabilities
Unit 3, Floor 3
Radisson Court
219 Long Lane
London SE1 4PR
Tel/textphone: 020 7450 0620
Information service: 0800 328 5050
Information service textphone: 18001 0800 328 5050
info@skill.org.uk
www.skill.org.uk

Skill produces a number of booklets and information sheets.

UKCISA (UK Council for International Student Affairs)
9–17 St Albans Place
London N1 0NX
Tel: 020 7288 4330
Advice Line: 020 7107 9922
1–4pm, Monday to Friday
www.ukcisa.org.uk

UKCISA provides advice and information for overseas students.

Support for learning

Arts and Humanities Research Council
Polaris House
North Star Avenue
Swindon SN2 1FL
Tel: 01793 416 000
enquiries@ahrc.ac.uk
www.ahrc.ac.uk

Biotechnology and Biological Sciences Research Council
Polaris House
North Star Avenue
Swindon SN2 1UH
Tel: 01793 413 200
www.bbsrc.ac.uk

Care Council for Wales
Southgate House
Wood Street
Cardiff CF10 1EW
Tel: 029 2022 6257
info@ccwales.org.uk
www.ccwales.org.uk

The CCW provides bursary support to undergraduate social work students in Wales.

Dance and drama awards
www.direct.gov.uk/danceanddrama

Department for Business, Innovation and Skills
1 Victoria Street
London SW1H 0ET
Tel: 020 7215 5000
www.bis.gov.uk

Responsible for student support for higher education in England and for adult learners in further education in England.

Department for Children, Education, Lifelong Learning and Skills
Tel: 0845 010 3300 or 0300 060 3300
dcells.enquiries@wales.gsi.gov.uk
http://wales.gov.uk/about/civilservice/departments/dcells

Responsible for education funding in Wales.

Department for Education
Castle View House
East Lane
Runcorn
Cheshire WA7 2GJ
Tel: 0870 000 2288
Textphone/minicom: 18001 0870 000 2288
www.education.gov.uk

Responsible for learner support for 16–19-year-olds in England.

Department for Employment and Learning

Student Finance Branch
4th Floor
Adelaide House
39–49 Adelaide Street
Belfast BT2 8FD
Tel: 028 9025 7710
Fax: 028 9025 7747
studentfinance@delni.gov.uk
www.delni.gov.uk

Responsible for student financial support in Northern Ireland.

Department of Health

Department of Health
Richmond House
79 Whitehall
London SW1A 2NS
Tel: 020 7210 4850
Textphone: 020 7210 5025
www.dh.gov.uk

Responsible for NHS-funded students in England.

Department of Health, Social Services and Public Safety

Social Work Student Incentive Scheme
Bursary Administration Section
Office of Social Services
Castle Buildings
Stormont
Belfast BT4 3SQ
Tel: 028 9052 0517
www.dhsspsni.gov.uk

Provides bursaries for social work students in Northern Ireland.

Economic and Social Research Council

Polaris House
North Star Avenue
Swindon SN2 1UJ
Tel: 01793 413 000
www.esrc.ac.uk

Educational Guidance Service for Adults

4th Floor
40 Linenhall Street
Belfast BT2 8BA
Tel: 028 9024 4274
www.egsa.org.uk

Engineering and Physical Sciences Research Council

Polaris House
North Star Avenue
Swindon SN2 1ET
Tel: 01793 444 000
studentships@epsrc.ac.uk
www.epsrc.ac.uk

Medical Research Council

20 Park Crescent
London W1B 1AL
Tel: 020 7636 5422
mrcgrants@ssc.rcuk.ac.uk
www.mrc.ac.uk

Natural Environment Research Council

Polaris House
North Star Avenue
Swindon SN2 1EU
Tel: 01793 411 500
www.nerc.ac.uk

NHS Business Services Authority
NHS Student Bursaries
Hesketh House
200–220 Broadway
Fleetwood Lancashire FY7 8SS
Tel: 0845 358 6655
bursary@nhspa.gov.uk
www.nhsbsa.nhs.uk/students

Provides information on funding
and assessments for students
undertaking allied health
professions courses in England.

Social Work Bursary
Sandyford House
Newcastle Upon Tyne NE2 1DB
Tel: 0845 610 1122
swb@ppa.nhs.uk
www.nhsbsa.nhs.uk/students

Administers social work bursaries for
all social work students in England.

NHS Careers Helpline
Tel: 0345 6060 655
www.nhscareers.nhs.uk

Provides information about entering
into careers in the healthcare
professions in the NHS in England.

NHS Wales Student Awards Unit
3rd Floor
14 Cathedral Road
Cardiff CF11 9LJ
Tel: 029 2019 6167
www.nliah.wales.nhs.uk

Provides information and
assessments for students
undertaking allied health
professions courses in Wales.

**Professional and career development
loans**
Tel: 0800 585 505
www.direct.gov.uk/cdl

**Science and Technology Facilities
Council**
Polaris House
North Star Avenue
Swindon SN2 1SZ
Tel: 01793 442 000
enquiries@stfc.ac.uk
www.scitech.ac.uk

Skills Funding Agency
Cheylesmore House
Quinton Road
Coventry CV1 2WT
Tel: 0845 377 5000
info@skillsfundingagency.bis.gov.uk
http://skillsfundingagency.bis.gov.uk

Allocates funding for adult further
education and skills training in
England.

Student Finance NI
County Hall
182 Galgorm Road
Ballymena
Co Antrim BT42 1HN
Tel: 0845 600 0662
www.studentfinanceni.co.uk

Provides financial support to
students who normally live in
Northern Ireland, in partnership
with the Department for
Employment and Learning, the
Student Loans Company and the five
education and library boards in
Northern Ireland.

Student Finance Services European Team

Student Finance Services European Team
PO Box 89
Darlington DL1 9AZ
Tel: 0141 243 3570
eu_team@slc.co.uk
www.direct.gov.uk/studentfinance-EU

Provides information about applications by European Union students for fee payment support in England.

Student Finance Wales

Tel: 0845 602 8845
Minicom: 0845 603 1693
www.studentfinancewales.co.uk

Student Finance Wales is a Welsh Assembly Government-led partnership responsible for administering student financial support to students who normally live in Wales.

Student Loans Company

100 Bothwell Street
Glasgow G2 7JD
Tel: 0845 300 5090
Minicom: 0845 604 4434
www.slc.co.uk
www.direct.gov.uk/studentfinance
www.studentfinancewales.co.uk
www.studentfinanceni.co.uk

Responsible for administering government-funded loans and grants throughout the UK. Guides and information leaflets about financial support available for students are available from www.direct.gov.uk/studentfinance. They include:

- *Bridging the Gap: a guide for the disabled students' allowances (DSAs) in higher education in 2010/11*
- *Childcare Grant and Other Support for Full-time Student Parents in Higher Education 2010/11*
- *A Guide to Financial Support for Higher Education Students in 2010/11*
- *A Guide to Financial Support for Part-time Students in Higher Education 2010/11*

Training and Development Agency for Schools

151 Buckingham Palace Road
London SW1W 9SZ
Tel: 0845 600 0991 (for English speakers)
Tel: 0845 600 0992 (for Welsh speakers)
www.tda.gov.uk

Responsible for teacher training in England and Wales.

Universities and Colleges Admissions Service

Rose Hill
New Barn Lane
Cheltenham
Gloucestershire GL52 3LZ
Tel: 0871 468 0468
Text relay service:
18001 0871 468 0468
enquiries:@ucas.ac.uk
www.ucas.com

Contact UCAS for information on applying to higher education, or to obtain copies of two useful booklets:
- *The Parent Guide*
- *Student Finance*

Young People's Learning Agency
  Cheylesmore House
  Quinton Road
  Coventry CV1 2WT
  Tel: 0845 337 2000
  enquiries@ypla.gov.uk
  www.ypla.gov.uk

Supports the delivery of training and education to 16–19-year-olds in England.

Benefits and tax credits

Benefit Enquiry Line
  2nd Floor
  Red Rose House
  Lancaster Road
  Preston
  Lancashire PR1 1HB
  Tel: 0800 882 200
  Textphone : 0800 243 355
  BEL-Customer-Services@dwp.gsi.gov.uk
  www.direct.gov.uk/disability-money

Child Tax Credit and Working Tax Credit Helpline
  Tel: 0845 300 3900
  Textphone: 0845 300 3909
  www.hmrc.gov.uk/taxcredits

Department for Social Development
  www.dsdni.gov.uk

Responsible for social security in Northern Ireland.

Department for Work and Pensions
  Caxton House
  Tothill Street
  London SW1H 9DA
  enquiries@dwp.gsi.gov.uk
  www.dwp.gov.uk

Responsible for social security in England, Wales and Scotland. The DWP website has information on general entitlement to benefits and provides advisers with the *Decision Makers' Guide*.

Local Government Ombudsman
  PO Box 4771
  Coventry CV4 0EH
  Tel: 0300 061 0614 or 0845 602 1983
  advice@lgo.org.uk
  www.lgo.org.uk

The Local Government Ombudsman can investigate claims of maladministration by local authorities in England in respect of benefit claims or student support applications.

Northern Ireland Ombudsman's Office
  Freepost BEL 1478
  Belfast BT1 6BR
  Tel: 0800 343 424
  ombudsman@ni-ombudsman.org.uk
  www.ni-ombudsman.org.uk

The Northern Ireland Ombudsman's Office can investigate claims of maladministration by local authorities in Northern Ireland in respect of benefit claims or student support applications.

Public Services Ombudsman for Wales
  1 Ffordd yr Hen Gae
  Pencoed CF35 5LJ
  Tel: 01656 641 150
  ask@ombudsman-wales.org.uk
  www.ombudsman-wales.org.uk

The Public Services Ombudsman for Wales can investigate claims of maladministration by local authorities in Wales in respect of benefit claims or student support applications.

Other issues

Department of Health Publications
PO Box 777
London SE1 6XH
Tel: 0300 123 1002
Minicom: 0300 123 1003
Fax: 01623 724 524
www.orderline.dh.gov.uk

For bulk orders of HC1 forms – eg, for students' union advice centres.

HM Revenue and Customs
www.hmrc.gov.uk/students

For information on claiming tax back:
www.hmrc.gov.uk/taxback
For the address of your nearest HMRC office:
www.hmrc.gov.uk/menus/contactus.shtml

NHS Business Services Authority Help with Health Costs
Tel: 0845 850 1166
lis1@ppa.nhs.uk
www.nhsbsa.nhs.uk/healthcosts

The NHS Business Services Authority Help with Health Costs advises students on low-income scheme claims.

Appendix 3

Abbreviations used in the notes

General abbreviations

Art(s)	Article(s)
EWCA	England and Wales Court of Appeal
EWHC	England and Wales High Court
para(s)	paragraph(s)
reg(s)	regulation(s)
s(s)	Section(s)
Sch(s)	Schedule(s)

Acts of Parliament

Acts of Parliament can be ordered from TSO Customer Services, PO Box 29, Norwich NR3 1GN (tel: 0870 600 5522; textphone: 0870 240 3701). Recent Acts are available at www.tsoshop.co.uk.

CA 1989	Children Act 1989
C(LC)A 2000	Children (Leaving Care) Act 2000
C(LC)A(NI) 2002	Children (Leaving Care) Act (Northern Ireland) 2002
EA 1996	Education Act 1996
ESA 2008	Education and Skills Act 2008
ETA 1973	Employment and Training Act 1973
FA 2010	Finance Act 2010
HEA 2004	Higher Education Act 2004
HSCA 2008	Health and Social Care Act 2008
ITA 2007	Income Tax Act 2007
IT(EP)A 2003	Income Tax (Earnings and Pensions) Act 2003
IT(TOI)A 2005	Income Tax (Trading and Other Income) Act 2005
JSA 1995	Jobseeker's Act 1995
LGA 2003	Local Government Act 2003
LGFA 1992	Local Government Finance Act 1992
NICA 2002	National Insurance Contributions Act 2002
SSA 1998	Social Security Act 1998
SSAA 1992	Social Security Administration Act 1992

SSCBA 1992	Social Security Contributions and Benefits Act 1992
TCA 2002	Tax Credits Act 2002
WRA 2007	Welfare Reform Act 2007

Regulations

Regulations can be ordered from TSO Customer Services, PO Box 29, Norwich NR3 1GN (tel: 0870 600 5522; textphone: 0870 240 3701). Recent Acts are available at www.tsoshop.co.uk. Each set of Regulations has a statutory instrument (SI) number and a date. You ask for them by giving their date and number.

ALGL(HE)(W) Regs	The Assembly Learning Grants and Loans (Higher Education)(Wales) Regulations 2009 No.2737
CB Regs	The Child Benefit (General) Regulations 2006 No.223
CBGA(A) Regs	The Child Benefit and Guardian's Allowance (Administration) Regulations 2003 No.492
C(LC)(E) Regs	The Children (Leaving Care) (England) Regulations 2001 No.2874
C(LC)(W) Regs	The Children (Leaving Care) (Wales) Regulations 2001 No.1855
CT(DD)O	The Council Tax (Discount Disregards) Order 1992 No.548
CT(ED)O	The Council Tax (Exempt Dwellings) Order 1992 No.558
CTB Regs	The Council Tax Benefit (General) Regulations 2006 No.215
CTC Regs	The Child Tax Credit Regulations 2002 No.2007
E(ALGS)(W) Regs	The Education (Assembly Learning Grant Scheme) (Wales) Regulations 2002 No.1857
E(G)(DD)(E) Regs	The Education (Grants, etc.) (Dance and Drama) (England) Regulations 2001 No.2857
ESA Regs	The Employment and Support Allowance Regulations 2008 No. 794
ESA(TP) Regs	The Employment and Support Allowance (Transitional Provisions) Regulations 2008 No.795
E(SL) Regs 1998	The Education (Student Loan) Regulations 1998 No. 211
E(SL)(R) Regs	The Education (Student Loans) (Repayment) Regulations 2009 No. 470
E(SS) Regs	The Education (Student Support) Regulations 2009 No.1555
E(SS)(NI) Regs	The Education (Student Support) (No.2) Regulations (Northern Ireland) 2009 No.373
E(WMTTIS) Regs	The Education (Welsh Medium Teacher Training Incentive Supplement) Regulations 1990 No.1208
HB Regs	The Housing Benefit (General) Regulations 2006 No.213
HSS&WF(A) Regs	The Healthy Start Scheme and Welfare Food (Amendment) Regulations 2005 No.3262

ILA (W) Regs	Individual Learning Accounts (Wales) Regulations 2003, No.918
IS Regs	The Income Support (General) Regulations 1987 No.1967
IT(I)(No.4)O	The Income Tax (Indexation) (No.4) Order 2008 No.3024
IT(PAYE) Regs	The Income Tax (Pay As You Earn) Regulations 2003 No.2682
JSA Regs	The Jobseeker's Allowance Regulations 1996 No.207
NHS(CDA) Regs	The National Health Service (Charges for Drugs and Appliances) Regulations 2000 No.620
NHS(DC) Regs	The National Health Service (Dental Charges) Regulations 2005 No.3477
NHS(DC) (W) Regs	The National Health Service (Dental Charges) (Wales) Regulations 2006 No.491
NHS(FP&CDA)(W) Regs	The National Health Service (Free Prescriptions and Charges for Drugs and Appliances) (Wales) Regulations 2007 No.121
NHS(GOS) Regs	The National Health Service (General Ophthalmic Services) Regulations 1986 No.975
NHS(OCP) Regs	The National Health Service (Optical Charges and Payments) Regulations 1997 No.818
NHS(TERC) Regs	The National Health Service (Travel Expenses and Remission of Charges) Regulations 2003 No.2382
NHS(TERC)(W) Regs	The National Health Service (Travelling Expenses and Remission of Charges) (Wales) Regulations 2007 No.1104
PAL Regs	The Paternity and Adoption Leave Regulations 2002 No.2788
SF(AR) Regs	The Social Fund (Application for Review) Regulations 1988 No. 34
SFCWP(G) Regs	The Social Fund Cold Weather Payments (General) Regulations 1988 No.1724
SFM&FE Regs	The Social Fund Maternity and Funeral Expenses (General) Regulations 2005 No.3061
SPPSAP(WR) Regs	The Statutory Paternity Pay and Statutory Adoption Pay (Weekly Rates) Regulations 2002 No.2818
SPPSAP(G) Regs	The Statutory Paternity and Statutory Adoption Pay (General) Regulations 2002 No.2822
SS(C) Regs	The Social Security (Contributions) Regulations 2001 No.1004
SS(C&P) Regs	The Social Security (Claims and Payments) Regulations 1987 No.1968
SS(DLA) Regs	The Social Security (Disability Living Allowance) Regulations 1991 No.2890
SS(IB) Regs	The Social Security (Incapacity Benefit) Regulations 1994 No.2946

SS(ICA) Regs	The Social Security (Invalid Care Allowance) Regulations 1976 No.409
TC(CN) Regs	The Tax Credits (Claims and Notifications) Regulations 2002 No.2014
TC(DCI) Regs	The Tax Credits (Definition and Calculation of Income) Regulations 2002 No.2006
TC(I) Regs	The Tax Credits (Immigration) Regulations 2003 No.653
TC(ITDR) Regs	The Tax Credits (Income Thresholds and Determination of Rates) Regulations 2002 No.2008
TC(R) Regs	The Tax Credits (Residence) Regulations 2003 No.654
WTC(EMR) Regs	The Working Tax Credit (Entitlement and Maximum Rate) Regulations 2002 No.2005

Other abbreviations

ALG Guidance	Adult Learning Grant Guidance
DMG	Decision Makers Guide
EIM	Employment Income Manual
GM	The Housing Benefit and Council Tax Benefit Guidance Manual
OFFA	Office for Fair Access
SF Dir	Social Fund Directive
TCTM	Tax Credits Technical Manual

See Appendix 1 for more details.

References like CIS/142/1990 and R(SB) 3/89 are references to commissioners' decisions.

Index

Training at CPAG

CPAG courses provide comprehensive rights training for advisers and detailed coverage of up-to-the minute legislative changes. Our tutors are expert in their areas of work and draw on the extensive training experience of CPAG's own welfare rights specialists. Courses include:

- An introduction to welfare rights
- Students and benefits – eligibility and definitions
- Students and benefits – treatment of student income
- Students and benefits – an update for experienced advisers
- Students and debt
- Students and debt – tactics for experienced advisers

For full course information and online booking please see our website (details below). Our courses can also be tailored to meet the needs of specific groups, including those not normally concerned with welfare rights. To assess your training needs, we are happy to discuss your requirements for 'in-house' training to meet the internal needs of your organisation.

CPAG's London-based courses are Law Society and Bar Council accredited and carry continuing education points. They are also approved by The Institute of Legal Executives and the UK College of Family Mediators. Courses in Scotland have Law Society Scotland accreditation.

Contact for further information:

Judy Allen, Training Co-ordinator

tel: 020 7812 5228

email: jallen@cpag.org.uk

website: www.cpag.org.uk/training